The Diachrony of Definiteness in North Germanic

Brill's Studies in Historical Linguistics

Series Editor

Jóhanna Barðdal
(Ghent University)

Consulting Editor

Spike Gildea
(University of Oregon)

Editorial Board

Joan Bybee (*University of New Mexico*) – Lyle Campbell (*University of Hawai'i Manoa*) – Nicholas Evans (*The Australian National University*) Bjarke Frellesvig (*University of Oxford*) – Mirjam Fried (*Czech Academy of Sciences*) – Russel Gray (*University of Auckland*) – Tom Guldemann (*Humboldt-Universität zu Berlin*) – Alice Harris (*University of Massachusetts*) Brian D. Joseph (*The Ohio State University*) – Ritsuko Kikusawa (*National Museum of Ethnology*) – Silvia Luraghi (*Università di Pavia*) Joseph Salmons (*University of Wisconsin*) – Søren Wichmann (*MPI/EVA*)

VOLUME 14

The titles published in this series are listed at *brill.com/bshl*

The Diachrony of Definiteness in North Germanic

By

Dominika Skrzypek
Alicja Piotrowska
Rafał Jaworski

BRILL

LEIDEN | BOSTON

This is an open access title distributed under the terms of the CC BY-NC-ND 4.0 license, which permits any non-commercial use, distribution, and reproduction in any medium, provided no alterations are made and the original author(s) and source are credited. Further information and the complete license text can be found at https://creativecommons.org/licenses/by-nc-nd/4.0/

The terms of the CC license apply only to the original material. The use of material from other sources (indicated by a reference) such as diagrams, illustrations, photos and text samples may require further permission from the respective copyright holder.

The research presented in this monograph was financed by a research grant from the Polish National Science Centre (NCN) entitled Diachrony of definiteness in Scandinavian languages, number 2015/19/B/HS2/00143. The authors gratefully acknowledge this support.

The Library of Congress Cataloging-in-Publication Data is available online at http://catalog.loc.gov
LC record available at http://lccn.loc.gov/2021012844

Typeface for the Latin, Greek, and Cyrillic scripts: "Brill". See and download: brill.com/brill-typeface.

ISSN 2211-4904
ISBN 978-90-04-43603-9 (hardback)
ISBN 978-90-04-46368-4 (e-book)

Copyright 2021 by D. Skrzypek, A. Piotrowska, and R. Jaworski. Published by Koninklijke Brill NV, Leiden, The Netherlands.
Koninklijke Brill NV incorporates the imprints Brill, Brill Hes & De Graaf, Brill Nijhoff, Brill Rodopi, Brill Sense, Hotei Publishing, mentis Verlag, Verlag Ferdinand Schöningh and Wilhelm Fink Verlag.
Koninklijke Brill NV reserves the right to protect this publication against unauthorized use.

This book is printed on acid-free paper and produced in a sustainable manner.

Contents

List of Tables and Figures IX
Abbreviations XII

1 **Introduction** 1
   1.1 Introductory Remarks 1
   1.2 Definiteness in the Modern North Germanic 3
      1.2.1 *The Definite Article in Modern North Germanic Languages* 4
         1.2.1.1 Insular Languages 4
         1.2.1.2 Continental Languages 7
      1.2.2 *The Indefinite Article in Modern North Germanic Languages* 9
         1.2.2.1 Insular Languages 9
         1.2.2.2 Continental Languages 9
   1.3 Aims, Scope and Organization of the Book 10

2 **Reference in Discourse and Models of Article Grammaticalization** 12
   2.1 Introductory Remarks 12
   2.2 The Rise of the Definite Article 13
      2.2.1 *Types of Reference/Definite Article Use* 14
         2.2.1.1 Direct Anaphora 15
         2.2.1.2 Indirect Anaphora 16
         2.2.1.3 Larger Situation Use 23
      2.2.2 *The Etymology of the Definite Article* 25
      2.2.3 *Demonstratives vs. Articles* 26
      2.2.4 *From a Demonstrative to a Definite Article* 27
      2.2.5 *The Meaning of Definiteness* 31
         2.2.5.1 Definite Articles in Fering and German 31
         2.2.5.2 The Problem of Indirect Anaphora 35
      2.2.6 *Grammaticalization of the Definite Article and Strong–Weak Definite Article Semantics* 36
      2.2.7 *Final Stages of the Grammaticalization of the Definite Article* 38
   2.3 The Rise of the Indefinite Article 39
      2.3.1 *Types of Indefinite Article Use* 39
      2.3.2 *From a Numeral 'One' to an Indefinite Article* 40
   2.4 Previous Studies on the Grammaticalization of the Definite Article in North Germanic 41

- 2.4.1 *General Studies* 42
  - 2.4.1.1 The Development of Double Definiteness in North Germanic 51
- 2.4.2 *Definite Article in Old Norse and Icelandic: Johnsen (1975), Faarlund (2009), van Gelderen (2007)* 54
- 2.4.3 *Definite Article in Danish: Skafte Jensen (2007a)* 57
- 2.4.4 *Definite Article in Swedish: Larm (1936), Skrzypek (2012), Dahl (2004 and 2015), Stroh-Wollin (2016)* 58
- 2.5 Previous Studies on the Grammaticalization of the Indefinite Article in North Germanic 64
  - 2.5.1 *Indefinite Article in Icelandic: Leijström (1934)* 64
  - 2.5.2 *Indefinite Article in Danish: Skafte Jensen (2016)* 64
  - 2.5.3 *Indefinite Article in Swedish: Brandtler and Delsing (2010), Skrzypek (2012), Stendahl (2013)* 65
- 2.6 Summary 67

3 Sources, Methods and Tools 70
- 3.1 Periodization of the North Germanic Languages 70
- 3.2 The Corpus 73
  - 3.2.1 *Period I (1200–1350)* 76
    - 3.2.1.1 Swedish 76
    - 3.2.1.2 Danish 77
    - 3.2.1.3 Icelandic 78
  - 3.2.2 *Period II (1350–1450)* 80
    - 3.2.2.1 Swedish 80
    - 3.2.2.2 Danish 80
    - 3.2.2.3 Icelandic 82
  - 3.2.3 *Period III (1450–1550)* 83
    - 3.2.3.1 Swedish 83
    - 3.2.3.2 Danish 83
    - 3.2.3.3 Icelandic 84
- 3.3 The DiaDef Tool and Its Benefits for the Study 85
  - 3.3.1 *Tool Overview* 85
  - 3.3.2 *Multi-Level Tagging* 85
  - 3.3.3 *Automatically Generated Suggestions* 89
  - 3.3.4 *Collected Data* 90
  - 3.3.5 *Statistics Generator* 90
  - 3.3.6 *Regression Analysis* 92
- 3.4 Annotation Issues 93
- 3.5 Summary 96

CONTENTS   VII

4 **The Diachrony of (In)definiteness—A Quantitative Study** 98
   4.1 Introduction 98
   4.2 General Data 98
   4.3 Definiteness and Number 101
   4.4 Definiteness and Gender 104
       4.4.1 *Results by Gender* 106
   4.5 Definiteness and Case 110
       4.5.1 *Case and the Definite Article* 113
       4.5.2 *Case and the Indefinite Article* 118
   4.6 Definiteness, Subjecthood and Objecthood 120
       4.6.1 *Syntactic Functions and Definiteness* 121
   4.7 Definiteness and Animacy 128
   4.8 Definiteness and Type of Reference 132
   4.9 All Factors—A Refined Analysis 139
       4.9.1 *The Definite Article* 140
       4.9.2 *The Indefinite Article* 144
       4.9.3 *The Definite Article vs. Bare Nouns—Classification Tree Analysis* 144
   4.10 Summary 156

5 **Grammaticalization Models Revisited—A Qualitative Analysis** 158
   5.1 Introductory Remarks 158
   5.2 On Models of Grammaticalization 158
   5.3 Grammaticalization of the Definite Article 160
       5.3.1 *From Deixis to Direct Anaphora* 160
            5.3.1.1 Accessibility Marking Scale 161
            5.3.1.2 Direct Anaphors in the Corpus 163
            5.3.1.3 Interim Summary 168
            5.3.1.4 Anaphoric Marking in Anaphoric Chains 169
            5.3.1.5 From Deixis to Direct Anaphora—A Brief Summary 172
       5.3.2 *From Direct Anaphora to Indirect Anaphora* 172
            5.3.2.1 Indirect Anaphors—Typology 176
            5.3.2.2 Semantic Types: Meronymic Relations 179
            5.3.2.3 Thematic Types 182
            5.3.2.4 Inference-Based Conceptual Types 184
            5.3.2.5 Summary 185
       5.3.3 *From Indirect Anaphora to Larger Situation Use* 185
       5.3.4 *Summary—A Review of the Grammaticalization Chain of the Definite Article* 190

- 5.4 Grammaticalization of the Indefinite Article   193
  - 5.4.1 *The Presentative Marker*   193
  - 5.4.2 *The Specificity Marker*   197
  - 5.4.3 *The Non-specificity Marker*   200
  - 5.4.4 *Summary*   201
- 5.5 Grammaticalization of Definiteness—A Larger Chain   202
- 5.6 *Excursus*: The Incipient Indefinite Article in Icelandic beyond 1500   204
  - 5.6.1 *Cardinal Uses*   211
  - 5.6.2 *Potential Cardinal Use*   212
  - 5.6.3 *Temporal Adverbials and Presentative Marker*   213
  - 5.6.4 *Marker of Specificity*   214
  - 5.6.5 *Marker of Non-specificity*   215
  - 5.6.6 *Other Types of Non-specific Contexts*   217
  - 5.6.7 *Generic Reference*   220
- 5.7 Summary   221

6 **Discussion and Conclusions**   223
- 6.1 Introduction   223
- 6.2 Grammaticalization of the Definite Article   223
- 6.3 Grammaticalization of the Indefinite Article   229
- 6.4 The Puzzles Revisited   231
- 6.5 Concluding Remarks   235

Sources   237
References   241
Index   257

Tables and Figures

Tables

1. An overview of NPs in North Germanic   5
2. Icelandic case inflection in bare nouns and definite nouns   6
3. Faroese case inflection in bare nouns and definite nouns   6
4. Stages and contexts in the grammaticalization of the definite article (after Skrzypek 2012:49)   30
5. The definite article paradigms in Fering (Ebert 1971b:159)   32
6. The suggested global cycle of definite articles (Carlier and Simonenko 2016:10)   37
7. Stages and contexts in the grammaticalization of the indefinite article (after Skrzypek 2012:53)   42
8. The inflectional paradigm of (*h*)*inn*   46
9. Definite nouns in Old Swedish (adapted from Skrzypek 2012:67)   46
10. Proposed dating of the cliticization of *hinn* in North Germanic (adapted from Skrzypek 2012:74)   48
11. The inflectional paradigm of *sá* in Old Norse   50
12. Double definiteness development in Norwegian after Stroh-Wollin (2015:132)   53
13. Double definiteness development in Swedish after Stroh-Wollin (2015:133)   53
14. Periodization of the North Germanic languages before 1100   71
15. Periodization of Old West Nordic after 1100   71
16. Periodization of Old East Nordic after 1100   72
17. Periodization used in the present study   72
18. Length of the texts in the corpus (total word counts)   74
19. Number of NPs tagged in the corpus   74
20. The annotation tags defined for the present project   87
21. Overall numbers of annotated words in the DiaDef system   90
22. The definite nouns in the corpus—an overview   99
23. Indefinite nouns in the corpus—an overview   99
24. Singular and plural nouns in the corpus (total frequencies)   102
25. Singular and plural nouns with -IN   103
26. The inflectional paradigm of the demonstrative *hinn* 'yon' in the singular   105
27. The inflectional paradigm of the numeral *enn* 'one'   105
28. The proportions of all genders in the corpus   106
29. Definiteness and the masculine gender   107
30. Indefiniteness and the masculine gender   107

31	Definiteness and the feminine gender 108	
32	Indefiniteness and the feminine gender 109	
33	Definiteness and the neuter gender 109	
34	Indefiniteness and the neuter gender 110	
35	Example declination of weak nouns: *bondi* 'yeoman' and *kirkja* 'church' 112	
36	Proportions of cases in the corpus 113	
37	Proportions of cases among definite NPs 115	
38	The nominative and definiteness 115	
39	The accusative and definiteness 116	
40	The dative and definiteness 117	
41	The genitive and definiteness 117	
42	Proportions of cases among indefinite NPs 119	
43	The main syntactic functions of NPs in the corpus 121	
44	Definite subjects in the corpus 126	
45	Indefinite subjects in the corpus 126	
46	Definite objects in the corpus 127	
47	Indefinite objects in the corpus 128	
48	Animate and inanimate NPs in the corpus 129	
49	Animate and inanimate definite NPs (-IN) in the corpus 130	
50	Animate and inanimate indefinite NPs (EN) in the corpus 130	
51	Animate NPs in definite form—a comparison with all nouns 131	
52	Animate NPs in indefinite form—a comparison with all nouns 131	
53	Expressions of direct anaphora in the corpus 133	
54	Expressions of indirect anaphora in the corpus 137	
55	Expressions of larger situation use in the corpus 138	
56	Variables influencing the selection of the definite article (-IN) in Period I 141	
57	Variables influencing the selection of the definite article (-IN) in Period II 142	
58	Variables influencing the selection of the definite article (-IN) in Period III 143	
59	Variables influencing the selection of the indefinite article (EN) in Period I 145	
60	Variables influencing the selection of the indefinite article (EN) in Period II 146	
61	Variables influencing the selection of the indefinite article (EN) in Period III 148	
62	Short and long definite descriptions in direct anaphoric contexts 167	
63	*Einn* in four Sagas of Icelanders, after Beier (2015) 208	
64	*Einn* in the supplementary Icelandic corpus (Kliś 2019:57) 210	

Figures

1. Sentence splitting in DiaDef 86
2. An example of an annotated sentence in DiaDef 86
3. Automatically generated tagging suggestions in DiaDef 89
4. The search window for simple statistics in DiaDef 91
5. An example of simple statistics generated in DiaDef—the dative case in Old Swedish 91
6. An example of collocation statistics search in DiaDef 92
7. An example of proportional statistics generated in DiaDef—animate singular referents within referents with postposed definite article 92
8. Proportions of definite subjects and objects in Danish 125
9. Proportions of definite subjects and objects in Swedish 125
10. Proportions of definite subjects and objects in Icelandic 126
11. Classification tree for Period I (1200–1350) 150
12. The importance of each independent variable in Period I 151
13. Classification tree for Period II (1350–1450) 152
14. The importance of each independent variable in Period II 153
15. Classification tree for Period III (1450–1550) 154
16. The importance of each independent variable in Period III 155

Abbreviations

Abbreviations Used for Corpus Texts

SV_AVL	Äldre Västgötalagen
SV_Bur	Codex Bureanus
SV_Did	Didrik af Bern
SV_DL	Dalalagen
SV_HML	Helga manna lefverne
SV_Järt	Järteckensboken
SV_KM	Karl Magnus
SV_Kris	Kristoffers Landslag
SV_Linc	Linköpingslegendariet, Legenden om Sankt Amalberga
SV_OgL	Östgötalagen
SV_Pent	Pentateukparafrasen
SV_ST	Själens tröst
SV_SVM	Sju vise mästare
SV_Troja	Historia Trojana
SV_YVL	Yngre Västgötalagen
DA_ErL	Eriks Lov
DA_GD	Gesta danorum
DA_Jer	Af Jeronimi levned
DA_Jesu	Jesu Barndoms Bog
DA_Kat	Af Katerine legende
DA_Kerst	Aff Sancte Kerstine hennis pyne
DA_KM	Karl Magnus Krønike
DA_Mar	Aff Sancta Marina
DA_MK	Mariaklagen
DA_ML	Marialegende
DA_SKL	Skånske Kirkelov
DA_SL	Skånske Lov
DA_SMB	Skriftemålsbøn
DA_ST	Sjalens trost
DA_Pouel	Huoel Sancte Pouel vort pint
DA_VL	Valdemars Lov
IS_Arna	Árna saga biskups
IS_Band	Bandamanna saga

IS_Did	Þiðreks saga af Bern
IS_Egil	Þetubrot Egils Sögu
IS_Finn	Finnboga saga ramma
IS_Ge	Geirmundar þáttr heljarskinns
IS_Gis	Gísla saga Súrssonar
IS_Gragas	Grágás. Lagasafn íslenska þjóðveldisins
IS_Gret	Grettis saga Ásmundarsonar
IS_Gun	Gunnars saga Keldugnúpsfífls
IS_Jarl	Jarlmanns saga og Hermanns
IS_Jart	Jarteinabók
IS_Marta	Mörtu saga og Maríu Magdalenu
IS_Torlak	Þorláks saga Helga
IS_To	Þorsteins saga hvíta
IS_Vig	Víglundar saga
IS_Vil	Vilhjálms saga Sjóðs

Abbreviations Used in the Present Study

BN	bare noun
defNP	definite noun phrase
DEN	proximal demonstrative
DEM	other determiners
dir-a	direct anaphora
EN	incipient indefinite article
-IN	incipient definite article
indefNP	indefinite noun phrase
N	overall number of nouns in the dataset
POSS-GEN	possessive-genitive
possNP	possessive noun phrase
POSS-PRO	possessive pronouns
POSS-REFL	possessive reflexive pronoun

Abbreviations Used in Glosses

2	second person
ACC	accusative
CONJ	conjunctive
DAT	dative

DEF	definite
DEP	deponent
EN	incipient indefinite article
F	feminine
GEN	genitive
IMPERS	impersonal construction
INDF	indefinite
INSTR	instrumental
M	masculine
N	neuter
NOM	nominative
OBL	oblique
PL	plural
PTCP	participle
REFL	reflexive
SG	singular
ST	strong form
UTR	common 'utrum' gender
WK	weak form

CHAPTER 1

Introduction

1.1　Introductory Remarks

The rise of definite and indefinite articles continues to puzzle historical linguists, despite a vast, and growing, body of literature on the subject. Interest in grammaticalization of (in)definiteness is partly fueled by interest in the category of definiteness itself, and partly by the relatively large number of sources—there are a number of languages that have developed articles in their literate histories, leaving us with corpora of texts in which the process may be observed. In this sense the morphologization of (in)definiteness, by which we understand the rise of its morphological exponents in the form of articles, either or both definite and indefinite, differs from the morphologization of case, which seems to predate extant sources, making its study a reconstruction rather than an analysis of data.

In this respect, the northern branch of the Germanic languages, today comprising Danish, Faroese, Icelandic, Norwegian and Swedish, presents a promising field of study. These closely related languages, with a common ancestor—Old Nordic—located in the not-too-distant past, at ca. 500–800 AD (Bandle et al. 2002), have all developed the definite article, and, with the exception of Icelandic, they have all developed the indefinite article too. However, the grammaticalization processes belong only partly to their common history; most have taken place in their individual histories, leading to slightly different scopes of use of the articles in each language, and different patterns of noun phrases, both definite and indefinite. The extant texts, although limited in size and stylistic variation to begin with, are of good enough quality to make the diachronic study of (in)definiteness possible, at least for Danish and Swedish (the eastern division) and for Icelandic (the western division). Not only do the texts exhibit the gradual rise of articles, they also illustrate the common elements of the process as well as its more isolated aspects, i.e., those limited to one language only.

Grammaticalization of (in)definiteness has been the subject of a number of studies, both theoretical and empirical, concerned with one language or language family. A fairly universal model of the grammaticalization of the indefinite article was proposed by Heine in 1997 (based to some extent on Givón 1981, see also Herslund 2012). The model was tested and confirmed against data from a number of languages (among them Danish, Swedish and Spanish, Pozas-Loyo 2010). As regards the definite article, some proposals have been put forward (beginning with Greenberg 1978), though so far none has been fully successful in identifying the transition from one stage of grammaticalization of the article to the next. The questions that remain to be answered are:

1. What makes the numeral 'one' and the deictic 'that' (or its like) such good candidates for the role of articles? In other words, why, in spite of there being other potential articles in the making, do these two universally form the first stage of grammaticalization of (in)definiteness? We will refer to this question as 'the puzzle of uniformity of sources'.
2. What makes these forms so successful, even when, at least to begin with, they are in competition with other forms, such as possessive or indefinite pronouns? In other words, how does the competition against other potential candidates unfold? We will refer to this question as 'the puzzle of success'.
3. Why does the order of events (grammaticalizations) seem to be universally 'definite first, indefinite second'? The studies of grammaticalization of (in)definiteness are for the most part concerned with either the rise of the definite or the rise of the indefinite article; however, the two developments are undoubtedly connected. In what ways does the rise of the definite article prepare the way for the rise of the indefinite article? But also, why is it not necessary for a language to develop both articles, as is the case with Icelandic? We will refer to this question as 'the puzzle of definite first'.
4. What is the diachronic bridge between the use of the definite article with anaphora and its use with unique referents (in more recent terms: between strong and weak definite articles)? Why can a demonstrative replace the definite article in the former context but not in the latter? And how are we to treat a context that is neither strong nor weak, i.e., indirect anaphora? This context itself is understudied diachronically, to say the least, and yet it seems to be crucial in the grammaticalization of the definite article. We will refer to this question as 'the puzzle of indirect anaphora'.

This list of puzzles is by no means exhaustive, and each would require a full-scale research project, in particular one taking into consideration languages from different language families. In the present study, we will focus in particular on the last puzzle, basing our study on a corpus of texts written in Danish, Icelandic and Swedish between 1200 and 1550. By limiting the scope of the study to one aspect of grammaticalization, we aim to shed more light on the process and somewhat elaborate on the model of grammaticalization. By focusing on a group of closely related languages, we aim to demonstrate both the universality and the individuality of the process.

1.2 Definiteness in the Modern North Germanic

Modern North Germanic languages include the so-called Continental or Mainland languages: Danish, Norwegian (in two official varieties, *bokmål* and *nynorsk*) and Swedish; and the so-called Insular languages: Faroese and Icelandic. All of these languages have developed the definite article; all but Icelandic have also developed the indefinite. Articles have evolved in all of the modern Germanic languages, English, German, Dutch and Frisian (see McColl Millar 2000 on the development of the definite article in English). Although the developments are common, they do not belong to the Proto-Germanic period, since no articles are attested in the most conservative texts, i.e., Runic inscriptions from before 800 AD. The now extinct Gothic exhibits some advancement in the formation of at least the definite article (Kovari 1984). It is, however, a matter of some debate to what extent this was the influence of the Greek original from which the only extant text, the New Testament, was translated (Askedal 2012). The northern branch of the Germanic language family has undergone clearly different developments than the rest, as the definite article in these languages is a suffix, while in other Germanic languages it is a free form, including the semi-article in Gothic.

The fundamental opposition in the article systems in North Germanic is one between definite and indefinite (as opposed to other potential articles, such as the partitive in French). The articles are either free lexemes (the indefinite and the preposed definite articles) or suffixes (the postposed definite article). The articles are inflected for number, gender and, in the Insular languages, case (Delsing, Vangsnes and Holmberg 2003).

The morphologization of (in)definiteness, i.e., the formation of morphological exponents in the form of articles, is typically a lengthy process with multiple stages, and this is also the case in North Germanic. The definite article seems to develop before the indefinite, and the preposed definite develops at a later stage than the postposed. It takes some time before the noun phrase acquires its modern form (slightly different in each language, Delsing 1993, Julien 2005). Also, the status of bare nouns (BNs) changes from being a marked alternative to an incipient definite article to being a marked alternative to a DP. The fact that the morphologization of (in)definiteness belongs at least partly to the individual history of each language is reflected in the variation of the NP structure, the functions of articles and the status of BNs among the languages.

In the modern North Germanic languages, the definite article is a suffix, always attached enclitically to the noun (in the Insular Scandinavian languages Icelandic and Faroese, to the case-inflected form of the noun). Its origins are to be sought in the distal demonstrative *hinn* 'yon'. Apart from the postpositional article, in the Mainland Scandinavian languages (Danish, Norwegian, Swedish) and Faroese there is a preposed article *den* 'that', which can co-occur with the postpositional one (so-called *double definiteness* in Faroese, Norwegian and Swedish, see Börjars 1994 and LaCara 2011) or be in complementary distribution with it (Danish). Also, in all North Germanic languages apart from Icelandic, there is an indefinite article, related with the numeral *en* (Danish, Swedish, Norwegian *bokmål*), *ein* (Faroese, Norwegian *nynorsk*) or *einn* (Icelandic) 'one', etymologically PGmc (and early Proto-Nordic) **ainaz*. An overview of the forms of NPs in North Germanic is given in Table 1.

1.2.1 *The Definite Article in Modern North Germanic Languages*
1.2.1.1 Insular Languages

Icelandic and Faroese, the Insular North Germanic languages, have both developed the postposed definite article. In both languages, but in particular in Icelandic, the morphology of the article reflects a relatively conservative stage of development (Askedal 2012:73), as the article is inflected for case, independent of the case morphology of the noun. Consider the following examples from Icelandic (Table 2).

Table 2 presents the inflectional paradigms of three Icelandic nouns: *hestur* 'horse' (masculine), *bók* 'book' (feminine) and *barn* 'child' (neuter). The second, fourth and sixth columns show the bare nouns inflected for case and number, the third, fifth and seventh the nouns in the definite, also inflected for case and number. The hyphens mark morph boundaries. In the majority of the forms, the separate case inflection of the noun and the definite suffix is still clearly visible.

One form that is not as easy to segment as the others is the plural dative ending in *-unum* in all genders. Originally, the form consisted of the segment *-uminum*, with two dative endings *-um*, one of the noun, one of the article. This form has been reduced in both western and eastern branches of North Germanic: in the west to *-unum* as found in Icelandic, in the east to *-omen* as found in Old Danish and Old Swedish (in both languages the category of case was later reduced, and with it the plural definite dative).

The Faroese definite forms, as presented in Table 3, are of similar construction as the Icelandic ones, with double case inflection within one form. The difference is that, due to a more advanced process of case reduction, the genitive has become almost obsolete in modern Faroese, rendering the genitive definite forms relic forms rather than productive ones (Askedal 2012:76).

TABLE 1 An overview of NPs in North Germanic

Context	Article	Form	Languages
Single noun NP 'the house'	Definite article postposed	hus-et house-DEF	Danish, Norwegian, Swedish
		hús-ið house-DEF	Faroese, Icelandic
NP with an adjective and noun 'the big house'	Definite article preposed only	det stor-e hus DEF big-WK house	Danish
	Double definiteness (preposed and postposed definite articles)	det stor-e hus-et DEF big-WK house-DEF	Norwegian
		det stora hus-et DEF big-WK house-DEF	Swedish
		hið/tað stór-a hús-ið DEF big-WK house-DEF	Faroese
	Definite article postposed only	stór-a hús-ið big-WK house-DEF	Icelandic
Single noun NP 'a house'	Indefinite article	et hus INDF house	Danish, Norwegian
		ett hus INDF house	Swedish
		eitt hús INDF house	Faroese
	No indefinite article	hús house	Icelandic

TABLE 2   Icelandic case inflection in bare nouns and definite nouns

Case	*hestur* 'horse'		*bók* 'book'		*barn* 'child'	
SG	BN	definite	BN	definite	BN	definite
NOM	hest-ur	hest-ur-in-n	bók	bók-in	barn	barn-ið
ACC	hest	hest-in-n	bók	bók-in-a	barn	barn-ið
DAT	hest-i	hest-i-n-um	bók	bók-in-ni	barn-i	barn-i-n-u
GEN	hest-s	hest-s-in-s	bók-ar	bók-ar-in-nar	barn-s	barn-s-in-s
PL	BN	definite	BN	definite	BN	definite
NOM	hest-ar	hest-ar-n-ir	bæk-ur	bæk-ur-n-ar	börn	börn-in
ACC	hest-a	hest-a-n-a	bæk-ur	bæk-ur-n-ar	börn	börn-in
DAT	hest-um	hest-u-n-um	bók-um	bók-u-n-um	börn-um	börn-u-n-um
GEN	hest-a	hest-a-n-na	bók-a	bók-a-n-na	barn-a	barn-a-n-na

TABLE 3   Faroese case inflection in bare nouns and definite nouns

Case	*armur* 'arm'		*hurð* 'door'		*barn* 'child'	
SG	BN	definite	BN	definite	BN	definite
NOM	arm-ur	arm-ur-in	hurð	hurð-in	barn	barn-ið
ACC	arm	arm-in	hurð	hurð-ina	barn	barn-ið
DAT	arm-i	arm-i-n-um	hurð	hurð-ini	barni	barn-i-n-um
GEN	arm-s	arm-s-in-s*	hurðar	hurð-ar-in-nar	barns	barn-s-in-s
PL	BN	definite	BN	definite	BN	definite
NOM	arm-ar	arm-ar-nir	hurðar	hurð-ar-na-r	børn	børn-in-i
ACC	arm-ar	arm-ar-nar	hurðar	hurð-ar-na-r	børn	børn-in-i
DAT	ørm-um	ørm-u-n-um	hurðum	hurð-u-n-um	børnum	børn-u-n-um
GEN	arm-a	arm-a-n-na	hurða	hurð-a-n-na	barna	barn-a-n-na

* Thráinsson et al. note that *forms of this kind may also be simplified to arm-ins, marking the genitive only on the article, but they are very rarely used anyway* (2012:94).
AFTER THRÁINSSON ET AL. 2012:94–95

The two definite articles, the pre- and the postposed, are in complementary distribution in NPs with adjectival modifiers in Icelandic, i.e., they do not occur within one NP (examples in 1). The adjective in the definite NP is usually in the so-called weak inflection, although a combination of strong adjective and definite noun within one NP is still possible (example 2).

Icelandic (Askedal 2012:74)
(1) a. *fljót-i   hestur-inn*
       quick-WK horse-DEF
       'the quick horse'

   b. *hinn fljót-i   hestur (considered more formal)*
       DEF quick-WK horse
       'the quick horse'

Icelandic (Thráinsson 2007:3)
(2) **Rautt/??rauð-a nef-ið**   *á honum glóði   í myrkr-inu.*
    red.ST/??red-WK nose-DEF on him   glowed in dark-DEF
    'His red nose glowed in the dark.'

The ungrammaticality of the weak form of the adjective in (2) lies in the fact that it would imply that the person had more than one nose and it was the red one that glowed in the dark, or at least that there is a contrast between the red nose and some other nose. As the strong form does not imply the existence of a similar contrast, it is preferred in this context. In Faroese, on the other hand, the two definite articles occur within one NP if the NP includes an adjectival modifier, a phenomenon known as double definiteness, as in (3).

Faroese
(3) *tann reyð-a bil-in*
    DEF red-WK car-DEF
    'the red car'

1.2.1.2   Continental Languages

The article morphology of the Continental languages is simplified in comparison to the Insular languages. Case was lost by the 15th century (earlier in Danish, later in Swedish and Norwegian), which resulted in the loss of the so-called double inflection of the noun and the cliticized article, which we find in modern Insular languages. Also, the number of genders has been reduced from three to two in Danish, Swedish and some varieties of Norwegian (while other varieties retain the three-fold gender). Remnants of the older stage of language development can be found in fairly infrequent fossilized phrases such as *havsens bunn* 'the bottom of the sea' (Norwegian) or *livsens rot* 'the root of life' (Swedish).

As mentioned in section 1.2, definiteness in modern North Germanic languages can be realized both pre-nominally (with a definite article) and post-nominally (with a definite suffix on the head noun). All of the Continental languages have developed both pre- and postposed definite articles. The preposed article is used with adjectival modifiers. Languages differ in whether they allow the two articles to co-occur within one definite NP: Norwegian, Swedish and Faroese allow the so-called *overbestemdhet* 'over-definiteness' with both articles present, as in example (4), while in Danish the two articles are in complementary distribution, as in (5). Icelandic has not really developed the preposed definite article. The construction with preposed *hinn* is considered literary and stylistically marked (e.g., Sigurðsson 2006). However, recent research suggests that *hinn* has largely the same syntactic status in Modern Icelandic as Swedish *den*, in spite of different etymologies and developments (Pfaff 2015, 2017, Harðarson 2017).

Swedish

(4) *den vackr-a dag-en*
    DEF beautiful-WK day-DEF
    'the beautiful day'

Danish

(5) a. *den smukk-e dag*
       DEF beautiful-WK day
       'the beautiful day'

   b. **den smukk-e dag-en*
      *DEF beautiful-WK day-DEF
      'the beautiful day'

For authors who consider both the pre- and the post-nominal determiners to be definite articles, the North Germanic languages become a natural object of study in terms of weak–strong definite semantics dichotomy. In this spirit, Ingason (2016a, 2016b) discusses Icelandic and Goodwin Davies (2016) discusses Swedish.

1.2.2 *The Indefinite Article in Modern North Germanic Languages*
1.2.2.1 Insular Languages

Among the five modern North Germanic languages, only Icelandic has not developed the indefinite article. There seem to have been some tendencies towards the grammaticalization of the numeral 'one' into an indefinite article in the 16th century (Kliś 2019). Why this development never truly became established, or whether it was perhaps suppressed, remains an open question and makes for a potentially fascinating field of study.

Faroese, on the other hand, has a fully formed indefinite article, just like the other Germanic languages (example 6). In contrast to the indefinite article in other Germanic languages, the Faroese indefinite has a plural form as well as a singular, as in (7), although its presence is limited to plurals denoting items typically found in pairs, such as shoes (Askedal 2012:75).[1] Otherwise, the plural indefinite NP is bare or includes the equivalent of *nakrir* 'some' (plural of *nakar*), as in (8).

Faroese

(6) *ein reyð-ur   hest-ur*
    INDF red-NOM.SG.ST horse-NOM.SG
    'a red horse'

Faroese

(7) *ein-ir   skógv-ar*
    one-NOM.PL shoe-NOM.PL
    'a pair of shoes'

Faroese (Thráinsson et. al. 2012:132)

(8) *Hann var heima **nakrar**   dag-ar.*
    he   was home some.ACC.PL.M day-ACC.PL.M
    'He was at home for a few days.'

1.2.2.2 Continental Languages

All of the Continental languages have grammaticalized indefinite articles, etymologically continuations of the numeral 'one'. The indefinite article is a free preposed lexeme. In indefinite NPs it is combined with the strong form of the adjective if an adjectival modifier is present, as in (9).

---

1 One reviewer points out that *einir* has also survived as a pluralia-tantum numeral in Icelandic (alongside *tvennir, þrennir, fernir*), in numeral uses (with plural nouns and nouns denoting natural pairs) only.

Swedish

(9) en snabb bil
    INDF fast.ST car
    'a fast car'

Similarly to Faroese, the article has only a singular form, and plural indefinite NPs are either bare or include indefinite pronouns: Swedish *några*, Danish *nogle*, Norwegian *noen*, all meaning 'some'.

1.3 Aims, Scope and Organization of the Book

The book is organized as follows: in Chapter 2 we present current views on the grammaticalization of (in)definiteness and the models of grammaticalization proposed in the literature, with particular reference to studies of the rise of articles in North Germanic languages. In Chapter 3 we present the selection of texts used in the study and the tool used to annotate the texts, DiaDef. Chapter 4 presents data harvested from the corpus and its statistical analysis. In Chapter 5 we investigate the context of indirect anaphora in a diachronic perspective, presenting a revised model of the grammaticalization of the definite article. Closing remarks are given in Chapter 6.

The analyses presented in Chapters 4 and 5 are methodologically quite different. We have chosen to include both analyses in our study, since each has merits of its own. Statistical analysis allows us a more global view of the process of grammaticalization, making use of the fact that many sources have been digitalized in recent years. An in-depth analysis of longer text passages, on the other hand, offers a chance to study each form in a broader context. For reasons of practicality, such analysis can be conducted only on a limited text sample; therefore, a statistical analysis of a larger database makes the results more substantial.

A qualitative approach is and has long been a desideratum in diachronic linguistics. It is indispensable when dealing with limited data or when consideration of a larger text fragment is necessary to make sense of the data. However, the qualitative approach is perhaps at its best when dealing with clear cases—well-formed and well-defined categories. Jenset and McGillivray (2017) cite the case of English *in* and *at*, which can clearly function as prepositions, as opposed to *concerning*, *regarding*, *following* and *given*, which may be treated as prepositions in certain contexts or under certain circumstances, but hardly in the majority of cases (Jenset and McGillivray 2017:4). To deal with less prototypical cases, a probabilistic model based on quantitative rather than qualitative studies may be applied. Moreover, in the case of a category under development, in this instance (in)definiteness, such a model lets us escape the clear-cut dichotomy of demonstrative vs. definite article or numeral vs. indefinite article, allowing us to reveal the degree of 'articleness' of a given form rather than imposing a final taxonomy upon it. Our goal has been to study the grammaticalization of definite and indefinite articles by means of two different types of models: quantitative and qualitative (a 'model parallelization'; Zuidema and de Boer 2014) with the aim of gaining new, and richer, insights into the morphologization of the category of (in)definiteness.

The results from both studies focus on the factors favouring the use of the (incipient) articles. These include types of nouns (such as countable vs. mass, singular vs. plural), their functions (subject, object, etc.), and the type of reference: i.e., whether the noun is marked as new (indefinite) or known (definite) because the discourse referent is known from the previous text, or rather because it is assumed to be universally known. We will specifically use the following terms throughout the book: *direct anaphora* to denote instances when the definite repeats a discourse referent introduced earlier, *indirect anaphora* for instances when the definite is a new discourse referent grounded in previous discourse, *unique reference* for instances when the discourse status of the referent is neutral, since the referent is known to both speaker and hearer based on their general knowledge ('larger situation use'; Hawkins 1978), and finally, *generic reference* to denote instances of article use with reference to kinds and not individuals.

As this study is a diachronic one, we wished to avoid labeling the grammaticalizing forms as definite or indefinite articles, since we study them at different stages of their development. In the more theoretically oriented Chapters 1 and 2, we will therefore refer to the forms as incipient articles. In the chapters devoted to the study of the grammaticalizing articles in North Germanic we will use the notation -IN (in capitals) to refer to the incipient definite article and EN for the incipient indefinite article. The notations hint at the etymologies of the present-day articles (see Chapter 2).

CHAPTER 2

Reference in Discourse and Models of Article Grammaticalization

2.1   Introductory Remarks

The rise of articles, both definite and indefinite, is an example of a process of grammaticalization, i.e., a type of language change whereby lexical items gain grammatical meanings or grammatical items gain more grammatical meanings while being subject to certain changes, such as erosion of phonetic and semantic substance, acquisition of a more fixed position in the phrase or loss of independence, as in cliticization or affixation (see Kuryłowicz 1965, Lehmann 1995, Heine 2002, Hopper and Traugott 2003, Lehmann 2004). The process of grammaticalization of the articles has been studied within grammaticalization studies, among others Greenberg (1978), Givón (1981), Heine (1997), Dahl (2004), De Mulder and Carlier (2011), Skrzypek (2012, 2013), to name but a few. Another approach to grammaticalization of the articles has been couched in generative terms, and its foremost proponents with respect to North Germanic include van Gelderen (2007), Faarlund (2007, 2009) and Stroh-Wollin (2009, 2015, 2016).

In the following, we adopt the grammaticalization studies approach, discussing the model of the rise of the definite article first and the model of the rise of the indefinite second, concluding with an attempt at joining them. The grammaticalization processes which result in the formation of articles are not universal, yet they exhibit cross-linguistic regularities, with respect to both the etymologies of the articles and their later developments. Our study focuses on a group of closely related languages; nevertheless, we aim to develop a model that may have a more universal application in diachronic studies of (in)definiteness. In this chapter, the theoretical and terminological discussions are limited to the terms, concepts and hypotheses crucial for the study of grammaticalization of articles only, omitting a wider discussion of reference in general.

2.2 The Rise of the Definite Article

The first study of the development of the definite article, on which later studies of its grammaticalization are based, is Greenberg (1978). In that paper on the rise of gender markers, Greenberg proposes a development from a demonstrative through a definite article, which in later stages of grammaticalization turns into a nominal marker signaling the gender of the noun. Greenberg does not analyze the transition from a demonstrative to an article in any more detail. In later studies, notably De Mulder and Carlier (2011), the grammaticalization chain from a demonstrative to a definite article is described as consisting of at least three crucial stages: 1) the incipient article used as a direct anaphoric marker, 2) the incipient article used as an indirect anaphoric marker, and 3) the incipient article used as a unique marker.

Virtually all studies of definiteness, either synchronic or diachronic, stress the fact that the definite article has a wide range of uses, which are difficult to subsume under one semantic category or notion. Thus, anaphora is regarded as an instance of familiarity, when the hearer is 'reminded' by means of the definite article that the discourse referent has already been introduced into the discourse. On the other hand, the use of the definite article with referents such as *sun* is regarded as being due to their uniqueness, which renders previous mentions unnecessary for their successful resolution. Numerous attempts have been made to define all uses as building on either the familiarity or the uniqueness of the discourse referent, always with a proviso that the category in question is weakened; in fact, Roberts (2003), a proponent of the familiarity hypothesis, does term some definite article uses as instances of 'weak familiarity'. In recent years, one senses that such attempts have been given up, and many authors work instead with the idea that there are in fact two types of definiteness in article languages, beginning perhaps with the famous paper by Sebastian Löbner (1985), who distinguishes between semantic and pragmatic definiteness. This view has received strong support from empirical studies of languages with more than one definite article, notably North Frisian (Fering) and some German dialects (Ebert 1971a, Hartmann 1967), and has subsequently been developed into a systematic typology of definites as either strong or weak (Schwarz F. 2009 and later). In his monographic study of definiteness, Christopher Lyons postulates two types of definiteness: textual-situational (including anaphoric and immediate situation uses) and all other uses of the definite article (Lyons C. 1999:198). The most successful of the theoretical proposals in recent years is that of F. Schwarz (2009), whose concept of definiteness builds directly on the familiarity vs. uniqueness opposition.

Irrespective of the differences between the three proposals, their common denominator is that they do not attempt to reconcile all uses of the definite article under one banner, and that they propose two types of definiteness and not more. Florian Schwarz (2009), whose main inspiration comes from empirical studies of languages with more than one definite article, also acknowledges that we do find contexts in which either of the articles, strong or weak, may be successfully used, revealing that the distinction is not absolute or discrete.

Before we present the current model of the grammaticalization of the definite article, we will first consider a typology of definite article uses. We take the typology proposed by Hawkins (1978) as our point of departure, paying particular attention to the so-called bridging uses of the definite article, in Hawkins' terminology *associative anaphora*, which we refer to as *indirect anaphora*. We will then attempt to classify each definite article use as representing definiteness based on either uniqueness or familiarity.

2.2.1   *Types of Reference/Definite Article Use*

In his now classic book on definiteness, Hawkins differentiates between four major uses of the definite article. These are:

1. immediate situation use
2. anaphoric use
3. larger situation use
4. associative anaphoric use

The types may be illustrated by the following examples:

(10) Type 1. **the desk** (in a room with exactly one desk or accompanied by a pointing gesture)

(11) Type 2. **the book** (when previous sentence or text included the phrase 'a book' with the same referent)

(12) Type 3. **the Queen** (in the UK)

(13) Type 4. John bought a book today. **The front page** was torn. / **The author** was French.
(after Hawkins 1978 and Schwarz F. 2009)

In the remaining text we will use the following terminology:

Deictical use (Hawkins' type 1) to describe a deictic use of the definite article.

Direct anaphora (Hawkins' type 2) to describe the use of the definite article with a discourse referent previously introduced in the text.

Indirect anaphora (Hawkins' type 4) to describe the use of the definite article with a discourse referent new in the discourse, but connected to some entity, process or event described earlier in the text. This entity, process or event is termed *the anchor* (Fraurud 1990).

Larger situation use (Hawkins' type 3) to describe the use of the definite article with a discourse referent not introduced previously, directly or indirectly, which the hearer may identify building on his general knowledge.

It is possible to differentiate each type further. Therefore, we will now discuss each type of definite article use in turn.

2.2.1.1   Direct Anaphora

Anaphora is a discourse phenomenon, a relation between two linguistic elements: an antecedent and an anaphor, as in the following example:

(14)   I came into *a spacious room*. It was sparsely decorated and rather gloomy.

A typical antecedent is an indefinite NP, and a typical anaphor is a pronoun or a definite NP. The simplicity of example (14) is of course misleading, for anaphora is a complex linguistic and cognitive phenomenon, which has duly received a great deal of attention, both within linguistic paradigms and in other domains, such as (language) philosophy, psychology, cognitive science and artificial intelligence studies.

In the present study, we differentiate between two very different types of anaphora, which we term direct and indirect. The indirect type corresponds to Hawkins' associative anaphora. The crucial difference between the two is that while both types of anaphora need an antecedent of sorts, the antecedent and the anaphor are co-referring in direct anaphora and not co-referring in indirect anaphora.

In historical linguistics, (direct) anaphora is singled out as the first context of the incipient definite article. Originally a deictic element (see Lyons C. 1999), it begins to be used to point not only in physical context, but also in text (anaphora, see e.g., Anderson and Keenan 1985), which constitutes the first stage of grammaticalization. The use of a demonstrative to point within text involves a shift from situational to textual deixis (Lyons J. 1975). In itself, such use is not sufficient to imply that a grammaticalization of the definite article has begun. This can first be asserted when the original demonstrative comes to be used in the second type of anaphora: indirect anaphora.

Direct anaphoric use includes prototypical examples, such as (15), in which the same discourse referent is described by identical lexical means, but also uses such as (16–17), in which the same discourse referent is presented together with some new lexical information.

(15) Fred was discussing *an interesting book* in his class. I went to discuss **the book** with him afterwards. (Hawkins 1978:86)

(16) Fred was wearing *trousers*. **The pants** had a big patch on them. (Hawkins 1978:107)

(17) Fred bought *a new house*. **The extravagant purchase** / **This extravagant purchase** drained him of all money.

Note that the more new information is added the less natural the definite article becomes. In (17) the demonstrative seems to be a better option (stylistically).

The direct anaphora is based on co-reference of the first and the subsequent mentions of the discourse referent. There is a wide variety of elements which can serve as anaphors and both demonstratives and definite articles can be used anaphorically. However, this interchangeability of demonstratives and articles may be limited by among others stylistic reasons. For more discussion of direct anaphora and its exponents see in particular Kibrik (2011) and Huang (2000).

2.2.1.2   Indirect Anaphora

Indirect anaphora shares some properties both with direct anaphora—its successful resolution relies on information included in the discourse—and also, with larger situation use—the discourse itself does not provide all the information necessary for the successful resolution of the anaphor, which must be supplied by the hearer from their encyclopaedic knowledge. It is a type of reference called bridging reference, understood as a relationship between two objects or events introduced in a text or by a text. The relationship is not spelled out, and yet constitutes an essential part of the content of the text, in the sense that without this information the lack of connection between the objects or events would render the text incoherent (Asher and Lascarides 1998). Let us consider the following examples:

(18) I met two interesting people last night at a party. **The woman** was a member of Clinton's Cabinet.

(19) In the groups there was one person missing. **It was Mary** who left.

(20) John partied all night yesterday. He's going to get drunk **again** today.

(21) Jack was going to commit suicide. He got **a rope**.

(22) Jack locked himself out again. He had left **his keys** on the kitchen table. (examples 18–21 after Asher and Lascarides 1998:83, 22 after Skrzypek 2020)

There is a variety of expressions forming bridging relations with other expressions in the text, including, but not limited to, a definite NP. We can further note that there is some variation as to which form may be used; it would be perfectly possible to substitute a definite article for the possessive pronoun in (22), as well as for the indefinite article in (21), although both substitutions would result in slightly different nuances of the meaning of the NPs.

For the purpose of the present study, we will focus on (nominal) indirect anaphora, the type of bridging that involves anaphoric NPs: examples such as (18), (21) and (22), disregarding other types. It will be of interest to investigate what types of NPs can be used in this context throughout the periods studied, when the definite NPs gain ground, and how their competition against possessive NPs, BNs and other types of NPs plays out.

An unequivocal difference between direct and indirect anaphora is that while the former relies on an antecedent, i.e., a previous mention of the discourse referent, the latter does not. Instead, we are for the most part able to identify some connected entity, event, activity, scenario or frame in the preceding discourse that seems to serve a similar function (*two interesting people—the woman, suicide—a rope, locked himself out—his keys*). This 'antecedent' need not be nominal, thus differing from the antecedent in direct anaphora. In the literature it is referred to as a *trigger* (Hawkins 1978) or an *anchor* (Fraurud 1990). In the present study we will use the term *anchor* to refer to all antecedents of indirect anaphors.

There are a number of possible relations between the anchor and the (indirect) anaphor. The two major types of indirect anaphora are part–whole relations, on the one hand, and semantic roles, on the other. Some authors limit the scope of indirect anaphora to these two (e.g., Irmer 2011), while others identify a third subtype, inferential relations.

(23) a book—the cover (part–whole relation)

(24) a book—the author (semantic roles, nominal anchor)

(25) to read—the book (semantic roles, non-nominal anchor)

(26) an event—a seemingly unconnected entity, see example (49)

Perhaps the simplest indirect anaphoric relations involve all types of meronymy, i.e., part–whole relations, e.g., *watch—battery* in example (27).

(27) *My watch* has stopped. **The battery** must be dead.

A number of other semantic relations are also possible, such as producer—product (*author—the book*), object—component (*joke—the punchline*), collective—member (*deck—the card*), mass—portion (*pie—the slice*), object—material (*bike—the steel*), activity—episode (*shopping—the payment*), region—area (*Florida—the Everglades*). In these types there is a semantic or lexical relation between the anchor and the indirect anaphor, i.e., the knowledge necessary for the resolution of the anaphor is stored in our mental lexicon (Schwarz-Friesel 2007:9).

The meronymic types are further subdivided by Clark (1983) into types describing necessary, probable and inducible parts, as in the following examples.

Necessary parts:

(28) I looked into the room. The ceiling was very high.

(29) I hit a home run. The swing had been a good one.

(30) I looked into the room. The size was overwhelming.

Probable parts:

(31) I walked into the room. The windows looked out to the bay.

(32) I went shopping yesterday. The walk did me good.

(33) I left at 8 p.m. The darkness made me jumpy.

Inducible parts:

(34) I walked into the room. The chandeliers sparkled brightly.

(35) I went shopping yesterday. The climb did me good.

(36) I left at 8 p.m. The haste was necessary given the circumstances.
(Clark 1983, see also Kołaczek 2019)

As the examples quoted indicate, the interpretation of the anaphors, while in each case dependent on the anchor, differs with respect to how natural or stereotypical a part of the aforementioned whole they make.

Another subtype of indirect anaphora is the lexical/thematic type (in Clark's terminology *indirect reference by characterisation*), which is based on the thematic roles such as instrument, object, agent, etc. The interpretation of indirect anaphors depends on the activation of knowledge in the mental lexicon (Schwarz-Friesel 2007:8). In her extensive study of indirect anaphors in a corpus of authentic texts, M. Schwarz (2000:100 f.) presents the following examples to illustrate this subtype:

(37) Nachdem sie das Lokal verlassen hatten, so der Mann, habe die Frau ohne Vorwarnung auf ihn geschossen. Die Pistole habe sie plötzlich aus der Handtasche gezogen.
'After they had left the venue, the man said, the woman had shot at him without any warning. She had suddenly drawn the gun out of her handbag.'

(38) Der Sohn des Englischen Geheimagenten Tarrant wurde entführt. Die Kidnapper fordern ein Lösegeld von einer Million Pfund.
'The son of the English secret agent Tarrant was kidnapped. The kidnappers demand a ransom of one million pounds.'

(39) Er angelte seit Stunden. Aber die Fische wollten und wollten nicht anbeißen.
'He was fishing for hours. But the fish didn't want to take the bait.'

(40) Um sieben Uhr fuhr Tschanz zu Bärlach in den Altenberg […] Es regnet, und der schnelle Polizeiwagen kam in der Kurve ins Schleudern.
'At seven o'clock Tschanz went to Bärlach in the Altenberg […] It rains and the fast police car skidded in the curve.'

The roles illustrated by these examples are as follows: in (37) *the gun* is the instrument of shooting; in (38) *the kidnappers* are the agents of the action of kidnapping; in (39) *the fish* is the object of the action of fishing, and in (40) *the fast police car* is the means of transport connected with the action of going somewhere. The common denominator for the examples is a lexical connection between the anchor and the indirect anaphor, e.g., *to shoot—a gun*. With the lexical/thematic type a more refined categorization is possible, dividing the roles into necessary and optional.

Necessary roles:

(41) John was murdered yesterday. The murderer got away.

(42) I went shopping yesterday. The time I started was 3 p.m.

(43) I trucked the goods to New York. The truck was full.

Optional roles:

(44) John died yesterday. The murderer got away.

(45) John was murdered yesterday. The knife lay nearby.

(46) John went walking at noon. The park was beautiful. (Clark 1983:418)

Clark's classification is basically bi-partite, with parts and roles as the major types of indirect anaphora. M. Schwarz proposes two further subtypes, i.e., scheme-based conceptual types and inference-based conceptual types.

The scheme-based conceptual types are similar to the lexical/thematic type, but as M. Schwarz points out they cannot be interpreted just through the semantic relation (activation of knowledge in the mental lexicon), because the relation between the anaphor and its anchor forms a wider network of associations and connections and involves the processing of the more general world knowledge. Thus, anchors such as *restaurant* activate a mental frame which includes elements such as waiters, food, menus, bill, as in (47) and (48), and *hospital* will activate a mental frame with elements such as doctors, nurses, bed, medicine, operating theatre and so on (Schwarz M. 2000:111 ff., Schwarz-Friesel 2007:10).

(47) Ich kenne ein schönes Restaurant in Refrath. Das Essen ist köstlich, und der Kellner ganz besonders nett.
 'I know a nice restaurant in Refrath. The food is delicious and the waiter quite especially nice.' (Schwarz M. 2000:111)

(48) To kill some time I walked over to Greenwich Street, to the Elephant and Castle, *a restaurant* where my mother and I ate sometimes when we were downtown. But the instant I stepped in, I realized my mistake. The mismatched china elephants, even **the ponytailed waitress** in a black T-shirt who approached me, smiling: it was too overwhelming, I could see **the corner table** where my mother and I had eaten lunch the last time we were there, I had to mumble an excuse and back out the door.[1]

The most complex relations are found between anaphors and anchors in indirect anaphors of the inference-based conceptual type. They are typically founded on inferences and deductions and are parts of very specific situations. Therefore, they are most often found in punchlines of jokes (Schwarz M. 2000:114). M. Schwarz illustrates the type by means of the joke quoted below.

(49) Nachts stürzt ein Mann auf die Polizeiwache und berichtet erregt, daß er soeben im Dunkeln an seiner Gartenpforte niedergeschlagen worden sei. Ein Polizist wird beauftragt, am Ort des Überfalls Spuren zu sichern. Kurz darauf kommt er mit einer Riesenbeule am Kopf zurück: „Ich habe den Fall aufgeklärt." „Bravo", sagt sein Chef, „und wie?" „Ich bin auch auf **die Harke** getreten!"
'At night a man plunges into the police station and reports with agitation that he has just been knocked down in the dark at his garden gate. One policeman is instructed to secure the scene of the attack. Shortly after he comes back with a huge bump on his head. 'I have solved the case'. 'Bravo' says the chief 'and how?' 'I stepped on **the rake**, too!'' (Schwarz M. 2000:114).

The use of the definite article in the NP 'the rake' is only understandable if we realize that the object is also the 'perpetrator' of the alleged attack on the complainant.

It should be noted that the inference-based conceptual type is not universally regarded as an instance of indirect anaphora; see Irmer (2011). On the other hand, the typology of indirect anaphors as proposed in Clark (1983) may seem too limited, as observed elsewhere.

> [W]e remain agnostic as to whether Clark's taxonomy of bridging provides an exhaustive list of plausible bridging relations. There may be rich

---

1 Tartt, Donna. 2013. *The Goldfinch*. New York: Little, Brown and Company, Chapter 3, para. xii.

discourse context in which world knowledge permits a plausible bridging relation that lies outside this taxonomy. (Asher and Lascarides 1998:97)

In the context of the present study, we find that the inference-based conceptual type merits closer scrutiny, as far as this is possible in a historical corpus.

Finally, we should also note that one entity can serve as anchor for a number of different indirect anaphors, also within one text. Consider the following examples:

(50) a. Hanna hat Hans *erschossen*. **Der Knall** war bis nach Galdbach zu hören.
'Hanna shot Hans. The report could be heard all the way to Galdbach.'
b. Hanna hat Hans *erschossen*. **Die Wunde** blutet furchtbar.
'Hanna shot Hans. The wound is bleeding awfully.'
c. Hanna hat Hans *erschossen*. **Das Motiv** war Eifersucht.
'Hanna shot Hans. The motive was jealousy.'
d. Hanna hat Hans *erschossen*. **Die Polizei** fand **die Waffe** im Küchenschrank.
'Hanna shot Hans. The police found the weapon in the kitchen cabinet.'
(Schwarz M. 2000:38; she calls the collection of entities and processes activated by the same trigger 'konzeptuell Skopus'.)

Before we continue to discuss other uses of the definite article, we would like to return to some of the first examples of bridging that we quoted in this section, i.e., (18–22). In (22) a possNP was used ('his keys'), in a context in which a defNP would be equally acceptable and correct. It has been observed before that in some uses of the definite article, variation between the article and other items is possible—in direct anaphoric use with a demonstrative,[2] and in indirect anaphoric use with a possessive.

(51) Beside the barn there is *a little cottage*. The/**This** cottage was built in 1875. (but *Its cottage)

---

[2] This is naturally a simplification. To what extent the demonstratives and the definite article may be interchangeable in a certain context is dependent on a number of factors, including the level of the definite article grammaticalization. Furthermore, proximal and distal demonstratives may behave differently—while in many direct anaphoric contexts the distal demonstrative can be used, the proximal is less felicitous. Consider e.g. the so-called donkey anaphora in English. It is possible to use either the definite article or the distal demonstrative here, e.g. *Every farmer who owns a donkey beats **the animal/that animal***, but *Every farmer who owns a donkey beats ***this animal*** (see also Abbott 2002).

(52) Beside the barn there is *a little cottage*. The/**Its** roof is leaking.[3]
(but *This roof)
(Skrzypek 2012:45, after Fraurud 2001:246)

However, not all types of indirect anaphora allow this variation freely. In part–whole relations the necessary and probable parts can possibly be expressed by possNPs (compare with examples 28, 31, *its ceiling, its windows*), but are less acceptable with inducible parts (?*its chandeliers*, example 34). Lexical/thematic types may allow possNPs occasionally (e.g., *his murderer* instead of *the murderer*), but the inferential conceptual types probably never do. Thus, the variation between different NP types can also be taken as an argument in favour of the proposed taxonomy of indirect anaphors, whose complexity mirrors that of indirect anaphora itself.

2.2.1.3 Larger Situation Use

Larger situation use is the next type of definite article use identified in Hawkins (1978). Similarly to indirect anaphora, in this type of context the hearer must also rely on their encyclopaedic knowledge (specific or general) for a successful resolution of the definite, as in (53).

(53) *The Prime Minister* has just resigned. (Hawkins 1978:116)

Larger situation uses are different from direct anaphora, which is an immediate situation use, i.e., the referent is then present, though not necessarily visible, in the situation in which the utterance is made. The referent of the direct anaphor may be present physically or mentally, by having been mentioned previously. In larger situation use, on the other hand, people in the same village can talk about *the church, the pub, the village green*; members of the same nation can talk about *the Queen, the navy, the Prime Minister*; all people can talk about *the sun, the moon, the planets*. These larger situations can be of varying size, but they will all have as their focal, defining point the immediate situation of utterance in which the speech act is taking place (Hawkins 1978:115). In this sense the definite article retains its link with the original demonstrative. Depending on the size of the situation, the definite reference may be made based on specific knowledge (we are in a village we know, we know there is a church in it,

---

3 One reviewer points out that the possessive is a better option, even though the definite article is not incorrect. It seems that for the definite article more context would make it more acceptable, e.g. a sentence 'The cottage is in poor shape' or 'It needs some renovations' before the problem with the roof is presented.

we can talk about the church), or on general knowledge (we do not know the church, but it is part of our knowledge that there usually is one in a village). This context may allow determiners other than the definite article, especially possessives; however, the variation is limited to some sub-types (especially to larger situation uses based on specific rather than general knowledge, e.g., *our Prime Minister, our village pub*) and it may be subject to stylistic considerations.

Larger situation use is entirely dependent on the size of the situation and may be crudely subdivided into local and global larger situation uses, which form a continuum rather than discrete categories. In examples (54–58), we can discern how the utterance situation gradually becomes larger: from a very local one (a room), in which the definite *the sofa* does not preclude that there are other sofas in rooms nearby, to the most global one, comprising the whole world, which has only one sun.

(54) the sofa (in a room)

(55) the kitchen (in a flat)

(56) the church (in a village)

(57) the King (in a kingdom)

(58) the sun (in our solar system)

It is not a coincidence that the different definite article uses have been presented in this order. We may observe how the different types of definite article use overlap: indirect anaphora seems to be located in between direct anaphora and larger situation use, sharing some features with both. On the one hand, it is anchored in the text, just as direct anaphora is; on the other, it relies on some knowledge from outside the text, as larger situation uses do. We may also conclude that some types of direct anaphora resemble indirect anaphora in this respect, i.e., even though the discourse referent is the same, it is presented by means of a new, or more detailed description, e.g., *a book—the magnificent volume* and not by mere repetition as in *a book—the book*. To successfully understand this, the hearer must be able to equate the volume with the book. Also, since indirect anaphors may be anchored in the text by means of other elements than just nominal ones, even genres themselves, one could extend the notion of context to include the (physical) context of the utterance, e.g., a conversation taking place in a courthouse, where the use of the defNP *the judge* would be entirely natural. Let us imagine a person entering the courthouse and being greeted by the phrase *Welcome to the courthouse. The judge will see you shortly*, or by the phrase *Good day. The judge will see you shortly*. If we are rigorous, we would need to classify the two uses as two different types of definite article use: indirect anaphora in the first example (with a definite anchor *the courthouse*) and larger situation use in the second (as there is no anchor in the text, the definiteness is a result of the situation of the utterance, i.e., being in a courthouse).

The model of definite article grammaticalization proposed in the literature stipulates that the incipient definite article will begin with direct anaphoric use and gradually spread through indirect anaphora to larger situation use. Before we discuss the model in detail, we will present the common sources of definite articles and main differences between definite articles and demonstratives.

2.2.2   The Etymology of the Definite Article

The origins of the definite article lie in deictic elements, most typically in demonstrative pronouns. This applies to Germanic languages, such as English (*the*), German (*der*) and Swedish (the clitic *-in*, stemming from demonstrative *hinn* 'yon'), Romance languages (French *le/la*, Italian *il/la*, Spanish *el/la*, Portuguese *o/a* are descendants of Latin *ille* 'that'), and Slavic languages (the Bulgarian clitic article *-ta* from demonstrative *ta* 'this'), but also to non-Indo-European languages such as Bizkaian Basque *a* or Hungarian *az* (Heine and Kuteva 2002:109–110). In his discussion of the sources of the definite article, C. Lyons (1999) demonstrates that in languages where the definite originates in an element different from a demonstrative it can still be regarded as deictic, similar to the verb *behold* in contexts such as *Behold the Walls of Moria*, which can correspond to Latin *ecce* or Slavic *oto* (Lyons C. 1999:331 quotes the definite article in Sissala as originating in a verb of a similar meaning). Heine and Kuteva (2002:110) establish demonstratives as the major source of definite articles.

Even though the deictic origin of the definite article seems nigh on universal, Fraurud (2001) demonstrates how definites can develop out of possessive pronouns, discussing Uralic languages as an example of such a process. It should be noted, as Fraurud herself observes, that the scope of the use of the articles which have arisen out of deictic and possessive elements is not identical. Similar ideas are found in Bechert (1993):

> [...] in this continuum (between the possessive and the emerging definite article-DS), the end seems to be never reached, at the eastern margins of Europe and in Northern Asia, the definite article remains a category in statu nascendi. It might even be the case that this category in Eurasian

languages is a product of our Eurocentric perspective. If we reverse the perspective, we can view the European category of the definite article as a special case of a category of belonging which is denoted indirectly, in Europe, by weakened demonstratives and would be more aptly expressed by possessive suffixes, as it is in Northern Asia and its western outskirts. (Bechert 1993:37 f.)

In the case of the North Germanic languages the source of the definite is deictic and the model of grammaticalization has a demonstrative as its source.[4] We will therefore concentrate on the potential of the demonstrative to grammaticalize into a definite article.

2.2.3 *Demonstratives vs. Articles*

One of the fundamental properties of articles is the necessity of their use. In an article language, such as English, it is only in a limited number of contexts that one may omit the article and use a bare noun instead. There is, however, a certain degree of variation, which allows the speaker to use a different determiner instead, e.g., a possessive or a demonstrative pronoun in place of a definite article, as we have illustrated in discussion of different definite article uses, in particular indirect anaphora. Two examples can be quoted after Fraurud (2001) (with modifications).

(59) We came to a little village. This/*Its/The village was underpopulated. *This/Its/The church was old. *This/*Its/The sun was shining.

There are three types of reference in this brief story: a direct anaphoric reference (*a village—the village*) and an indirect anaphoric reference (*a village—the church*), both textually founded, and a unique reference (*the sun*), whose definiteness is independent of the previous discourse. In each type the definite article can be used, and is perhaps the preferred option. If it is not used it can be exchanged for a demonstrative in direct anaphoric reference or a possessive in indirect anaphoric reference; none of these will work, however, with unique reference. Therefore, there does seem to exist a difference between the demonstrative, in which the definite article originates, and the definite article itself. This difference, however, is not clear-cut, and therefore the stages of

---

4 It should be noted that some scholars have considered an alternative source of the definite article in personal pronoun *han* 'he' (Gjerdman 1924; Perridon 1996). This idea has not won support.

grammaticalization are not discrete. In other words, the development forms a continuum from a purely deictic element to a distinct definite article. The grammaticalizing entity gradually turns into an article; we expect to find that at some point in the course of this process it may exhibit features of both the demonstrative and the article. It is therefore important to define what these features may be in order to classify the form found in the texts as either one or the other, or perhaps as the incipient article.

In many languages demonstratives form a complex group of entities, which among others differ with respect to the distance from the speaker that they encode. While a demonstrative is usually regarded as a linguistic counterpart of a pointing gesture, there may be additional information on the location of the referent pointed at, such as its proximity to the speaker (e.g., English *this*) or its remoteness from the speaker and possibly also the hearer (e.g., English *that*). No such information is conveyed by means of the definite article; therefore, the loss of such a distinction is regarded as one of the first hallmarks of grammaticalization, even though the distinctions may persist for some time (Lyons C. 1999:55).

From the examples quoted above we may further note that the demonstrative is not allowed in a number of contexts in which the definite article is the default option. These include generic reference (not mentioned above, but easily illustrated with sentences such as *The/*This/*That lion is a mammal*) and unique reference (which Hawkins 1978 calls *larger situation use*, in which no textual context is necessary to make the definite form, and the identification of the referent, felicitous), but also indirect anaphora, which we believe to be of crucial importance in the development of definiteness marking.

Finally, it should be noted that there may be differences among demonstratives themselves. In English, for instance, in some contexts the distal *that* is allowed while the proximal *this* is not, e.g., *That/The/*This hominid who discovered fire was a genius* (King 2001). As one reviewer points out, a similar pattern can be found in Icelandic in which the proximal *þæssi* cannot be used, but a non-proximal *sá* can.

2.2.4 *From a Demonstrative to a Definite Article*

The most commonly identified first stage in definite article grammaticalization is the use of the form in direct anaphoric contexts (see in particular Lyons J. 1975, also Diessel 1999). At this stage, the deictic use of the demonstrative is extended to include textual, and not only situational deixis. In many languages that have not developed articles, such use of demonstratives is perfectly normal without its grammaticalizing into the definite article (see also Chapter 5). C. Lyons notes that in anaphoric contexts either proximal or distal demonstratives can be used (if both are available) with no apparent difference in meaning (see also De Mulder and Carlier 2011:526). Thus, the semantic difference between them is blurred, which is the first step in the grammaticalization process.

It has been observed, however, mainly through empirical studies on Romance languages (Epstein 1993 on Old French, Selig 1992, Vincent 1997 and Carlier and De Mulder 2010 on Late Latin, and Faingold 2003 on the evolution from Latin to Spanish, Portuguese and Romanian), that the anaphoric use of demonstratives is originally not neutral, but involves topicalized or focused discourse referents, usually highly individuated, typically human and agentive.

The next, highly debated, stage of definite article grammaticalization is the use of the incipient article in indirect anaphoric contexts. This is the use typical of a definite article, in which no variation with the demonstrative is possible. The definite article's function in this context is to instruct the hearer to retrieve the discourse referent indirectly, i.e., via its anchor (see 2.2). This is the crucial shift in the use of the original demonstrative (or other deictic element) and has so far not been fully accounted for (see also De Mulder and Carlier 2011:527).

The final stage of grammaticalization of the definite article is its appearance in larger situation use, including the most global uses, such as *the sun*. In contrast to the previous two stages, this stage is characterized by the fact that the definite article is used independently of the textual information. There is no antecedent or anchor, nothing to ground the discourse referent in the text; the definite form may be used out of the blue, so to speak.

The development described above can also be formulated in terms of types of context, according to Heine (2002). Heine (also Diewald 2002 and 2006, although in different terms) describes the new contexts acquired by the grammaticalizing form in terms of their connection with the form's original meaning. Heine focuses on the affinity in meaning between consecutive forms as the grammaticalization proceeds. Reflexes of the original semantics are present in the fully grammaticalized form, allowing its use in the original contexts, such as those of a future marker formed from the verbs 'to wish' or 'to want', although in some grammaticalizations this connection may be severed, as with the negation marker in French. Heine argues that there are two meanings available for the form in the stages of grammaticalization which he terms *bridging* and *switch contexts*: as the source and as the target.

– bridging contexts: trigger an inferential mechanism to the effect that, rather than the source meaning, there is another meaning, the target meaning; it is most likely to be inferred but is cancellable (Grice 1967) which means that an interpretation in terms of the source meaning cannot be ruled out; a given linguistic form may be associated with a number of contexts.

- switch contexts: incompatible or in conflict with some salient property of the source meaning; interpretation in terms of the source meaning is ruled out; the target meaning provides the only possible interpretation.
- conventionalization: meanings that need no contextual support, turn into 'normal', 'inherent', 'usual' or 'semantic' meanings. That a target meaning has been conventionalized may be seen when it can be used in new contexts, other than bridging or switch, which may violate the source semantics. (Heine 2002:84–85)

In Table 4 we present a model of grammaticalization of the definite article formulated in terms of Heine's context typology.

It should also be noted that the grammaticalization of the definite article may proceed beyond the final stage identified here, when the definite article turns into a specificity marker, from where it may proceed even further to noun marker and primary exponent of the category gender, as in (60) (as first proposed by Greenberg 1978, note that the stages in Table 4 and (60) do not match as two different models are discussed here).

(60) Stage 0   Stage I   Stage II   Stage III
     demonstrative > definite article >   specific article >   noun marker
     (after Greenberg 1978, see also De Mulder and Carlier 2011:525)

Greenberg (1991) observes that the development is more likely to proceed to stage II and beyond in a language that has no indefinite article (Greenberg 1991, cf. De Mulder and Carlier 2011:525). This observation merits its own study. Here we may note that if there is an indefinite (or an incipient indefinite) article in a language with a definite article, the two forms will be in competition in contexts based on specificity. Conversely, in absence of an indefinite article, the definite may come to be used with specific (not necessarily definite) reference and thus proceed to Greenberg's Stage II of the grammaticalization.

The implicit conclusion of the model is that articles may be lost as well as formed. The model does not predict the definite article turning into morphological zero, but rather illustrates that the expansion beyond Stage I and especially beyond Stage II entails the article acquiring non-definite uses, and thus becoming something other than a definite article (Lyons C. 1999:337). Such development is attested in Voltaic languages Gurma and Gangam and in Eastern Aramaic. Greenberg's model finds support in Schuh (1983), a study of the development of the definite determiners in the Chadic languages. Schuh notes that a form that was once the definite article in some dialects of Bade is now found in contexts in which it can only be interpreted as signalling indefinite-

TABLE 4   Stages and contexts in the grammaticalization of the definite article (after Skrzypek 2012:49)

Stage in grammaticalization	Context	Demonstrative/definite article—function
Stage I	Original context	Deixis
Stage II	Bridging context	Direct anaphora (textual deixis)
Stage III	Bridging context/ Switch context	Indirect anaphora (textual)
Stage IV	Extended switch context	Unique reference (non-textual)
Stage V	Conventionalization	Generics (non-textual)

ness. Greenberg's model presents the development as potentially cyclical (see also van Gelderen 2007).[5]

The model takes a deictic element as its starting point. As noted above, there has been some evidence of possessives grammaticalizing into definite articles, e.g., in Bantu and Oceanic languages (see also Bechert 1993). However, the possessives never seem to reach the full range of definite uses associated with definite articles with deictic sources. The model still leaves a number of questions unanswered, in particular the switch from direct to indirect anaphora and from indirect anaphora to larger situation use. We will consider these questions on the basis of North Germanic data in Chapter 5.

Finally, empirical studies of article languages have revealed that in languages with two definite articles (such as some German dialects or Fering; see 2.4), their scope of use differs in that one definite article is used with direct anaphora and the other with referents in larger situation use, with indirect anaphors represented by either (but not necessarily in free variation). This fact would suggest that in some languages the grammaticalization process may involve more than one item at a time, resulting in a system with two definite articles, while in other languages one grammaticalizing item covers all uses, both

---

5 As one reviewer points out, given the long history of human language it is unlikely that the emergence of (definite) articles is merely a recent development; on the contrary, we may assume that over the course of human (language) history, articles have emerged many times without leaving traces until writing made it possible to document these developments. On the other hand, the interdependencies between articles and literacy merit a separate (diachronic) study.

corresponding to weak and to strong definite article. We will consider this hypothesis in the next section.

2.2.5 The Meaning of Definiteness

The discussion of the gradual spread of the incipient definite article to new contexts can be founded on the concepts of familiarity and uniqueness, which we will briefly present here. It is a part of the discussion of the meaning of definiteness, which dates back at least to Frege's (1892) classic example *The Morning Star is the Evening Star*, has mainly focused on why some discourse referents may be definite, with two major concepts emerging: the discourse referents are definite either because they are familiar or because they are unique. A number of attempts have been made either to subsume all uses of the definite article under one or the other (e.g., Christophersen 1939 opts for familiarity in all definite article uses) or to reconcile the notions by widening the scope of their meaning, as in weak familiarity (Roberts 2003). A common denominator for most theoretical literature on definite descriptions has been an explicit goal of providing a universal analysis of all types of their uses in natural languages. Empirical studies, on the other hand, have provided linguists with new insights into the meaning of definiteness. With the benefit of field studies of languages with more than one definite article, a number of authors have suggested that the two notions cannot be reconciled and that there are instead two types of definiteness: expressed by weak and strong definite articles (roughly corresponding to the original uniqueness and familiarity respectively), in terms proposed in particular by F. Schwarz (2009) and developed in his later publications. Essentially, strong definite articles are based on familiarity and the typical use of a strong definite article is direct anaphora, while weak definite articles are based on uniqueness, and are used with uniquely identifiable referents, e.g., in larger situation uses. The dichotomy is reflected in some languages with two definite articles that are in complementary distribution in certain contexts, e.g., the Fering dialect described in Ebert (1971a) (see examples in 61 below) and a number of German dialects, such as the dialects of the Rhineland (Heinrichs 1954), the Mönchen-Gladbach dialect (Hartmann 1982), the Cologne dialect (Himmelmann 1997) and Bavarian (Scheutz 1988, Schwager 2007). Since some languages have developed two semantically different definite articles, perhaps the notion of a unified account should be abandoned—this is the position taken in a growing body of literature on definiteness.

2.2.5.1 Definite Articles in Fering and German

Fering is one of the first languages with two definite articles for which different patterns of their distribution were observed and analysed. A number of

TABLE 5 The definite article paradigms in Fering (Ebert 1971b:159)

Article form	M.SG	F.SG	N.SG	PL
A-form (weak article)	a	at	at	a
D-form (strong article)	di	det (jü)	det	dön (dö)

German dialects share the same pattern, and Standard German exhibits an interesting variation in the use of the definite article in its full or contracted form (after a preposition). This variation is the cornerstone of the weak–strong definite semantics hypothesis (Schwarz F. 2009), which will be the subject of the following section. Here, we will briefly discuss the article system in Fering and the German variation.

In Table 5 the definite article paradigms in Fering are presented, followed by some examples of their use. Both articles are descendants of demonstratives, *di* is cognate with the North Germanic *den*, English *the* and *a* are most likely cognates of North Germanic *inn* and English *yon* 'that' from Proto-Germanic **jaino-*.

Fering (Ebert 1971b:161)
(61) a. *Ik skal deel tu a / *di kuupmaan.*
    I must down to DEF.WK / DEF.ST grocer
    'I have to go down to the grocer.'

   b. *Oki hee an hingst keeft. *A/Di hingst haaltet*
    Oki has INDF horse bought DEF.WK/DEF.ST horse limps
    'Oki has bought a horse. The horse limps.'

The same distributional restrictions apply to the definite article in German when it is a part of a prepositional object (Hartmann 1980, Schwarz F. 2009). The article is used in its full form in phrases with familiar reference, and in a contracted form in phrases with unique reference.

(62) *Hans ging zum Haus.*
    Hans went to.DEF.WK house
    'Hans went to the house.'

(63) *Hans ging zu dem Haus.*
    Hans went to DEF.ST house
    'Hans went to the house.' (Schwarz F. 2009:7)

Even when both articles can seemingly be used, there is a difference in meaning, or more specifically, in the reason for the definiteness of the NP. Consider the two examples given in Ebert (1971a).

Ebert example 38a
(64) A   hunj hee tuswark.
     DEF.WK dog has toothache
     'The dog has a toothache.'

Ebert example 38b
(65) Di   hunj hee tuswark.
     DEF.ST dog has toothache
     'The dog has a toothache.' (Ebert 1971a:83)

Beide Äußerungen setzen voraus, daß der Hörer bereits weiß, welcher Hund gemeint ist. Die Voraussetzungen sind aber für [(38a)] und [(38b)] verschiedener Art. [(38b)] ist eine adäquate Äußerung, wenn der Hund im vorhergehenden Text speziziert wurde; der D-Artikel weist dann anaphorisch auf den Textreferenten. [(38a)] setzt voraus, daß der gemeinte Hund nicht näher spezifiziert zu werden braucht, weil zur Zeit und am Ort des Sprechaktes nur ein einziger Hund als Referent in Frage kommt.

Both utterances presuppose that the hearer already knows which dog is meant. But the presuppositions (for the two forms) are of a different nature. [(38b)] is an adequate utterance if the dog was specified in the preceding text; the (strong; FS) D-article then refers anaphorically to the text referent. [(38a)] presupposes that the intended dog does not need to be specified any further, because there is only one dog at the time and place of the speech act that could be meant. (Ebert 1971a:83, translation Schwarz F. 2009:38)

This is not to say that the two articles are in complementary distribution. The two articles are interchangeable in some contexts. F. Schwarz (2009) quotes examples of weak definite articles used in direct anaphoric contexts.

(66) *Meyer har sich   ein   Haus   mit Garten gekauft. Im   Haus*
     Meyer has REFL   INDF   house with yard   bought   in.THE.WK   house
     selber halt sich Meyer tagsüber   nur selten auf. Er arbeitet
     itself stays REFL Meyer during.the.day just rarely on   he works

    gerne ***im***   *Garten.*
    happily in.the.WK yard
    'Meyer has bought a house with a yard. He rarely stays in the house in the daytime. He likes to work in the yard.' (Hartmann 1978:78, quoted after Schwarz F. 2009:44)

(67) *Der Gaustadvatnet ist ein   See in Norwegen.* ***Am***   *See liegt*
    DEF Gaustadvatnet is INDF lake in Norway   on.the.WK lake lies
    der Ort   Korsvegen
    DEF town Korsvegen
    'The Gaustadvatnet is a lake in Norway. The town Korsvegen lies on the lake.' (http://de.wikipedia.org/wiki/Gaustadvatnet, quoted after Schwarz F. 2009:44)

The same example retrieved in 2020 shows the referent of *am See* introduced not as a predicative but as a modifier, though this is not likely to have influenced the choice of form.

(68) *Gaustadvatnet* [...] *ist der Name eine-s   See-s   in Norwegen.*
    Gaustadvatnet   is DEF name INDF-GEN lake-GEN in Norway
    Am   *See liegt der Ort   Korsvegen.*
    on.the.WK lake lies DEF town Korsvegen
    'Gaustadvatnet is the name of a lake in Norway. The town Korsvegen lies on the lake.'

Familiarity as a basis of definiteness builds on the insight that the speakers use definite descriptions to refer to discourse referents that are in some way known to the hearer, because they have either been mentioned before or are visible to the hearer (or at least present in the context of the utterance). Uniqueness, on the other hand, stresses that speakers may use definite descriptions that have not been mentioned earlier and are not visible or present in the immediate utterance situation, but can be identified by the hearer because they have a role or property that is unique (at least within some domain). It is of course possible that a referent is both present in the immediate situation and is one of a kind.

    However, uniqueness must have some reference frame. Is the referent unique in the whole universe? On the continent? In the country? In our town? In our apartment? The fact that sentences like *The couch needs to be cleaned* are felicitous despite there being hundreds of thousands of couches demonstrates that either the definite descriptions are incomplete (and the missing content must be supplied by the hearer) or that the uniqueness is not absolute, but the referent may be unique with respect to some domain only. This is consistent with Hawkins' larger situation use in its local version. Similarly, familiarity has also been nuanced, differentiating between strong and weak familiarity (Roberts 2003), with the former consistent with the referent being used anaphorically, and the latter with the referent being familiar by virtue of 'being perpetually accessible to the discourse participants' (after Schwarz F. 2009:3).

2.2.5.2 The Problem of Indirect Anaphora

While it has been relatively easy to map two uses of the definite article—direct anaphora and larger situation use—onto the strong–weak (or familiar–unique) distinction, it is not as easy to do so with indirect anaphoric use. Turning once again to a language with two distinct definite articles, Fering, we note that this use can be represented by either of the articles.

Fering (Ebert 1971a:118, after Schwarz F. 2009:62)
(69) Wi foon   a   sark   uun a   maden faan't taarep. A
     We found DEF church in   DEF middle of.the village   DEF.WK
     törem stän wat   skiaf
     Tower stood a little crooked
     'We found the church in the middle of the village. The tower was a little crooked.'

Fering (after Schwarz F. 2009:62)
(70) Peetji hee uun Hamboreg an   bilj   keeft. Di   mooler hee
     Peter has in Hamburg   INDF painting bought DEF.ST painter has
     ham an   guden pris   maaget.
     him INDF good price   made.
     'Peter bought a painting in Hamburg. The painter made him a good deal.'

This type of definite article use cannot be easily classified as either weak or strong, as its use is in fact based on both familiarity (by virtue of the definite being anchored in previous discourse) and general knowledge. Furthermore, there are a number of ways to anchor a referent and a number of semantic relations between the anchor and the indirect anaphor. On the basis of the Fering data and his own questionnaire, F. Schwarz finds that the type of indirect anaphora which involves part–whole relations is realized by strong definites, while the type which involves semantic relations such as product–producer is realized by weak ones (Schwarz F. 2009).

Finally, a few words on the definite reference and the concept of totality. The motivation (of the speaker) for using definite description is one matter; another is the effect the definite description has on the hearer. A phenomenon that has been widely discussed in the literature, both linguistic and philosophical, is the so-called uniqueness effect. On hearing a definite description, the hearer will automatically assume that there is only one referent of that description, whether known or unknown to the hearer. With plural or mass referents, the hearer will interpret the definite description so that it corresponds to 'all of', giving a sense of completeness, Hawkins' totality, as exemplified in the quote below.

> Consider the following data.
> 3.172 Bring *the wickets* in after the game of cricket.
>
> Would I be satisfied if the hearer brought me only four or five of the six wickets? I would not. *The wickets* refers to all six.
>
> 3.173 I must ask you to move *the sand* from my gateway.
>
> Would I be satisfied if only some were moved? As before, I would not. If my hearer only moved part of the sand away I would be justified in complaining: *I thought I asked you to*. (Hawkins 1978:159)

Observe that the uniqueness-effect with singular count nouns limits the potential discourse referents to one. In this, we find a parallel with the origins of the indefinite article, which are invariably found in numeral 'one'. As we will argue below, the grammaticalization of the indefinite article at its early stages mirrors that of the definite article. Here we may find a clue to the puzzle of universality of sources we named in Chapter 1. The definite article emphasizes the singularity of the discourse referent and the indefinite article, at the early stages of grammaticalization, also states that there is one discourse referent, of which more will be said (see 5.4.1).

2.2.6 *Grammaticalization of the Definite Article and Strong–Weak Definite Article Semantics*

The strong–weak dichotomy has consequences for the diachronic account of definite article grammaticalization. As we have noted above, in languages with two definite articles which are used in different contexts, we may assume that the process of grammaticalization consists of two sub-processes, each concerning one form, which are mutually interdependent and which influence each

TABLE 6   The suggested global cycle of definite articles (Carlier and Simonenko 2016:10)

	Late Latin	Old French	Preclassical French	Modern French
Direct anaphora	ille	li	le	ce
Relative clauses	ille	li	le	le/ce
Relational nouns	o	li	le	le
Mass nouns	o	o	le	le
Abstract nouns	o	o	le	le

other resulting in a system such as for example the Fering one, in which two definite articles are used differently.[6] However, in the languages included in the present study one definite article has emerged, whose use encompasses both those based on familiarity and on uniqueness.[7] Part of the grammaticalization process is, therefore, the shift of the incipient definite article from strong to weak semantics.

In their 2016 work, Carlier and Simonenko test this hypothesis for the Old French definite article, suggesting that while strong definite semantics include the requirement that there be a salient individual in a given situation, the requirement for weak definite semantics is that there be a unique, not necessarily salient, individual in a given situation.

> With a change from strong to weak semantics, the l-forms are expected to expand onto the contexts typically satisfying the uniqueness/maximality presupposition and previously left to the zero article. (Carlier and Simonenko 2016)

The passage from strong to weak definite semantics in the history of the French definite article was shown in the distribution of the forms to be compatible with this hypothesis.

---

6 In the case of North Germanic, Dahl (2004:178) argues that there are in fact two separate grammaticalization processes.

7 It could be claimed that there are in fact two distinct definite articles, at least in the Mainland languages in the sample, Danish and Swedish, *den* and *-en*, with different etymologies and position in the NP. However, their distribution is not dependent on the type of discourse reference as is the case in Fering (see also Chapter 1 for an overview of definite article distribution). Nevertheless, some authors (notably Julien (2005) and Lohrmann (2010)) argue that they do encode different referential properties (e.g. discourse reference vs. specificity).

The authors include an intuitive interpretation of the etymology of the definite typically lying in the distal (and not proximal) demonstrative, as this fact seems to allow the hearer to draw on some additional descriptive content in order to retrieve a referent normally not present in the physical context of the utterance (ibid., compare also De Mulder and Carlier 2011).

2.2.7 *Final Stages of the Grammaticalization of the Definite Article*

As the original demonstrative gradually loses some of its semantic and phonological content and moves towards the definite article, gaining new functions, it appears in more and more contexts that are not accessible to demonstratives proper, such as (some types of) indirect anaphora and larger situation uses. Gradually it forces out potential competitors, such as possessive pronouns and bare nouns, to become the only 'correct' form to be used in these contexts. We argue, alongside many other scholars of grammaticalization, that although the grammaticalization cline is a universal model, i.e., the development in unrelated languages proceeds through the same or at least similar stages, different languages may develop definite articles to varying degrees. In other words, the grammaticalization may halt at any point. Therefore, there are languages with definite articles that are, for instance, only used with direct anaphoric reference. It is also common for a language to have a definite article that is not used with generic reference.

Generics are notoriously difficult to describe in terms of form. Many article languages allow great formal variation in this type of reference; in North Germanic five different forms may be used: bare noun singular, definite singular, definite plural, indefinite singular, bare plural. Although all five forms are allowed (except in Icelandic, which does not have an indefinite article), they are not fully interchangeable; at times one or two forms are preferred over the other three or four. The factors behind the choice of one form rather than another are understudied, although it seems that both animacy and countability of the referent play an important role (see also Pettersson 1976, Carlsson 2012 for Swedish, Kurek-Przybilski 2020 for Norwegian, Skrzypek and Kurek 2018, Skrzypek, Kurek-Przybilski and Piotrowska 2020 for a comparison between the Continental North Germanic languages). We may therefore conclude that the grammaticalization of both the definite and the indefinite articles has not reached the stage in which one or the other is considered to be a generic marker, which is a relatively common property of articles in all of the Germanic languages.

2.3 The Rise of the Indefinite Article

In 2.2.5 (The meaning of definiteness) we have noted that the variety of uses of the definite article has led to numerous efforts to explain the seeming disparity in the meaning of definiteness. We have also chosen to follow F. Schwarz in his strong–weak dichotomy. The meaning of indefiniteness does not seem to have generated similar debates. However, it has been recognized that the indefinite article can be used in two types of contexts: specific and non-specific.[8]

2.3.1 *Types of Indefinite Article Use*

Specificity is the traditional heading under which specific and non-specific uses of the indefinite article are discussed. The difference between them can be illustrated by the following examples:

(71) I bought **a car** this morning.

(72) Pass me **a book**.

Neither of the referents is identifiable to the hearer, but in the first example the speaker is familiar with it, the referent is specific, while in the second, neither the hearer nor the speaker is familiar with the referent of the indefinite NP *a book* (Lyons C. 1999:165). This double nature of the indefinite article is also known as referential opacity (Quine 1940, 1953). In its specific uses, the indefinite article is referentially transparent; in others it is referentially opaque and requires more context to be interpreted as either specific (74a) or non-specific (74b).

(73) John married **a rich woman**.

(74) John wanted to marry **a rich woman**,
 a. ... but *she* refused him.
 b. ... but he couldn't find *any*. (Quine 1953, quoted after Skrzypek 2012:51)

---

8 One reviewer points out that the uses of the indefinite article could be divided into more subtypes. Haspelmath (1997) distinguishes three types, i.e. non-specific (*She wanted something to eat*), specific unknown (*She got something to eat (I don't know what it was.)*) and specific known (*She got something for her birthday. (Can you guess what it was?)*). These subtypes may have separate morphological representations. In the present study we limit the classification to specific vs. non-specific uses of the indefinite article.

The opacity is created by a logical operator, such as negation. A number of other contexts render the indefinite opaque, such as conditionals, verbs of volition and propositional attitude, questions, modals and future tense.

2.3.2 *From a Numeral 'One' to an Indefinite Article*

A model of indefinite article grammaticalization was proposed by Givón (1981). We begin with a more detailed model proposed by Heine (1997).

The first stage of the grammaticalization of the indefinite article is the so-called presentative use of the incipient indefinite article. In this use the numeral 'one' serves as a presentation marker for a new discourse referent, which is salient in the discourse. In discussions of indefinite article grammaticalization this use is often likened to the use of the proximal demonstrative 'this' in English, studied in Prince (1981a, 1981b).

(75) **This man** came and wanted to speak to the manager.

What is characteristic for this use is that it raises the hearer's expectations with regard to the new discourse referent, and the hearer is expecting to hear more about it, since it has been marked as salient. This use of the incipient indefinite article is limited to introducing most important discourse referents, to which further reference will be made. As the first article-like use of the demonstrative was anaphoric, this first article-like use of the numeral is in a sense cataphoric.

It should be noted that at this stage there may be a number of competing forms, i.e., other presentative markers in use in the language, such as indefinite pronouns like 'some', 'any' or adjectives like 'certain', but invariably it is the numeral that grammaticalizes into the indefinite article (see, e.g., an interesting study of Old Tuscan by Stark 2002, who studied the competing forms at the onset of article grammaticalization).

In spoken discourse any ambiguity in interpretation between the numeral and the presentative and specific markers is often resolved by the presence or absence of stress. In diachronic studies no such disambiguation is possible; however, other tests are available. Previous studies of indefinite article grammaticalization in Swedish reveal that, at the onset of the grammaticalization, the original numeral 'one' is used with new discourse referents which are picked up by at least one anaphoric expression (Skrzypek 2012, 2013). There is a tendency to place them clause-initially (stylistically indefinites are not preferred in initial position in modern Swedish); they are also predominantly subjects. However, this may be a language-specific idiosyncrasy.

The second stage of indefinite article grammaticalization is the use of the incipient article with all new discourse referents, irrespective of their salience.

In this use we find also backgrounded referents introduced as indefNPs, referents which are mentioned only once in the text and to which no anaphoric reference is made. The presentative marker is in fact a subtype of the specific marker, as it is also used to introduce new referents into the discourse. However, any competing forms appear only at the presentative stage. Hopper and Martin (1987), in a study of the rise of the indefinite article in Old English, note that there is some variation in this context between the numeral *an* and *sum* and that the variation seems to be quite systematic: while *sum* introduces new and salient referents with numerous subsequent mentions and is located at the beginning of the text, *an* introduces less salient referents with fewer subsequent mentions and can appear anywhere in the text, not just at the beginning. Both uses fall under the category of the specific use of the indefinite article. The development beyond this stage involves the use of the incipient indefinite article also in non-specific contexts, such as in questions and conditionals and under the scope of negation, verbs of volition and verbs of propositional attitude.

The final stage of indefinite article grammaticalization is the use of the original numeral 'one' in generic NPs.

(76) Model of grammaticalization of the indefinite article according to Heine (1997:72–73)
 Stage I: the numeral 'one'
 Stage II: presentative marker
 Stage III: specific marker
 Stage IV: nonspecific marker
 Stage V: generalized article

As with the definite article, we place the consecutive stages of grammaticalization in Heine's typology of context (Heine 2002); see Table 7.

The final stage of indefinite article grammaticalization, the generalized article, is in fact identical with the final stage of the definite article grammaticalization, i.e., the article can be used generically.

2.4 Previous Studies on the Grammaticalization of the Definite Article in North Germanic

The rise of articles in North Germanic, in particular that of the definite article, has been the subject of a number of studies using different theoretical approaches. It is not realistic to do all of them justice; nevertheless, in

TABLE 7 Stages and contexts in the grammaticalization of the indefinite article (after Skrzypek 2012:53)

Stage in grammaticalization	Context	Numeral 'one'/indefinite article
Stage I	Original context	Numeral
Stage II	Bridging context	Presentation marker
Stage III	Bridging context/ Switch context	Marker of specific reference
Stage IV	Extended switch context	Marker of non-specific reference
Stage V	Conventionalization	Generalized article

this section we present a brief overview of selected publications that have either influenced a number of scholars or have a direct bearing on the present study.

2.4.1 *General Studies*

The subject of the evolution of the definite article in North Germanic has attracted much attention. The structure of the defNP in modern North Germanic languages mirrors three layers of linguistic innovation: the grammaticalization of the weak adjectival declension (the origins of which most likely are to be found in a coalescence of the adjective with an original demonstrative particle, e.g., Heinrichs 1954:67), the grammaticalization of the postposed, suffixed definite article, and the grammaticalization of the preposed definite article. The origins of each process are found in the extended use of demonstratives.

The formation of the weak adjectival declension belongs to the Proto-Germanic period (Prokosch 1939, Ringe 2006) and is common to all Germanic languages, as well as some Baltic and Slavic ones. It has been studied mainly in the Indo-European context, with the weak form of the adjective seen as the first tool of definiteness marking.

> Diese 'schwachen' n-Bildungen haben ursprünglich individualisierenden Charakter, wie etwa griech. στράβων, ‚Schieler' (eigentl. ‚der schielende') neben στραβός ‚schielend'; sie werden daher—im Gegensatz zum starken Adj.—mit dem bestimmten Artikel verbunden, wie noch heute der gute Mann im Gegensatz zu (ein) guter Mann usw. (Krahe 1948:81)

> 'These 'weak' n-formations have originally an individualizing character, as in Greek στράβων, 'squinter' (actually 'the squinting') next to στράβός 'cross-eyed'; they are therefore—in contrast to the strong adjectives—connected to the definite article, as in today's contrast between *der gute Mann* 'the good-WK man' and (*ein*) *guter Mann* '(a) good-ST man'.'

The idea that the weak adjectival declension could have an individualizing function goes back at least to Osthoff (1876).

In modern North Germanic the weak form of the adjective is used if the NP is definite, and the strong when it is indefinite. In the period studied it was possible to use the strong form in in definite contexts, as illustrated below.

(77) *hans siuk-t ben*
 his sick-ST leg

(78) *hans siuk-a ben*
 his sick-WK leg
 'his sick leg' (Delsing 1994)

Such productive use of the strong form of the adjective ascribes new characteristics to familiar referents, while the use of the weak form is understood to denote a known characteristic of the familiar referent (Skrzypek 2012:60–61). Although no longer grammatically correct in the Continental languages,[9] this use is still found in Modern Icelandic (Naert 1969, Sigurðsson 2006, Thráinsson 2007), where the following NP patterns are possible.

(79) *góð-ur maður*
 good-ST man

(80) *góð-i maður*
 good-WK man

(81) *góð-i maður-inn*
 good-WK man-DEF

---

9 With the exception of the adjective *egen* 'own', which appears in the strong form after possessives, e.g. *mitt ege-t/*egn-a hus* 'my own-STR/*own-WK house', but in weak form in defNPs, e.g. *det egn-a hus-et* 'the own-WK house-DEF' (see Lohrmann 2010 for further discussion).

(82) *góð-ur   maður-inn*
good-ST man-DEF
(based on Naert 1969)

The combination of the strong form of the adjective and the definite article implies an attributive reading of the adjective, while the weak form has a contrastive function.

(83) *Ég horfði upp í   **blá-an** himin-inn.*
I   looked up into blue-ST sky-DEF
'I looked at the sky that was blue.'

(84) *Ég horfði á **blá-a**   bíl-inn.*
I   looked at blue-WK car-DEF
'I looked at the blue car [and not the red].' (after Thráinsson 2007:3)

Skrzypek (2012) quotes a similar use from *Yngre Västgötalagen*, a Swedish legal text from ca. 1280.

(85) *Konæ   firigiær manni fællir   hana **luct***
woman kills   man   charge her   closed.NOM.F.ST
hæræznæmpð-in.
jury-DEF
'If a woman kills a man, she shall be charged by a closed jury.' (YVL FB:12; Skrzypek 2012:60)

In this example the intended meaning seems to be descriptive, i.e., 'a jury that is closed' and not contrastive 'the jury that is a closed one, out of a number of juries, some open'. Such variation in historical texts is studied in Delsing (1994), mainly in connection with possessives, as in (77–78). Naert (1969) is a study of Modern Icelandic.

While the formation of the weak adjectival paradigm belongs to the Proto-Germanic period, the grammaticalization of the postposed, cliticized definite article takes place in the common history of North Germanic (see Table 10 for an overview of proposed dates). As previously stated, the rise of the postposed, suffixed definite article has attracted by far the most attention. The older research, originating with Grimm (1898), focuses mainly on the unusual form of the article as compared to the West Germanic and Romance languages (apart from Romanian), and the main aim of these publications was to account for the processes that led to the definite article taking this particular form. More recent research, in particular Dahl (2004), Skafte Jensen (2006) and Skrzypek (2012), focuses more on the functional evolution of the original distal demonstrative, which is the source of the definite article in North Germanic.

Being an instance of grammaticalization, the rise of the definite article consists of two major ingredients: the formal development, in the course of which the original free lexeme loses its independence and is gradually cliticized to the preceding noun in its inflected form, and the functional development, which consists of a number of stages, in which the form begins to be used in new contexts. The two developments are not entirely simultaneous. Based on the textual evidence we may claim that the formal cliticization had begun before the oldest extant texts were written (excluding the Runic inscriptions, the majority of which are lapidary, although those that are longer and can be dated, such as the Rök inscription from ca. 800, exhibit no signs of either the definite article or the cliticization of the demonstrative). In the oldest Icelandic texts, we find examples of clitics, as we do in the oldest Danish and Swedish texts (which are about a century younger). However, the distribution of the form is not regular and is difficult to map. The functional development can be studied to a large extent in the available textual material. Thus, the grammaticalization of the definite article straddles the pre-textual and textual epochs in the history of the North Germanic languages.

Etymologically, the definite article originates in a distal demonstrative pronoun, which in the western sources (Icelandic and Norwegian) may appear as either *inn* (or *enn*) or *hinn*, and in the eastern ones (Danish and Swedish) as *hin* only.

When cliticized (to an inflected form of the noun) it invariably appears as *-in* and retains its own inflection for case, number and gender, which we illustrate in Table 9 with Swedish examples.

The formal development from a free lexeme to an enclitic and later to a suffix (for a debate on the status of -IN in modern North Germanic languages see Faarlund 2007, Stark et al. 2007, Börjars and Harries 2008) required the postposition of the demonstrative pronoun with respect to the noun. Two hypotheses have been put forward concerning the exact circumstances. The first, proposed by Grimm in 1898 and later developed by Delbrück in 1916, assumes that the demonstrative was part of the adjective phrase, and that its original role was to mark the adjective, not the noun, as definite. The other hypothesis, found in Nygaard (1905) and later developed by Pollack (1912), assumes the postposition of the demonstrative itself, without the adjective, possibly to mark a different reading from that of the preposed demonstrative (see also Polish examples of anaphora, 147–148 in section 5.3.1). Both hypotheses are illustrated in (86).

TABLE 8   The inflectional paradigm of (h)inn

		M	F	N
SG	NOM	hinn	hin	hit
	GEN	hins	hinnar	hins
	DAT	hinum	hinni	hinu
	ACC	hinn	hina	hit
PL	NOM	hinir	hinar	hin
	GEN	hinna	hinna	hinna
	DAT	hinum	hinum	hinum
	ACC	hina	hinar	hin

TABLE 9   Definite nouns in Old Swedish (adapted from Skrzypek 2012:67)

		M 'day'	F 'journey'	N 'ship'
SG	NOM	daghr-in	færþ-in	skip-it
	GEN	daghs-ins	færþ-inna(r)	skips-ins
	DAT	daghi-num	færþ-inne	skipi-nu
	ACC	dagh-in	færþ-ena	skip-it
PL	NOM	dagha-ni(r)	færþe-na(r)	skip-in
	GEN	dagha-nna	færþa-nna	skipa-nna
	DAT	daghum-in	færþom-in	skipum-in
	ACC	dagha-na	færþe-na(r)	skip-in

(86) a. N (*h*)*inn* Adj   →   N-*inn* Adj   (Grimm 1898, Delbrück 1916)
     b. N (*h*)*inn*   →   N-*inn*   (Nygaard 1905, Pollack 1912)

The two reconstructions paint a different picture: the second assumes postposition of the demonstrative, most likely motivated stylistically or serving to place more emphasis on the discourse referent, while the first assumes a connection between the demonstrative and the adjective, and the postposition as a by-product of the natural and grammatically correct postposition of the adjectival phrase.

Neither of the hypotheses is particularly well-documented, largely because the process predates the oldest extant sources. There is evidence of tendencies to postpose and cliticize grammatical material, visible, for instance, in the form of the morphological s-passive. Delbrück's model example, *maðr inn gamli* 'man that old-WK', finds support in a textual study by Musinowicz (1911), which is a cornerstone of the hypothesis. Critics, Pollack (1912) and Møller (1945) in particular, observe that the textual evidence consists largely of postposed epithets with proper names (e.g., **þiaurikʀ hin þurmuþi** 'Þjóðríkr—Theodoric the great, the valiant' in the Rök inscription, although new interpretations suggest that it may be an appellative after all, i.e., **rikʀ hin þurmuþi** 'man-NOM the valiant'; see Ralph 2007 and Holmberg 2015). This in itself does not exclude the possibility of cliticization, as demonstrated by the spelling of a name with epithet as *Erik-i-n-um hælghæ* 'Erik-DAT-DEF-DAT holy-WK' (Kock 1919:98–99, also quoted in Börjars and Harries 2008:297). On the other hand, data supporting the Nygaard–Pollack reconstruction are equally scarce, with one often-quoted example from the Strøm runic inscription, dated at ca. 600.

(87) *wate hali   hino horna*
     wet stone DET horn
     'Let the horn wet this stone!' (N KJ50)

Although the postposition of the demonstrative is by no means rare, there are few examples with the demonstrative hinn, the majority involving other demonstratives, sá 'this' or sjá 'this here', as in (88).

(88) *stein saR*
     stone DEM
     'stone this' (U 10)11

(89) *þoriR ok   hroða let-u ræisa stæin þennsa*
     þoriR and Hroða let-PL raise stone DEM
     'Thore and Hroda had this stone raised.' (U 429)

Although most researchers are in agreement as to the etymology of the definite article (one exception being Gjerdman 1924; see also Perridon 1989)—albeit with some differences with respect to the actual context (postposed demonstrative or postposed adjectival phrase)—the proposed timeframes of the cliticization of the postposed demonstrative are widely divergent. In Table 10 we present a concise overview of the proposed dates.

The earliest instances of the postposed, cliticized article come from Runic inscriptions from the 11th century, i.e., **mirk-it mikla** 'landmark-DEF great' (Sö 41) and **ant-ini** 'spirit-DEF' (U 669).

TABLE 10 Proposed dating of the cliticization of *hinn* in North Germanic (adapted from Skrzypek 2012:74)

Proposed dating	Author
Ancient Norse/Old Norse	Delbrück (1916), Neckel (1924)
500–1100	Syrett (2002)
Old Norse	Gjerdman (1924), Larm (1936), Barnes (2008) (cf. Börjars and Harries 2008:295 f.)
The Viking Age	Boor (and von Friesen) (1928)
(just before the legal texts were written)	Seip (1958)
1000–1150	Braunmüller (1982)
With the first written texts	Hansen (1927)
Ca. 1200	Delsing (2002)

As we have mentioned before, of the three processes leading to the formation of the defNP in North Germanic, it is the rise of the suffixed article that has been very much the focus of research, from Grimm (1898), Hodler (1954) to Stroh-Wollin (2016), with the older studies focusing on reconstructing the process of cliticization and the recent ones on its functional development.

The rise of the preposed definite article, on the other hand, which seems to be the most recent development, has mainly been considered in terms of the structure of the defNP, in particular in terms of what is called double definiteness: the co-occurrence of both pre- and postposed definite articles within one defNP; see the next section for a short discussion of this development (see also Hirvonen 1987, 1997). In recent years there have been a number of publications concerning the preposed article as an adjectival article, in particular Pfaff (2019), bringing this development into focus.

With respect to the Old Icelandic data, it has been proposed that the occasional variation between the preposed demonstrative *sá* and the cliticized *-inn* was free, that is, either form could be used to achieve the same effect (Nygaard 1905:31, Delbrück 1916; see also Møller 1945).

> Oft hat man den Eindruck, als könnte statt *inn* auch *sá* stehen und umgekehrt: Ld. 125.9 könnte statt *þingit* wohl auch *þingit þat* gebraucht sein, 124.10 statt *þinginu* auch *þeim þingi*, und andererseits Eb. 85.5 statt *til þeirar ferðar* auch *til ferðarinnar*. (Delbrück 1916:72)

'Often one has the impression that *inn* could be used instead of *sá* and vice versa: Ld. 125.9 could have used instead of *þingit* likewise *þingit þat*, 124.10 instead of *þinginu* even *þeim þingi*, and in other places Eb. 85.5 instead of *til þeirar ferðar* even *til ferðarinnar*.'

This belief is grounded in the fact that for those researchers the category of definiteness and its expressions in Old and Modern Icelandic constituted two completely different systems (see also Skafte Jensen 2007b for a theoretically motivated account similarly demarcating the Old and Modern Danish systems with respect to the function of the NP).

We have so far described the rise of the definite article as if it were common to the whole of Scandinavia. There is one area, however, where the preposed definite article is the only one that has grammaticalized, and the postposed definite is not to be found. It has long been noted that the Danish dialects of western Jutland have the preposed definite article only, similarly to the West Germanic languages, but in contrast to the North Germanic ones (Møller 1974).

Standard Danish
(90) hus-et
     house-DEF
     'the house'

West Jutland
(91) æ   hus
     DEF house
     'the house'

This peculiarity was attributed in older research to Low German influence, a notion that has been (quite convincingly) refuted in Møller (1945, 1974) and Perridon (1996, 2009). Perridon argues that the grammaticalization of definiteness in North Germanic began long before language contact with Middle Low German started to play a significant role in Scandinavia. The distinct pattern of the Jutlandic dialects is probably due to word order differences, i.e., preposition vs. postposition of attributes and demonstratives. It seems that the original postposition was the default order in Scandinavia long enough for the definite article to grammaticalize as a suffix, with the exception of Jutland where the order underwent a major change, resulting in the preposition of the attributes and determiners, before the grammaticalization process began. Møller (1945) gives an alternative account, also with respect to the etymology of the preposed article.

TABLE 11   The inflectional paradigm of *sá* in Old Norse

		M	F	N
SG	NOM	sá*	sú*	þat
	GEN	þess	þeir(r)ar	þess
	DAT	þeim	þeir(r)i	því
	ACC	þann	þá	þat
PL	NOM	þeir	þær	þau
	GEN	þeir(r)a	þeir(r)a	þeir(r)a
	DAT	þeim	þeim	þeim
	ACC	þá	þær	þau

* later replaced by the ACC forms *þæn, þa*

It has been widely accepted that the source of *æ* is the demonstrative *þæn* (the continuation of the nominative *sá*) (Hansen 1927).

This reconstruction implicitly makes the development of *sá* parallel with the grammaticalization of the same demonstrative as the preposed definite article, e.g., *den gamle man* and *den gamle mannen* 'the old man' in Standard Danish and Swedish respectively. In this reconstruction there would have been no cliticization of *hinn*, or it would have been so limited as not to become successfully established. Hansen (1927) quotes a number of examples with the cliticized *hinn*, all in the genitive case, from legal prose, e.g., *by-s-in-s logh* village-GEN-DEF-GEN law, 'the law of the village'. Møller (1945) refutes these examples, and is instead of the opinion that the origins of the preposed definite article in western Jutlandic dialects lie in the same demonstrative that gave rise to the cliticized definite in other parts of the country (and elsewhere in Scandinavian), i.e., *hinn*, or more accurately, one of its competitive forms, *inn* (Møller 1945:77–81). Even if the textual documentation is not conclusive for either reconstruction, Møller raises an important objection to the etymology of *æ* in *þæn*, namely the improbability of the phonological reduction of the initial *þ*.[10] If the source of the preposed definite is instead the demonstrative *inn*, its present form is quite easily understood. In this reconstruction he is not alone; similar ideas are presented in Boor (1928), Schütte (1922), and very explicitly in Thorsen (1901). For more recent accounts see also Perridon (1996) and Stroh-Wollin (2018).

---

10   As one reviewer points out this is not entirely impossible. Subordinator *at(t)/að* 'that' is most likely descendant of **þat*.

2.4.1.1 The Development of Double Definiteness in North Germanic

As mentioned in section 1.2, modern Swedish, Norwegian and Faroese exhibit double definiteness in NPs modified by adjectives or other prenominal modifiers. If the head noun is preceded by a modifier, the latter must be preceded by a preposed definite article, while the head noun itself is marked by a suffixed definite article, as in (92). In Danish the two definite articles are in complementary distribution, and only the preposed article is present in NPs modified by adjectives, as in (93); see also Table 1 in section 1.2. For a detailed analysis of differences between double definiteness in Swedish and Norwegian and the non-double structure in Danish from the generative point of view see Julien (2005). Icelandic exhibits a different pattern altogether, namely just the suffixed article appears on the head noun and usually no preposed article is used (see also examples in 1 in section 1.2.1.1).

Swedish/Norwegian
(92) den gaml-e mann-en
 DEF old-WK man-DEF
 'the old man'

Danish
(93) den gaml-e mand
 DEF old-WK man
 'the old man'

As demonstrated above, the origin of the suffixed definite article in North Germanic languages is to be sought in the distal demonstrative *hinn* (see Tables 8 and 9). The preposed definite article, on the other hand, has its origins in the demonstrative *sá* 'that' (see Table 11 above). While the suffixed definite article was cliticized to the head noun around the year 1000 (Stroh-Wollin 2015:102; see also Table 10 on various proposed dating), the preposed definite article is a later development that began establishing itself around the year 1400 (Stroh-Wollin 2015:134). The development of double definiteness has been discussed most notably by Larm (1936), Lundeby (1965), Hirvonen (1997), and more recently by Faarlund (2009), Stroh-Wollin (2015) and Pfaff (2019). Interestingly, the Swedish and the Norwegian way to double definiteness exhibit different patterns.

Firstly, as regards the Old West Nordic variety, as Faarlund (2009) and Stroh-Wollin (2015) demonstrate, the two demonstratives (*hinn* and *sá*) could co-occur in Old Icelandic and Old Norwegian, as in the following examples.

Old Icelandic (Heimskringla, ca. 1300)
(94) þau   in   stóru   skip
     those DEF large.WK   ship.PL
     '(those) the large ships' (Faarlund 2009:13)

Old Norwegian (Sankt Olavs järtecken i Norska homilieboken, ca. 1200)
(95) sá   hinn   helgi   maðr
     that DEF   holy.WK   man
     '(that) the holy man' (Stroh-Wollin 2015:117)

The possibility for the demonstrative and the definite article (*hinn*) to co-occur is attributed to the differences in their referential properties and semantic functions: while the incipient definite article renders the DP definite and specific, the demonstrative provides deictic properties and uniqueness interpretation of the DP (Faarlund 2009:14; Stroh-Wollin 2015:117). Preposed *hinn* is also tightly bound to the adjective. See example (96) where *hinn* appears before every adjective, while *sá* appears only once per phrase, *hinn* is thus often analysed as an adjectival article (Stroh-Wollin 2015; see especially Pfaff 2019 for a detailed account of the development of adjectival article in Icelandic).

Old Icelandic (Brennu Njáls saga, ca. 1350)
(96) skaða   þann   hinn   mikla   og   hinn   illa
     damage that (*sá*) DEF   extensive   and DEF   bad
     'that extensive and bad damage' (Pfaff 2019:27)

Further, as the demonstrative *sá* grammaticalizes into a definite article in Old Norwegian, the adjectival *hinn* becomes redundant, as the model in Table 12 illustrates with an example of the NP 'the holy man'. Since the structure with the preposed article but no suffixed article (of type *den gamle man* 'DEF old.WK man') was frequent in Old Norwegian (Lundeby 1965, Stroh-Wollin 2015), it is assumed that this structure in combination with the definite-marked noun (*mann-en* 'man-DEF') gave rise to double definiteness in Norwegian.

As regards Old Swedish, the preposed *hinn* is very early replaced by *þænn* (originally *sá*), and *hinn* does not occur in Old Swedish texts with the same frequency as it does in Old Norwegian and Old Icelandic. Stroh-Wollin (2015:133) demonstrates that in Old Swedish texts *þænn* could have two functions: either as an element equivalent to Norwegian and Icelandic pre-adjectival *hinn* (referred to as *þænn*$_1$ by Stroh-Wollin), or as a definite article equivalent to the Old Norwegian *sá* (*þænn*$_2$). Since *þænn* in Old Swedish is very early on combined with the definite-marked form of the noun, it is assumed to be an adjecti-

TABLE 12 Double definiteness development in Norwegian after Stroh-Wollin (2015:132)

Determiner	Adjective	Head noun
	hinn helgi	*maðr*
sá	*hinn helgi*	*maðr*
sá	*helgi*	*maðr*
den	*heilage*	*mannen*

TABLE 13 Double definiteness development in Swedish after Stroh-Wollin (2015:133)

Determiner	Adjective	Head noun
	þænn$_1$ gamli	*mannin*
	(þænn$_1$) gamli	*mannin*
þænn$_2$	*gamli*	*mannin*
den	*gamle*	*mannen*

val article (like *hinn*) rather than fully developed definite article. Because of this the adjectival *þænn$_1$* becomes optional at a later stage, until *þænn$_2$* becomes grammaticalized as a determiner and a fully productive preposed definite article (either through reanalysis of adjectival *þænn* or through broader usage of the demonstrative *þænn*); see the model in Table 13 with an example of the NP 'the old man'.

Thus, in Norwegian double definiteness was reached through a construction with just the preposed article and no suffixed article, namely *den gamle man > den gamle mannen*. In Swedish, on the other hand, double definiteness was reached through the structure with the suffixed definite article, namely *gamle mannen > den gamle mannen*. For a detailed diachronic study and a discussion of earlier approaches to this development see Stroh-Wollin (2015).

2.4.2 Definite Article in Old Norse and Icelandic: Johnsen (1975), Faarlund (2009), van Gelderen (2007)

Although the majority of studies of the rise of the definite article take into consideration the Old Norse data, there are a number of larger studies dedicated solely to the Old Norse and Icelandic material (Sprenger 1977), and a number of studies which focus on the eastern branch. The study by Johnsen (1975) is unusual in that she combines four types of source material: the mythological and heroic Eddaic lays, the sagas, and Runic inscriptions. The last of these is not often found in Old Norse studies; strictly speaking the inscriptions represent both eastern and western vernaculars, as the author did not restrict the corpus to Norwegian Runic inscriptions, which might have ensured more continuity with the Icelandic texts.

The review of Icelandic sources begins with Hárbarðsljóð 'Lay of Hárbarðr', an Eddic poem which is considered to be written in a colloquial style, most likely to represent the spoken variant of contemporary Icelandic (Johnsen 1975:60). From this passage Johnsen excerpted 26 definite forms with suffixed -*inn*, of which the majority are concrete, inanimate nouns that are prepositional objects (Johnsen 1975:61). Interestingly, Johnsen also analyses independent uses of *hinn* (her terminology), i.e., those without any noun, as in (97).

(97) **Hins** vil   ec nú   spyria, hvat þú heitir.
     This want I   now ask,   what you are.called
     'Now I want to ask this: what is your name.' (Johnsen 1975:62)

This use is hardly consistent with distal deixis ('that'), but rather signifies proximal deixis ('this'). This observation is of importance when considering the likely source of the definite article, which would be the distal rather than the proximal demonstrative. As regards the free form *inn*, which is also found in the text, it occurs only with adjectives, either as part of full NPs (98) or as nominalizations (99).

(98) Ec drap Þiaz-a,   **inn** þrúðmóðg-a iǫtun.
     I   killed Þiazi-ACC DEF heroic-WK   giant.ACC
     'I killed Þiazi, the heroic giant.'

(99) **ina**   línhvít-o
     DEF   linen.white-WK
     'the (one) white as linen' (Johnsen 1975:66)

Furthermore, Johnsen observes that in the *Þrymskviða* 'Þrym's poem' from Poetic Edda there appear to be no uses of the definite suffix and no postposed instances of *hinn* or *inn*. Instead, the examples found there are always pre-adjectival and used when the adjective modifier is separated from the noun it modifies, as in (100), while when it is adherent to the noun, the demonstrative *inn* is not used, as in (101).

(100) **in** arm-a   iǫtn-a   systir
       DEF   poor-WK giant-PL.GEN sister
       'the poor sister of giants'

(101) hring-a   rauð-a
       ring-PL.ACC red-WK
       'red rings' (Johnsen 1975:69)

The separation between the adjective and the noun may come in the form of an intervening element, but it can also be deduced from the metric conditions— the phrases are separated into parts by the caesurae which separate a long line into the traditional two half-lines of the *fornyrðislag*-metre. This function of *inn* is reminiscent of the linking article as proposed in Himmelmann (1997).

The conclusions presented in Johnsen's study are that the incipient definite article plays a role in emphasis, which is illustrated among other things by its higher frequency in depictions of dramatic incidents and with the historical present tense.

> The evidence reveals a form which, while relatively empty of content, began to be used for narrative stylistic purposes with substantives, and which persisted over a long period of time, in spite of first partially and then, beyond the scope of this paper, totally losing its independence of form and its strength of function. (Johnsen 1975:132–133)

Interestingly enough, Johnsen is also one of the few scholars who draw attention to the developments of *einn* 'one'. She mentions specifically the potential confusion that may arise from the formal similarities between *inn* (or its weakened variant *enn*) and the numeral *einn*, but also from a certain functional overlap between the two, namely the fact that both could appear in postposition with respect to a noun to make it more real or draw attention to it, and—a fact rarely noted—both *inn* and *einn* occur predominantly in the singular (Johnsen 1975:131).

Faarlund (2009) is concerned with the changes which the postposed article underwent in Norwegian, based on textual material gathered from Old Norse, as it was written (and presumably spoken) in Norway and Iceland in the 12th and 13th centuries, and from the *nynorsk* variety of Modern Norwegian. The focus of the text is the status of the definite article—which as Faarlund argues, is a clitic in Old Norse and an affix in Modern Norwegian—the process in which this change has taken place and its consequences for the Norwegian NP. The arguments in favour of the proposed classification include existence of free counterparts of clitics (*hinn* is no longer found in nynorsk), the ability of affixes to affect the host (argued on the basis of the plural definites in nynorsk), existence of arbitrary gaps (the definite article in nynorsk does not attach to nouns with final -*en*) and lack of inflection of affixes (Faarlund argues that the definite in nynorsk constitutes the noun's inflection, while in Old Norse it receives an inflectional ending of its own).

Much of the argumentation is founded on the observation that in Old Norse it is possible to combine demonstratives and incipient definite article, e.g., *þau in stóru skip* 'those the large ships' (Faarlund 2009:13), which is impossible in nynorsk, e.g., **dei dəi store skipa* 'those the large ships' (Faarlund 2009:18). The major focus of the text is the formal difference in status between clitic -*in* and affix -*in* and the functional aspects of the change are not pursued.

In her 2007 study of cyclicity of article development, Elly van Gelderen considers in detail three Germanic languages (groups of languages), including Old Norse and the consecutive developments in its daughter languages. The focus of the study is the development of a demonstrative into a definite article accompanied by loss of the proximal/distal distinction and a consecutive renewal of the demonstrative by e.g., locative markers (see e.g., Modern Swedish *den här* 'this here' and *den där* 'this there' which are examples of the same process), illustrating the cyclical nature of language change.

As has been long recognized, demonstratives are far more frequent in the world's languages than definite articles are. Van Gelderen stresses that while the former express definiteness and locality with respect to the speech event, the latter only express definiteness (van Gelderen 2007:304), however, the border between the two forms is often fuzzy and their classification difficult (van Gelderen 2007:276). In her account, the source of the definite article is a locative adverb *hinn/hitt* 'here' (*sic*, van Gelderen 2007:294), which becomes reanalysed as a head and becomes a clitic nominal marker in Old Norse, from which the modern definite article stems. Then the Old Norse locative marker is renewed through a demonstrative, such as *sá* 'that', which being a deictic element becomes incorporated as a specifier of the DP. These demonstratives correspond to *det* and *den* in modern Mainland Scandinavian.

2.4.3 Definite Article in Danish: Skafte Jensen (2007a)

Skafte Jensen (2007a) considers both definite and indefinite articles as well as the scope of the use of BNs in Old and Modern Danish. Of particular interest are comparisons between texts of similar age representing different genres, in which striking differences in the use of defNPs and BNs can be found. She quotes two examples, from a legal text (*Skånske Lov* from ca. 1350) and a religious narrative (*Sjælens Trøst* from ca. 1425).

SL, ca. 1350

(102) a. ***Barn** um føth warthæt tha scal thæt hafwæ **gud fathær** oc*
 child if born be then shall it have god father and
 ***gud mothær** a kyrkiu oc fa sin cristindom af præste.*
 god mother in church and get its baptism of priest

Translation to Modern Danish

 b. *Hvis et **barn** bliver født, da skal det have en*
 if INDF child becomes born then shall it have INDF
 ***gudfader** og en **gudmoder** i kirke-n og døb af*
 godfather and INDF godmother in church-DEF and baptism of
 en præst/præst-en.
 INDF priest/priest-DEF
 'If a child is born it shall have a godfather and a godmother in church and be baptized by a priest/the priest.' (after Skafte Jensen 2007a:300, translations to Modern Danish by Skafte Jensen)

ST, ca. 1425

(103) a. ***folk-it*** *spordhe hwat som honum var. Han swarathe*
 people-DEF asked what which him was he answered
 *hær hængr ofvir mek **en stor steen** oc vil vpa mek falla.*
 here hangs over me EN large stone and will upon me fall
 *The callatho thit **præst-in** at han skulde sek granliga*
 they called there priest-DEF that he should self properly
 skrifta. Han skriftathe sek som han bæst cvnne. tha
 confess he confessed self as he best could then
 *vligavæl blef **sten-in** hængande.*
 nevertheless remained stone-DEF hanging

Translation to Modern Danish

 b. ***folk-et*** *spurgte ham hvad der var med ham. Han*
 people-DEF asked him what there was with him he

svarede	'her hænger	**en**	stor	sten	over mig som	vil
answered	here hangs	EN	large	stone	over me	which will
falde ned	på mig'. De	hidkaldte	**præst-en**		for at	han
fall down	on me	they summoned	priest-DEF		for that	he
kunne skrifte.	Han skriftede	så godt han kunne, men				
could confess	he confessed	as well he could but				
alligevel	blev	**sten-en**	hængende.			
nevertheless	remained	stone-DEF	hanging			

'The people asked what was the matter with him. He answered: 'here hangs a large stone over me which will fall down on me'. They summoned the priest so that he could confess his sin. He confessed as well as he could but still the stone remained hanging.' (after Skafte Jensen 2007a:300, translations to Modern Danish by Skafte Jensen)

As illustrated by the examples, the more recent, religious text displays an article system identical to the modern Danish one and quite different from the Old Danish one as illustrated by examples (102a and b). Without unreservedly stating that a significant linguistic change has taken place within a relatively short period of time (an issue addressed also in Delsing 2014), Skafte Jensen continues to compare the two systems with particular reference to the scope of the use of BNs, an issue seldom addressed in diachronic linguistics.

2.4.4   *Definite Article in Swedish: Larm (1936), Skrzypek (2012), Dahl (2004 and 2015), Stroh-Wollin (2016)*

Larm (1936) is the first monographic study of definiteness in Swedish, following his 1933 article. It is based on a corpus of texts representing all genres. Even though it is atheoretical from the modern perspective, it includes ideas which could be incorporated in studies of grammaticalization, mainly that the rise of the definite article involves the spread of the form to new functions. Larm identifies what we would call textual uses as the first step in the development of the definite article.

Skrzypek (2012) is a study of both definite and indefinite articles in Old Swedish (1225–1526). Based on the grammaticalization models of Greenberg (1978) and Heine (1997), the study focuses on the functional development and the use of the original demonstrative in new contexts. The author differentiates between textual and non-textual uses, placing the anaphoric (direct and indirect) ones into the first category, and the larger situation uses and generics in the latter. The development clearly proceeds from the textual to non-textual uses, and indirect anaphora is singled out as the switch context (Heine 2002) in the development. The analysis of examples is completed by simple frequency analysis, which reveals a significant rise in the frequency of the definite suffix between 1350 and 1450, with lower values in the final part of the studied period, i.e., 1450–1526. The reason for this peak is, according to Skrzypek, the tendency to mark abstract nouns as definite, especially those referring to the Christian virtues and vices (examples 104–105). She terms such uses co-textual, arguing that their definiteness arises from the type of text in which they appear.

> It is interesting to note that they are not wholly disconnected from the texts, although they are not introduced (linguistically) by any other prior referents; they may be considered 'introduced' by the text genre—a collection of moralizing stories to be read in a convent or at a religious gathering or by a pious Christian on his or her own, but always in clear connection to religion. The definiteness of concepts such as *dygden* 'the virtue' or *sanningen* 'the truth' arises not out of the textual situation but a co-textual one—the context in which the text is produced and read. There are frequent references made to different virtues, like *ödmiukt* 'humility' and vices, like *högfärdhet* 'vanity', which are likewise regularly marked with -IN and cannot be explained on the basis of linguistic information in the texts. Neither is it easy to think of them as uniques or generics. (Skrzypek 2012:148)

(104) *Thu giuir var herra* **hugnadh-in** *til at lätta   os mz* **hop-ino**
you give our lord   mind-DEF to to relieve us with hope-DEF
at   vi skulum ey vanskas   oc   dröuils-in til ödhmiukt-in-na
that we shall   not run.short and grief-DEF to humility-DEF-GEN
gömilse
preservation
'You give your mind to the lord, to relieve us with hope so that we shall not falter and grief for the preservation of humility.' (Bo 11, ca. 1390)

(105) *ok   thikkir mik thän vara komin til höxsta oc   vansammasto*
and thinks me then be   come to highest and most.beautiful
fulcomlikhet-zs-in-s   *trappo*
perfection-GEN-DEF-GEN ladder
'And I think I am come to the highest and most beautiful ladder of perfection.' (Bo 31, ca. 1390; both examples after Skrzypek 2012:148–149)

Concrete nouns can also be found in this category possibly understood as instances of larger situation use, referring to objects familiar to readers of the text, as in (106).

(106) *Nw   tha   the   komo fore **stallit** som   är thz **skiulit** som   var*
       now that they came for   stable   which is this shed   which our
       herra var föddir ij
       lord   was   born   in
       'They now came to the stable, which is the shed that our Lord was born in.' (Bo 1, ca. 1390; Skrzypek 2012:145)

Östen Dahl's (2004) study is a contemporary review of the use of both pre- and postposed definite articles in non-standard varieties of Swedish, with some references to other North Germanic vernaculars. Despite the fact that it is not diachronic, it is highly relevant to the present study.

The point of departure is an observation of how widely varied the defNP is in modern North Germanic, where the two articles are in complementary distribution in certain contexts, and may sometimes appear in the same defNP (see also Chapter 1). The possibilities are even more varied when one considers, as Dahl does, the non-standard varieties, which in contrast to the standard ones—with their more or less clean-cut borders—form a dialect continuum. This variation, according to Dahl, is the result of two competing grammaticalizations, the older one, originating in the north, of the postposed suffixed article, and the more recent one, originating in the south, of the preposed definite article. The only area where the latter has undergone full grammaticalization is the south of Denmark (see Møller 1945); in other parts its development was frozen, at different stages, since it presumably had to compete against the older and better established postposed definite article. In the areas where grammaticalizations 'met', a compromise of sorts was reached, with both forms uniting within the same NP. In the north the postposed definite prevails, and its use is spread wider than in the south.

> The two main definite article types in Scandinavia—called here "P-articles" and "S-articles"—thus represent two separate grammaticalization processes represented in overlapping geographical areas with different "centres of gravity". The S-article (historically oldest in the area) has reached its fullest development in north-eastern Scandinavia. The P-article (a newcomer from the south) has been frozen at a relatively early stage and has left some areas virtually untouched. (Dahl 2004:178)

Examples quoted in the study illustrate among other things the advanced stage of grammaticalization of the suffixed article (Dahl's S-article) in the northern dialects, exceeding the use of the article in the standard variety of modern Swedish. They include low referentiality uses (107), which in Standard Swedish would most likely be expressed by BNs, and non-delimited NPs (108), which would most likely be modified by *lite* 'some'.

Low referentiality uses of the definite article:

Nederkalix (Norrbotten)
(107) Jä skå tåla   åom för dä,   måmme, åt jä ållti
       I   shall speak.INF   about for you.DAT mother that I   always
       veillt hå   i   kjaatt män hä gja   jo   ät
       want-SUP have INDF cat   but it go-PRS as.you.know   not
       håå   kjatta   når   man båo   ini i   höreshöus.
       have-INF   cat-DEF   when   one live-PRS in INDF rent-house
       'I want to tell you, Mother, that I have always wanted to have a cat—but it isn't possible to have a cat (lit. **the cat**) when you live in an apartment house.' (Cat Corpus; Dahl 2004:174)

Non-delimited NPs with definite articles:

Våmhus (Dalarna)
(108) Ja, bara i a   faið   in wi-ðn,   so ska   i werm
       yes only I have-PRS   get-SUP in firewood-DEF so shall I warm-INF
       miö-tsī   a   na.
       milk-DEF   for PRO.3SG.F.DAT
       '[Granny says:] As soon as I have put in the firewood, I'll warm **some milk** for it (the cat).' (Cat Corpus; Dahl 2004:172)

There are also instances of the definite article used in presentation constructions with the dummy subject, which in Standard Swedish would be indefinite.

Presentation constructions with the dummy subject:

Skellefteå (Västerbotten)
(109) Hä gick   skaplit att klaar   sä,   meda   'ä fanns
       it go-PST   okay   to survive REFL   as.long.as   it exist-PST
       rått-än   å   mus-än ...
       rat-DEF.PL   and   mouse-DEF.PL
       '[The cat thinks:] It was kind of OK [to live in the forest], as long as there were **rats and mice** ...' (Cat Corpus; Dahl 2004:173)

While Dahl (2003, 2004) reviews and analyses the non-canonical uses of the suffixed definite article and the competition between the two definite articles in contemporary Swedish dialects, Dahl (2015) not only further develops these studies, but also offers a diachronic insight into the source of the variation (in this the account is radically different from the other analyses of the variation in the structure of the defNP in North Germanic, e.g., La Cara 2011). In his discussion, he refers to two possible grammaticalization paths beyond the 'classical' final stage of grammaticalization of the definite article in its generic uses: Greenberg's model from 1978, in which the development results in general affixes whose informative value includes gender and number (the title of Greenberg's paper is in fact 'How does a language acquire gender markers?') but not definiteness, or the development into specific articles as witnessed in Austronesian languages (Dahl 2015:245). However, the dialectal data do not support either of these paths. Instead, the definite suffix in Northern Swedish dialects seems to have developed some extended uses which are commonly associated with BNs in standard varieties, i.e., non-delimited uses, uses with quantifiers and low-referentiality uses of singular count nouns (Dahl 2015:246). According to Dahl, these uses could have been mediated through the generic use of the definite suffix, which is more widespread in the Northern dialects than elsewhere (see also Skrzypek, Kurek-Przybilski and Piotrowska 2020 for an analysis of generic expressions in modern Danish, Norwegian and Swedish). Such mediation would come about in contexts in which it is possible to choose between a generic noun phrase and an indefinite one, for example in habitual contexts. This is illustrated in (110), where the definite form induces a habitual rather than a generic interpretation.

Sollerön (Ovansiljan)
(110) An drikk   **mjotji**.
       he drink.PRS milk.DEF
       'He drinks milk.' (Dahl 2015:247)

The spread to new functions could also have been facilitated by the form of the article, i.e., the fusion of the stem and the affix (Dahl 2015:201).

Stroh-Wollin (2016) gives a minimalist account of the rise of the definite article. In her contribution she highlights two aspects of the development that have received little treatment in the literature as yet, namely the variation between *hinn* and *enn*, and the internal order of the NP. It has been noted before that the demonstrative from which the definite article develops is spelled in the sources as either *hinn* or *enn*. The former is the only spelling found in the eastern languages (Danish and Swedish); the variation is found in the western sources (Norwegian and Icelandic). The presence of the initial *h-* has been taken to be a reinforcement of the deixis of the original *enn* (see especially Perridon 1989). The absence of *h* in definite forms, e.g., *fisk-in* and not **fisk-hin* 'fish-DEF', suggests that either it was lost in cliticization or the cliticized form was in fact *enn* and not *hinn*. In this vein, Skrzypek (2009) argues that it could in fact have been *enn* that gave rise to the definite article, while *hinn* is a later formation. Stroh-Wollin (2016) suggests that the definite suffix in the eastern and western varieties is derived from two variants of the demonstrative: *enn* in the west, *hinn* in the east.

(111) Mainland Scandinavian
dag-s hin-s > dag-s'(h)in-s > dag-s-in-s (> dag-en-s)

(112) Icelandic
dag-s en-s > dag-s'en-s > dag-s-in-s (Stroh-Wollin 2016:13)

Her account finds some support in the Runic data (which predate the oldest extant text written in the Latin alphabet by some centuries), although the evidence is hardly conclusive. Nevertheless, we believe a more problematized consideration of the etymology of the definite article to be of great value.

Secondly, Stroh-Wollin convincingly argues that the factors which had an influence on the rise of the definite article also included a change in the internal order of the NP.

> My hypothesis was that "noun first", as in *stein þenna* and *faður sinn*, was the unmarked word order and that fronting of a modifier was a means to emphasize it. [...] On the whole, the investigation supports the view that "noun first" is unmarked and fronting of a modifier is pragmatically motivated. (Stroh-Wollin 2016:14–15)

The purpose of this brief and selective overview of the current state of research into the grammaticalization of the definite article was to demonstrate that, despite the fact that the problem has received due attention in the literature, it continues to present puzzles, making it worthy of further research. More specifically, the diversity of NP forms and the differences in the scope of the use of the definite article in the modern vernaculars suggests that these differences, although rooted in a common past, have arisen in the histories of the individual languages.

2.5 Previous Studies on the Grammaticalization of the Indefinite Article in North Germanic

The rise of the indefinite article is surprisingly understudied in comparison with that of the definite article, although a number of larger studies, in particular concerning Swedish, have been published recently.

2.5.1 Indefinite Article in Icelandic: Leijström (1934)

Even though there is no indefinite article in Modern Icelandic, there are article-like uses of the numeral 'one' in Old Icelandic texts, which have attracted the attention of historical linguists. The most extensive study is that of Leijström (1934), who systematically compares the use of *einn* in two groups of sagas: the so-called family sagas, considered indigenous and free from foreign influence, and the so-called chivalric sagas, which were inspired by continental (mainly French) romances.

Leijström finds a number of instances in which *einn* is used as the indefinite article would be used, limited to three major types: presentation of a new discourse referent (individual), similes (*as a king*), and non-specific uses when there is some expectation of a potential referent (e.g., *ger grof eina* 'make a cavity'). None of the uses is obligatory. He further finds that the indefinite article in other North Germanic languages is a result of language contact with Middle Low German, and its absence in Icelandic can be explained by the isolation of the population (see also Heine and Kuteva 2005). We will return to Leijström's study and other smaller studies in section 5.6, when we consider the developments in Icelandic beyond 1550.

2.5.2 Indefinite Article in Danish: Skafte Jensen (2016)

In her 2016 article, Skafte Jensen considers the textual evidence from the oldest Danish texts (apart from Runic inscriptions), namely legal prose. She quotes examples clearly illustrating the lack of the indefinite article and the scope of the use of BNs in Danish.

(113) Varthær **kunu** døth. oc lifwær **barn** æftær. oc [...] um them
becomes woman dead and lives child after and if them
skil um. ath **barn** fic cristindom
divides about that child got Christianity
'If a woman dies and a child survives her, and [...] there is a disagreement as to whether the child was christened.' (SL, after Skafte Jensen 2016:264)

Interestingly, the earliest instances of the article-like use of the numeral 'one' are similar to those identified in Icelandic, i.e., presentative uses (examples 114–115) and similes (example 116), which can be found as early as ca. 1300, even though such uses are sporadic.

(114) *warthær swa at   en man sæctær annæn   um   sar*
      becomes so   that EN man sues   another about wound(s)
      'if it so happens that one man sues another about wound(s)' (ErL, ca. 1300)

(115) *Swa com   en røst af himæn*
      so   came EN voice of heaven
      'Then came a voice from Heaven' (SC, 14th century)

(116) *E   uar han sum eet lamb*
      always was he like EN lamb
      'Always he was like a lamb' (Lam, 14th century; Skafte Jensen 2016:269)

Examples like (114) may, according to Skafte Jensen, have constituted bridging contexts for the grammaticalization of the indefinite article. She further claims that by the 15th century the use of the indefinite article is very much as it is in Modern Danish (in this genre).

2.5.3   *Indefinite Article in Swedish: Brandtler and Delsing (2010), Skrzypek (2012), Stendahl (2013)*

The grammaticalization of the indefinite article in Swedish is well studied in comparison with other North Germanic languages. Apart from the references to the development found in Leijström (1934) and Terner (1922), there are a number of recent studies devoted to the issue.

Brandtler and Delsing (2010) is the first treatment of the subject where the rise of the indefinite article is studied against Heine's grammaticalization model. The study is based on four religious texts written between 1330 and 1450 and the authors' conclusion is a confirmation of the model's predictions, with the grammaticalization of the indefinite article more or less completed by the middle of the 15th century.

The development is studied in similar vein in Skrzypek (2012), where a larger and more mixed (in terms of genre) corpus exhibits the same timeline of the development and the gradual acquisition of new functions. It should also be noted that a more detailed inspection of the position and syntactic function of indefNPs reveals that at the onset of the grammaticalization, the presentative function is strongly associated with initially placed subjects. Skrzypek follows the same periodization of the textual data, i.e., period I: 1200–1350, period II: 1350–1450 and period III: 1450–1550. She finds that in period I the NPs containing *en* 'one' are (if *en* is not to be understood as a cardinal) overwhelmingly initially placed subjects, introducing new and persistent discourse referents (Heim 1988), with a number of subsequent mentions (Skrzypek 2012:161–170). She also finds such use to be cataphoric and parallel to the origins of the definite article (in terms of the marking of salient discourse referents first).

(117) *En vælburin ungar suen forlæt værud-ena ok folgþe*
       EN well.born young boy left world-DEF and followed
       andream: hans frændar vildo þøm baþa inne brænna ok
       Andreas his relatives wanted them both in burn and
       *tændo brand iui þera hærbærghe **Smasuenn-en** slækte balet*
       lit fire over their shelter small.boy-DEF quenched fire
       mz litlo vatne þa vildo þe kliva i hus-et ok
       with some water then wanted they step in house-DEF and
       wrþo alle iæmskyt blinde: þa øpte en at allom: vaþe
       became all suddenly blind then called one to all danger
       ær striþa viþ guþ som siæluan haldar mz andrea. ok
       is fight with God which self holds with Andreas and
       þøm hanom følgher hær af worþo mange cristne. ok
       them him follow this of became many Christian and
       troþo þy andreas prædicaþe
       believed this Andreas preached
       'A well-born young man left the world and followed Andreas. His relatives wanted to burn them (alive) and started a fire over their shelter. The young man put out the fire with some water. Then they wanted to enter the house and became all suddenly blind. Then one called to all: it is dangerous to fight against God himself who protects Andreas and all who follow him. Because of this many became Christian and believed what Andreas preached.' (Bur 133; Skrzypek 2012:164)

Stendahl (2013) is a monographic study of the grammaticalization of the indefinite article in Swedish which spans the same time as the two previous studies, but subdivides it into four periods, allowing an even more fine-grained picture. His choice of texts includes genres of high narrativity, and excludes legal prose, as the author treats lack of articles as a particular property of legal material (Stendahl 2013:90). He does not follow Heine's model, but groups the uses of *en* into categories, or strategies (for instance, to mark non-referential nouns as well). His interpretation of the results places the formation of the indefinite article in Swedish quite early, at the beginning of the 14th century; he also finds that any discrepant uses of *en*, or rather its absence, are due to stylistic factors rather than being a diagnostic of incomplete grammaticalization (Stendahl 2013:161). Even though the indefinite article in Swedish seems to be very well studied diachronically, there remain differences between authors as to the time at which its grammaticalization took place.

2.6 Summary

In this chapter, we have discussed functions of the definite and indefinite article cross-linguistically, as well as the models of their grammaticalization proposed in literature and earlier research into the rise of articles in North Germanic languages.

Definite articles regularly develop out of deictic elements and their origins can be traced in the earlier stages of grammaticalization, which involve the direct anaphoric reference, i.e., reference to a previously mentioned entity. It seems that rather than being confined to an immediate situation, the use of the original deictic element is extended to encompass textual deixis, direct anaphora. The grammaticalization then proceeds via indirect anaphoric use, in which the incipient definite article is used with new referents, which are grounded in earlier discourse, to the unique reference, in which the definite article is used as a marker of the uniqueness of the referent. The uniqueness corresponds to Hawkins' larger situation use, in which a referent can be identified as being the only one satisfying the description within a given situation. Such situations can be of varying size, from local, e.g., *a room*, to global, e.g., *the entire universe*. Existing models of definite article grammaticalization propose that in the course of the process these functions are gradually encompassed by the incipient definite article in this order, however, the bridging contexts from one definite article function to the next remain unclear.

Indefinite articles seem to universally stem from the numeral 'one'. As with the definite article, also the indefinite article appears in a multitude of functions, which do not arise simultaneously. The proposed grammaticalization models, which have been successfully tested on data from a number of languages, single out the presentative use as the onset of the development. The incipient indefinite article is used to present new and salient discourse referents. The consecutive stages involve the introduction of specific discourse referents, new, but not necessarily salient, and finally the non-specific use of the erstwhile numeral. The final stage of both grammaticalizations is the generic use of the articles, in which the known: new distinction, so pervasive in earlier stages of the process, becomes obliterated.

Dryer (1989) demonstrates that articles are present in only one-third of the world's languages. The definite article is more wide-spread than the indefinite, meaning that if a language has an indefinite article it is very likely to have the definite also (see also Moravcsik 1969, Heine 1997, Dryer 2013a, 2013b), although some exceptions have been found. Diachronically, it is easily observable that the definite article predates the indefinite, at least to some extent, i.e., the grammaticalization of the indefinite begins only when the grammaticalization of the definite is already well underway. In this sense, the discrepancy between the frequencies of the two articles in the world's languages can be understood as a result of complete grammaticalization of the definite article without the grammaticalization of the indefinite. In other words, the fact that the grammaticalization of the indefinite follows the grammaticalization of the definite does not imply that it must occur. A language may only develop one article and make use of zero determination to express the indefinite meanings. This is the case with Icelandic, one of the languages in our sample, although we will modify the claim of its not having developed the indefinite article somewhat in Chapter 5. Even when a language has grammaticalized both the definite and the indefinite article, it may still retain a residual domain of zero determination, which in turn may also undergo a grammaticalization process of its own.

The first stages of the grammaticalization of both definite and indefinite articles as identified in grammaticalization chains above are textual. The anaphoric use of the original demonstrative helps select a discourse referent known from previous discourse, especially one that has not been in focus for some time (De Mulder and Carlier 2011:527). The presentative use of the original numeral 'one' helps prepare the hearer for a new, salient discourse referent. We discern a certain symmetry in the earliest stages of both grammaticalization processes: discourse referents are presented by means of incipient articles for a stronger pragmatic impact. We may further say that while the original use of the definite article is anaphoric, the original use of the indefinite is cataphoric. At the same time, as the data from many languages indicate, it is not in any way necessary for a language to develop this symmetry. The incipient definite article may go on to grammaticalize successive functions without having any indefinite opposite number other than a bare noun.

In Chapters 4 and 5 we test the proposed models of article grammaticalization against data from a North Germanic corpus. Two approaches are combined: quantitative (Chapter 4) and qualitative (Chapter 5). Our aim is to verify the chronology of definite and indefinite article use in contexts identified as consecutive stages of grammaticalization, as well as to provide examples of contexts that may have been critical for the development.

CHAPTER 3

Sources, Methods and Tools

In this chapter, we present the corpora chosen for the present study and the criteria for their compilation. In order to do so, we begin with an overview of the adopted periodization of the history of the North Germanic languages. We proceed then to a detailed presentation of each text included in the corpus. In the second part of the chapter, we describe the programme used in the annotation of the corpora as well as the statistical toolkit. We conclude with a discussion of some issues that arose in the course of annotation and the decisions that were made, which have a bearing on the final analysis.

3.1 Periodization of the North Germanic Languages

North Germanic languages or Nordic languages developed and became distinguishable from other Germanic languages most likely around 200 AD, but the Old Nordic language first took form around 500 AD (Bandle et al. 2002). Around 800 AD internal differences became more pronounced, as is attested in runic inscriptions from that period, and Old Nordic split into two distinct branches, western and eastern, as presented in Table 14.

The periodization of Old West Nordic seems quite straightforward (see Table 15). The Old Norwegian period begins conventionally around 1100, which is the end of the Viking Age. The oldest manuscripts of legal texts, however, date from the second half of the 12th century (Bandle et al. 2002:788). The year of the Great Plague, 1350, marks the delimitation between Old Norwegian and Middle Norwegian, as significant changes in the language took place after that time (Bandle et al. 2002:788).

The Old Icelandic period begins with the oldest manuscript of the legal codex *Grágás* (ca. 1170). Old Icelandic is usually treated as one long period between the years 1100 and 1550. While the term Middle Icelandic is not often used, some scholars point out the importance of distinguishing a middle period in the history of Icelandic, as several important sound changes took place in the 14th century (Bandle et al. 2002:1086).

In the tradition of Swedish and Danish language history, a three- or four-way periodization is employed (see Table 16). What is commonly regarded as Old Nordic, in the Swedish and Danish tradition is often called the runsvenska 'Runic Swedish' and rundanska 'Runic Danish' respectively. The begin-

© D. SKRZYPEK, A. PIOTROWSKA, AND R. JAWORSKI, 2021 | DOI:10.1163/9789004463684_004
This is an open access chapter distributed under the terms of the CC BY-NC-ND 4.0 license.

TABLE 14   Periodization of the North Germanic languages before 1100

200–500	Proto-Nordic/Proto-Norse
500–800	Ancient/Old Nordic
800–1100	Old Nordic ca. 800 splits into:

Old West Nordic	Old East Nordic
(Iceland and Norway)	(Denmark and Sweden)

TABLE 15   Periodization of Old West Nordic after 1100

Old Nordic 800–1100

Old Icelandic	1100–1350	Old Norwegian	1100–1350
Middle Icelandic	1350–1550	Middle Norwegian	1350–1530

ning of the Old Swedish period is conventionally set at the time the oldest legal manuscript was composed, i.e., *Äldre Västgötalagen* in 1225. The Old Swedish epoch is generally divided into two periods, the classical period (1225–1375) and the younger period (1375–1526). The delimitation year is usually 1375 for Swedish (cf. Wessén 1941), as again the Great Plague had an influence on language changes. It has, however, become customary to further divide Younger Old Swedish into two periods at 1450. A division into three periods better reflects the linguistic development (cf. Hirvonen 1987, Håkansson 2008, Skrzypek 2012). 1526, the year of the first complete translation of the New Testament into Swedish, conventionally marks the move towards New Swedish.

The Old Danish period begins around 1100, as the first Danish laws were written ca. 1170 (Bandle et al. 2002:788). This period is often called Middle Danish by Danish linguists and historians, but for the sake of consistency with other Nordic languages we use the denomination Old Danish. The Old Danish period is usually subdivided into two periods at 1350, i.e., Older Old Danish and Younger Old Danish. The year 1350 is conventionally used, as after that time a strong Low German influence on the vocabulary is attested (Bandle et al. 2002:788), which is also true of Norwegian. 1537, the year of the Reformation, is traditionally taken as the beginning of New Danish.

To create a uniform periodization for the Old Swedish, Old Danish and Old Icelandic texts used in the present study, we had to compromise between the delimitations of periods described above. Throughout the study we use the

TABLE 16 Periodization of Old East Nordic after 1100

Runic Swedish	800–1225	**Runic Danish**	800–1100
Old Swedish:		Old Danish:	
Period I	1225–1375	Period I	1100–1350
Period II	1375–1450	Period II	1350–1537
Period III	1450–1526		

TABLE 17 Periodization used in the present study

Old Swedish, Old Danish, and Old Icelandic

Period I	1200–1350
Period II	1350–1450
Period III	1450–1550

periodization indicated in Table 17. As the oldest manuscripts used in the study were written in the early 13th century, the year 1200 is used as the beginning of Period I. The year 1350 is the beginning of Period II, as most Nordic languages use that year as the marker of language changes that took place due to rapid reductions in the morphological and syntactic systems (partly influenced by the Great Plague) and the influence of other languages (mostly Low German influence on Danish). In line with the Swedish tradition, we further distinguish Period III, beginning at 1450, in order to distinguish the most modern texts written after 1450, which demonstrate considerable differences compared with those from Period II.

At this point we should mention that Old Norwegian texts are not considered in the present study, for practical reasons. Firstly, Old West Nordic exhibits little variation between the two varieties (Icelandic and Norwegian) compared with Old East Nordic. Thus, in the literature the term Old Nordic or Old Norse is often synonymous with Old West Nordic (Bandle et al. 2002:34). Secondly, Old West Nordic is predominantly preserved in Icelandic texts, which are additionally much more diverse as regards text types than the text originating in Norway. It is thus not an easy task to find medieval texts from the 12th and 13th centuries that are unequivocally written in Old Norwegian and not in Old Icelandic, as they are often labelled as Old Nordic and often originate in Iceland. Further, it is assumed that there was a greater loss of manuscripts in Norway than in Iceland (Bandle et al. 2002:805). Naturally, there are available texts written in Old Norwegian, like the so-called *Landslǫg*, King Magnús Hákonarson's Norwegian Code from 1274, or the Norwegian didactic work from ca. 1250 *Konungs skuggsjá* ('The King's Mirror'). Old Norwegian texts from the period 1200–1350 are nonetheless few and are not easily available. Middle Norwegian, on the other hand, is well represented by diplomas, i.e., legal documents and letters. These, however, are not comparable to other texts included in the corpus, as Swedish, Danish and Icelandic diplomas were not included in the study (see section 3.2).

3.2 The Corpus

To make the present project possible, we decided to compile a new corpus of Old North Germanic texts from existing sources. Historic texts written in Nordic languages are well-documented and easily accessible thanks to such projects as *Fornsvenska textbanken* by Lars-Olof Delsing, which is the largest repository of Old Swedish texts,[1] and *Middelalder og renæssance* by Det Danske Sprog- og Litteraturselskab, which is the largest available corpus of Old Danish texts.[2] Another project that merits mentioning is *Medieval Nordic Text Archive* (Menota) led by Einar Haugen, which has the aim of preserving and publishing medieval texts and manuscripts written in Nordic languages.[3] Some of the Icelandic sagas were also obtained via *The Icelandic Parsed Historical Corpus* (IcePaHC, Wallenberg et al. 2011).[4] Thanks to these projects we were able to choose the texts and fragments of texts that we deemed most suitable for our project's objectives.

The corpus comprises Old Swedish, Old Danish and Old Icelandic texts written between 1200 and 1550. To make our analyses more nuanced and to make the texts more comparable across the three languages, we divided the studied epoch into three periods. Period I encompasses the texts written between 1200 and 1350, Period II the texts written between 1350 and 1450, and Period III the texts written between 1450 and 1550. The corpus consists of 280,024 words in total. The total length of the texts for each language and period is given in Table 18.

---

1 *Fornsvenska textbanken*, https://project2.sol.lu.se/fornsvenska/.
2 *Middelalder og renæssance*, https://dsl.dk/website?id=32.
3 *Medieval Nordic Text Archive*, https://menota.org/forside.xhtml.
4 *The Icelandic Parsed Historical Corpus*, https://linguist.is/icelandic_treebank/Icelandic_Parsed_Historical_Corpus_(IcePaHC).

TABLE 18   Length of the texts in the corpus (total word counts)

Period	Old Swedish	Old Danish	Old Icelandic
Period I (1200–1350)	47,434	13,231	56,761
Period II (1350–1450)	27,700	12,078	73,946
Period III (1450–1550)	12,027	7,813	29,034
Total	87,161	33,122	159,741

TABLE 19   Number of NPs tagged in the corpus

Period	Old Swedish	Old Danish	Old Icelandic
Period I (1200–1350)	1,194	1,097	1,536
Period II (1350–1450)	1,093	1,016	1,037
Period III (1450–1550)	635	787	648
Total	2,922	2,900	3,221

Admittedly, the length of the texts differs greatly between languages. Old Icelandic is represented by the longest texts, whereas in Old Danish much shorter texts are chosen for the corpus. The length of the texts, however, does not have a substantial bearing on the data analysed, as the entirety of texts was not analysed, but rather fragments chosen evenly for each language. Specifically, 9043 noun phrases were extracted from the corpus. In Table 19, we give the number of noun phrases tagged and analysed in each language and period.

The number of NPs analysed is quite evenly distributed, as we aimed to make the data commensurate, in particular so that each period would be comparable across the three languages. Thus, in Period I, the mean number of tagged NPs per language is 1276 (SD = 231), in Period II the mean number is 1049 (SD = 40), and in Period III the mean number is 690 (SD = 84).

The texts chosen for the corpus represent four major genres: legal prose, religious prose, profane prose and sagas. Sagas are specific to the Icelandic literary tradition. As they are prose narratives describing historical or local events or the lives and legends of saints, they are comparable to the other profane and religious prose texts available for the Continental Scandinavian languages of that time. Texts representing these four genres were chosen because they are examples of the oldest extant texts written in the respective languages (legal texts for Swedish and Danish, sagas for Icelandic), and because they include longer descriptive and narrative passages (especially profane prose and religious prose), which offer an abundance of different types of reference of NPs, e.g., specific, non-specific, unique or generic referents. Legal texts are the only ones written without foreign models, while prose texts are usually free translations from German or Latin. There might thus be some influence from the source languages. The only remaining genres of texts available from the Nordic countries during the studied period (from the 13th to the 16th century) are poetry and diplomas. The latter is a specific set of legal documents, mostly letters, which pertain to the history of a given Nordic country or, more locally, to a given province or settlement. We chose not to use diplomas in our corpus, as the documents and letters are usually short and do not contain many narratives. The genre is thus very distinct and not comparable to others. We also decided to omit poetry, as the form of these texts is often governed by metrics and rhyme. Previous studies have also indicated that poetry is not a reliable source material for research on definiteness. Poetry, usually including translations from German, exhibits a significantly higher proportion of preposed determinatives and a lower proportion of postposed articles (Haskå 1972). The fragments of texts in the corpus were for the most part chosen randomly. The only ground rule was to make sure that the excerpts chosen included longer narrative passages and be sufficiently self-contained that any potential referents introduced in the omitted fragments would not be missed. Thus, fragments containing many dialogues were often excluded. In the case of shorter texts, especially in the Old Danish corpus, the texts were studied in their entirety.

As regards the uniformity of the corpus, we strove to make the texts as comparable as possible, especially within one period. When working with medieval texts, however, it is not always possible to choose freely the texts to work with. Thus, the texts in our corpus are not entirely comparable across the three periods studied. In the first period, the majority of the texts are examples of hermetic legal prose. These are the oldest extant texts written in Nordic languages in Latin script, and for that reason they must be included in the study, even though they may be of a very specific genre. In the later periods there are no legal texts, but exclusively profane and religious prose, as these were the types of texts that were regularly translated and adapted from foreign models at that time, with the exception of the native Icelandic sagas. Whenever possible we included the same text in different variants or translations. For instance, the *Karl Magnus* saga is represented by fragments in both Old Swedish and Old Danish; there are also Old Swedish and Old Icelandic versions of *Didrikssagan*, as well as Old Swedish and Old Danish versions of the religious text *Själens tröst*. The sections below describe the texts used. The corpus texts are classified here first by period, then by language, and finally by genre.

3.2.1 Period I (1200–1350)
3.2.1.1 Swedish
Legal texts: *Äldre Västgötalagen* (AVL), *Östgötalagen* (OgL), *Dalalagen* (DL)

Äldre Västgötalagen is the oldest extant text written in Swedish using Latin script. The oldest fragment is dated to 1225, and the whole text comes from a later manuscript (Holm B 59) written around 1280. It is a legal codex of the province of Västergötland. It is divided into smaller parts dealing with different areas of law, e.g., criminal offences, marital and inheritance law, regulations on religious matters, etc. The fragments chosen for the study are *Af mandrapi*, § 1 ('On manslaughter') and *Ärvdabalken*, § 1–6 ('The inheritance codex'). The language in AVL is very archaic, even compared with other legal texts from the same period (Holmbäck and Wessén 1979, Skrzypek 2012:17).

Östgötalagen is a legal codex for the province of Östergötland written around 1280. The earliest preserved copy of the manuscript (Holm B 50) is dated to ca. 1350. Similarly to AVL it includes several codices; the fragments excerpted for the study include *Drapa balken*, § 1–2 ('The manslaughter codex') and *Gipta balken*, § 1–7 ('The marriage codex'). The language of OgL is considered among the most modern found in legal texts (Ståhle 1967).

Dalalagen, also known as *Äldre Västmannalagen*, was written at some time between 1200 and 1320, and the only preserved manuscript, Holm B 54, is from around 1350. Whether this legal codex was intended for the province of Dalarna or Västmanland is unclear. The fragment used for this study comes from *Kristnu balkar*, § 6–9 ('The church codex').

Religious prose: *Codex Bureanus* (Bur), *Pentateukparafrasen* (Pent)

Codex Bureanus is a collection of hagiographic legends, and is a free translation of *Legenda aurea* by Jacobus de Voragines. It was written between 1276 and 1307 (Jansson 1934:4); the manuscript used here, Holm A 34, is dated to ca. 1350. Apart from the legal texts described above, Codex Bureanus is the oldest text written in Old Swedish. The fragment chosen for the analysis is the first legend in the collection, *Af ioakim* ('On Joachim') on pages 3–7.

Pentateukparafrasen is a free translation of the five books of Moses. It was most likely written in Vadstena around 1330 (Klemming 1848:577). There are two extant manuscripts: the A manuscript is dated to 1430–1450, and the B manuscript to 1526. The latter manuscript, also called *Codex Thott*, is presumed to be more faithful to the original, as its text is less modernized than that of the earlier copy. The fragment chosen for the study comprises pages 156–159 and tells the story of Abraham.

3.2.1.2 Danish
Legal texts: *Eriks Lov* (ErL), *Valdemars Lov* (VL), *Skånske Kirkelov* (SKL), *Skånelagen* (SL)

Eriks Lov, also called *Eriks Sjællandske Lov*, is a legal codex for the province of Zealand. It consists of three parts: the inheritance law, the criminal law, and a supplement in which various laws are laid down, e.g., laws concerning the king. The fragments chosen for the study include chapters 1:13, 1:47, 2:4, 2:69, 3:1 and 3:23. *Valdemars Lov* is also a codex for the province of Zealand; it is an older law than *Eriks Lov*, and thus ErL is considered to be a continuation of VL. There are three extant editions of VL, the earliest of which is assumed to have been written before 1300. The language of VL is considered to be quite modern for its times, with properties of an oral text rather than formal legal prose. Chapters 12, 13, 27, 47 and 66 are included in the present study. The manuscript that contains both *Eriks Lov* and *Valdemars Lov* is coded as AM 455 12mo. It was written ca. 1300, most likely in the Sorø Kloster monastery on the Danish island of Zealand (VL, Skovgaard Boeck 2015).

Skånske Kirkelov (Scanian Church Law) is, despite its name, not an actual law but rather a legal agreement between the archdiocese of Lund and its inhabitants. The text was composed ca. 1200 and is preserved in around 30 manuscripts, the earliest of which is dated to 1300 (manuscript AM 28, 8vo). For the present study chapters 3, 5 and 11 were chosen; these include the codex on breaches of the law in church.

Skånelagen is another codex from the province of Scania (covering also the provinces of Halland, Blekinge and Bornholm). It has been preserved in many manuscripts both in Denmark and Sweden. The first Old Danish version of the law, written entirely in runes, is dated to 1203–1212, although the earliest manuscript, *Codex Runicus*, is from ca. 1350. In this study we make use of the Holm B 76 manuscript in Old Swedish and Latin script, which is dated to 1300. The paragraphs chosen are §1–5.

Religious prose: *Marialegende* (ML), *Skriftemålsbøn* (SMB), *Mariaklagen* (MK)

Marialegende and *Skriftemålsbøn* are religious texts found in one of the oldest manuscript fragments, dated to ca. 1300. The manuscript K 48 is fragmentary; it was split into two separate volumes early in its history, and a part of it is known as *Cambridgefragmentet* ('The Cambridge fragment'), as it was found and stored in Cambridge. *Marialegende* consists of two short stories relating miracles of St. Mary; the text is studied in its entirety. Following ML in the manuscript is the prayer *Skriftemålsbøn*. It is assumed to have been written later by a different author, as it has no connection to the preceding legends or the herb book that follows it in the manuscript. The relatively long prayer is studied in its entirety.

Mariaklagen is a short religious text relating the prayers and lament of St. Mary witnessing the crucifixion of her son. The text was first written in its entirety in runes; the text in Latin script (manuscript Cod. Holm. A120) is dated to 1325 (MK, Brøndum-Nielsen & Rohmann 1929). The text is studied in its entirety.

3.2.1.3   Icelandic
Legal texts: *Grágás* (Gragas)

Grágás is the only legal codex written in Old Icelandic included in our corpus. It is one of the longest Nordic legal codices from the Middle Ages. It is preserved in two major manuscripts: the so-called *Konungsbók* ('King's book', GKS 1157 fol.) dated to 1258–1262, and *Staðarhólsbók* ('Book of Stadarholm', AM 334 fol.) dated to 1262–1271. For the analysis only a short fragment was chosen, namely § 9, which describes the punishment for murder.

Sagas: *Þiðreks saga af Bern* (Did), *Geirmundar þáttr heljarskinns* (Ge), *Þorsteins saga hvíta* (To), *Þetubrot Egils Sögu* (Egil), *Grettis saga Ásmundarsonar* (Gret)

Þiðreks saga af Bern is based on the Old German story of Didrik of Bern. The Old Norse version was written ca. 1250 in Norway. It is preserved in several manuscripts, the earliest of which, Perg. fol. nr. 4 at the Royal Library in Stockholm, is dated to the late thirteenth century. For the analysis we chose chapters 82–86.

Geirmundar þáttr heljarskinns is a short saga from ca. 1300 describing the lives of Geirmund and his twin brother Håmund. They were the sons of a king, but were abandoned as infants due to their horrific appearance. The saga tells the story of their coming of age and successful Viking raids. It is preserved in the manuscript of the so-called *Sturlunga saga* (manuscript AM 122 a fol.), a collection of Icelandic sagas from the 13th and 14th centuries. Chapters 1–7 were selected for the corpus.

Þorsteins saga hvíta belongs to sagas of the Icelanders from the 13th century. It tells the story of the settlement of Iceland by Þorstein the white and his family. Dated to ca. 1230, it is only preserved in one manuscript, namely AM 496 qu from 1629.

Þetubrot Egils Sögu or simply *Egils saga* is a family saga by Snorri Sturluson tracing the lives of the clan of Egil Skallagrímsson in a period spanning the years 800–1000. The saga begins with Egil's grandfather settling in Iceland with his two sons following a conflict with the royal family. The text is preserved in several manuscripts. The oldest manuscript (AM 162 A θ fol.), often called the Theta manuscript, is dated to ca. 1250. The fragment of approximately 1300 words chosen for the study comes from the beginning of the Theta manuscript.

Grettis saga Ásmundarsonar portrays the life and family of an outlaw, Grettir Ásmundarson. The fragment chosen for the study, Chapters 14 and 15, describes Grettir's childhood and his immediate family. The saga is dated to ca. 1300–1320. The various fragments of the text are preserved in more than 50 manuscripts, most of them written in the 17th and 18th centuries. The oldest manuscripts, on which most printed editions are based, are dated to ca. 1400–1500 (AM 152 fol., AM 551a, AM 556a).

Religious sagas: *Þorláks saga helga* (Torlak), *Árna saga biskups* (Arna), *Jarteinabók* (Jart)

Þorláks saga Helga is a saga about the life of Saint Þorlákr Þórhallsson, the patron saint of Iceland. There are at least five major manuscripts of the texts. The earliest one is in Latin (manuscript AM 386 4to) and is dated to ca. 1200. The oldest Old Norse manuscript is dated at ca. 1350, and the remaining three manuscripts were written in the 14th to the 17th centuries. For the study, pages 111–117 are chosen.

Árna saga biskups is considered the primary source for the political and ecclesiastical history of Iceland during the episcopacy of Árni Þorláksson of Skálholt, i.e., in the years 1269–1298. The saga is dated to ca. 1325. The text is preserved in several manuscripts, the oldest of which, AM 220 VI fol., is dated to 1340–1360. For the study, the first 1100 words of the saga are chosen.

Jarteinabók is a religious saga which, together with Þorláks and Árna, makes up the so-called Bishop sagas (*Biskupa sögur*). It is a miracle collection composed in honour of Saint Þorlák, dated to ca. 1200–1220. Jartein is preserved in several manuscripts, the oldest being the so-called *Heilagramanna sögur* ('Legends of Saints', AM 645 4to) dated to 1220–1249. For the present study, chapters 1–6 of Jart are selected.

The Bishop sagas are in general the closest to the religious prose genre in Old Swedish and Old Danish, as they also relate miracles and legends of saints. They are, however, very much grounded in the Icelandic saga literary tradition.

3.2.2 *Period II (1350–1450)*
3.2.2.1 Swedish
Religious prose: *Järteckensboken* (Järt), *Helga manna leverne* (HML), *Själens tröst* (ST)

Järteckensboken is a religious text that comprises relatively short texts relating miracles connected with the host (the altar bread). It is dated to 1385, as is the manuscript from which the text is taken, the so-called *Codex Oxenstiernianus* (Holm A 110). The fragments used for the study are pages 3–12.

Helga manna leverne is a collection of short hagiographic texts; it is a translation of the Latin *Vitae Patrum*. It comes from the same manuscript as Jart; however, it is believed to have been written later than 1385 as the language and spelling are somewhat more modern (Mattsson 1957:232). For this study we chose the fragment on pages 185–189.

Själens tröst is a translation of the Low German *Seelenstrost*. It is a collection of legends written for the purpose of explaining the Ten Commandments. There is only one manuscript with the text preserved in Old Swedish, Holm A 108, written in Vadstena and dated to 1430–1450. The fragment on pages 326–330 was chosen for the study.

Profane prose: *Sju vise mästare* (SVM), *Karl Mangus* (KM)

Sju vise mästare is a collection of short stories with a Chinese box structure. The protagonists tell each other stories, each with a moral lesson, to convince the king either to save or to hang his son for his crimes. The text thus has an overarching main story and a number of shorter novellas woven into it. SVM is a translation from Latin or German, depending on which of the three manuscripts one considers. The most comprehensive and complete is manuscript A (Holm D 4), which is a translation from Latin, dated to 1430–1450. Pages 117–121 were chosen for the analysis.

The *Karl Magnus* saga is a Swedish translation of two tales of Charlemagne based on an earlier Norwegian version *Karlamagnús Saga*, which was based on a number of French poems (Skrzypek 2012:19). It was most likely translated at the end of the 14th and the beginning of the 15th century, and it is preserved in the same manuscript as SVM, dated to 1430–1450. The pages studied here are 265–270.

3.2.2.2 Danish
Religious prose: *Aff Sancte Kerstine hennis pyne* (Kerst), *Aff Sancta Marina* (Mar), *Huoel Sancte Pouel vort pint* (Pouel), *Sjalens trost* (ST)

Aff Sancte Kerstine hennis pyne is the Danish version of the Legend of St. Christina, a martyr who refused to worship pagan gods and suffered tortures at the hand of her father. The story focuses on various cruel tortures inflicted on her. There are two manuscripts in which fragments of the legend are preserved. The earlier manuscript dated to ca. 1300 contained only a short fragment of the legend (manuscript Cod. Upps. C871). The later manuscript, Cod. Holm. K4, often called *De hellige Kvinder* 'The holy women', is dated to ca. 1450. In the study we use the latter manuscript as it contains a longer, more comprehensive text. The pages used are 38–41.

Aff Sancta Marina is another legend about the life of a woman saint, Marina the Monk, who lived as a monk in an all-male monastery. *Huoel Sancte Pouel vort pint* is a gruesome tale of St. Paul descending into hell and witnessing the grotesque punishments and suffering of lost souls. It is based on the apocryphal story *Visio Pauli*, which was translated into many languages of Europe and beyond during the classical period and the Middle Ages (Bullitta 2017:1). Both texts are preserved in the same manuscript as Kerst, i.e., Cod. Holm K4, dated to ca. 1450. The text of Mar is studied in its entirety, while for Pouel pages 24–26 are chosen.

Sjalens trost is the Old Danish version of the Old Swedish ST, based on the same German source text. The Danish version is split into two parts; the first part is preserved in one manuscript (Cod. Ups. C 529) and the second in another manuscript (Cod. Holm A 109). Both manuscripts are dated to 1425. The latter manuscript is used in the present study, and the fragment on pages 68–72 was chosen.

Profane prose: *Gesta danorum* (GD)

Gesta danorum is one of the first attempts to record the history of Denmark in the mother tongue. It is a collection of brief descriptions of individual events in the history of the country, as well as a list and description of its kings. There is a particular focus on the information about the church, particularly the archdiocese in Lund. That fact, and the presence of linguistic traits typical of the Scanian dialect, lead researchers to conclude that the text might have originated in Lund (GD, Akhøj Nielsen 2015). The text is preserved in two manuscripts, both from ca. 1450. Manuscript C67 is used here. The text itself is dated to around 1380–1400. Chapters 1 (Humble), 4 (Guttorm), 6 (Halfdan) and 7 (Rolf Krake) were chosen for the study.

3.2.2.3 Icelandic
Religious sagas: *Mörtu saga og Maríu Magdalenu* (Marta)

Mörtu saga og Maríu Magdalenu is the Old Norse version of the apocryphal legend of the sisters of Lazarus, Martha and Mary of Bethany. The character of Mary of Bethany was later conflated with Mary Magdalen. The legends tell stories of the sisters' lives and miracles they performed or witnessed. The text was translated from Latin ca. 1350. It is preserved in five manuscripts. The oldest manuscript (NoRA 79 fragm.) is dated to 1350 and is considered to be the original compilation, on which other manuscripts are based (Van Deusen 2012:201). In the NoRA manuscript only a short fragment of the legend survived; for this reason, the edition of the saga used in the present study is based on manuscript AM 233a fol., dated to 1350–1375. The fragment chosen for the study is the first 1133 words of the saga text.

Sagas: *Víglundar saga* (Vig), *Bandamanna saga* (Band), *Gunnars saga Keldugnúpsfífls* (Gun), *Finnboga saga ramma* (Finn)

Víglundar saga tells the love story of Víglund and Ketilríð and their desire to marry despite the objections of her family. The saga is dated to ca. 1400 and is preserved in many manuscripts. One of the oldest manuscripts is AM 551 4to, dated to 1500. The fragment chosen for the corpus consists of the first 1462 words of the saga.

Bandamanna saga tells the story of Grettir's nephew Ospakr and his friend and protector Oddr. Oddr wants to help his less fortunate friend and invites Ospakr to live with him and lead his household, from which many family disputes arise. The saga was composed around 1350, although some scholars argue that it was created at the end of the 13th century (cf. Magerøy 1981). It is preserved in two major manuscripts: the so-called *Möðruvallabók* (AM 132 fol.) dated to ca. 1350, and the so-called *Konungsbók* (GKS 2845 4to) dated to ca. 1425.[5] In the present study chapters 1 and 2 are considered.

Gunnars saga Keldugnúpsfífls and *Finnboga saga ramma* are considered to be post-classical sagas, as they were composed later than the sagas previously described. Both sagas are dated to the late 14th century, Finn being a somewhat older saga than Gunnar. Finn is preserved, among others, in the manuscript *Möðruvallabók* (AM 132 fol.) and Gunnar survives only in quite late manuscripts

---

5 Note that this is a different manuscript than the earlier *Konungsbók* (GKS 1157 fol.) which contains a copy of *Grágás*.

from the 17th century (e.g., AM 572 c 4to). The fragments excerpted for the study are the first 1865 words of Gunnar and the first 2930 words of Finn.

3.2.3 Period III (1450–1550)

3.2.3.1 Swedish

Religious prose: *Linköpinglegendariet, Legenden om Sankta Amalberga* (Linc)

Linköpinglegendariet is a collection of hagiographic legends composed around 1520. In the first part of the work there are fifteen legends translated by Nils Ragvaldi, including the legend of St. Amalberga. The legend is preserved in the manuscript Linc B 70a, dated to the first half of the 16th century. For the present study pages 278–281 were chosen.

Profane prose: *Didrikssagan* (Did), *Historia Trojana* (Troja)

Didrikssagan is the Swedish translation of the Old German story of Didrik of Bern. The Swedish translation is dated to 1450 (Henning 1970:28) and is based on an earlier Old Norse version from ca. 1250 (Skrzypek 2012:21). The manuscript containing the text, Skokloster 115, 116, is dated to ca. 1500. For the analysis chapters 79–87 were chosen.

Historia Trojana is the Swedish translation from Latin of the story of the Trojan War. There is only one extant manuscript of the text, translated in 1529 and published in 1892 (Holm D 3a). Troja was chosen for the study as the last Old Swedish text, in line with many previous studies (Ståhle 1967:121, Hirvonen 1987:63, Delsing 1999, Håkansson 2008:21). Pages 1–6 are included in the analysis.

3.2.3.2 Danish

Religious prose: *Af Jeronimi levned* (Jer), *Af Katherine legende* (Kat), *Jesu Barndoms Bog* (Jesu)

Af Jeronimi levned and *Af Katherine legende* are legends about Saint Jerome and Saint Catherine of Siena respectively. Both texts are preserved in the manuscript called *Mariager Legende-Håndskrift*, dated to 1488. It was composed at the Saint Bridget monastery in Mariager in Denmark. For the present study chapters 2–4 (pages 341–345) of Jer and chapters 20–22 (pages 346–347) of Kat are chosen.

Jesu Barndoms Bog is an apocryphal story about the childhood of Jesus Christ and the miracles he performed. Stories about St. Mary, the birth of Christ, etc. also make up an important part of the book. The manuscript is based on a version by Gotfred af Ghemen from 1508. The stories are based on an apocryphal gospel by an unknown author. The Danish version is largely based on a German poem, *Marienleben* by a monk named Philip (Jesu, Skovgaard Boeck 2015). The chapters chosen for the present study are 4–7 (4: Abrathar, 5: Maria og Josef, 6: Bebudelsen, 7: Jesu fødsel).

Profane prose: *Karl Magnus Krønike* (KM)

Karl Magnus Krønike is the Danish version of the tales of Charlemagne and, like the earlier Swedish version, was based on the Old Norwegian *Karlamagnus Saga*. There are three Danish manuscripts; the oldest version, which we use in the present study, originated in 1480. The fragments chosen are pages 138–149.

3.2.3.3 Icelandic
Sagas: *Gísla saga Súrssonar* (Gis), *Vilhjálms saga Sjóðs* (Vil), *Jarlmanns saga og Hermanns* (Jarl)

Gísla saga Súrssonar is one of the sagas of the Icelanders. It tells the story of Gisli who is forced to kill his brother-in-law as a revenge for another brother-in-law's death. Gisli is then outlawed resulting in a thirteen years' long exile, until he is finally hunted down and killed. Although dated to ca. 1200, it is only available in manuscripts from the beginning of the 1400s.

Vilhjálms saga Sjóðs is a long chivalric saga. While probably inspired by translations of continental romances, it is an original Icelandic knightly saga. Vilhjálm's genre is quite distinct from that of the earlier classical sagas of Icelanders, as it does not focus so much on the history of Iceland, but rather on more exotic and romantic adventures of knights in distant countries. It is dated to the first half of the 15th century, and is preserved in many manuscripts from the 17th century. The earliest known manuscript is AM 548 4to, dated to 1543. The fragment chosen for the study encompasses the first 1039 words of the text.

Jarlmanns saga og Hermanns is another romance saga about the lives of two foster brothers, Hermann and Jarlmann, and their difficulties in finding wives. It is dated to the second half of the 15th century. The text of Jarlmann is preserved in numerous manuscripts, the earliest being the so-called *Eggertsbók* ('Book of Egert', AM 556b 4to) composed in the late 15th century. The fragment selected for the present study spans the first 1570 words of the text.

3.3 The DiaDef Tool and Its Benefits for the Study

3.3.1 *Tool Overview*

The process of collecting linguistic data was facilitated by computer software, the manual tagging system DiaDef (Diachrony of Definiteness), based on the open-source Tagger framework, available on the GitHub platform (https://github.com/rjawor/tagging). More information about systems of the Tagger family can be obtained at http://rjawor.vm.wmi.amu.edu.pl/wiki.

Similar systems are commonly used in contemporary linguistic research; see for instance Haig and Schnell (2015). Features of DiaDef include:
- import of texts in textual format (.txt or Microsoft Word) into documents;
- storing of information about the language of the document and the epoch in which it was written;
- automatic splitting of the text into sentences and individual words;
- manual assignment of tags to individual words.

The key functionality of the DiaDef tool is multi-level annotation of words and sentences in larger documents. The tool provides several features that improve the efficiency of use. For most annotation levels the system displays a context-sensitive list of prompts of available annotation tags. For a word under annotation the system displays a "prompt cloud", which consists of a set of tag suggestions.

DiaDef minimizes the cost of usage errors or system failure. Each annotation decision is saved automatically in a periodically backed-up database. There is no save button. This solution ensures protection against the loss of valuable annotations. The wide variety of configuration settings ensures the flexibility of the tagger, allowing it to be used in various scenarios. On request, DiaDef generates statistics concerning occurrences of specific classes of words and word collocations in a specified document or collection of documents.

3.3.2 *Multi-Level Tagging*

To begin the tagging process, the user uploads a text document into the system. Upon upload, the document is automatically split into sentences (see Figure 1).

The user can easily override the automatic sentence split (using "scissors" or "glue"; Fig. 1). The document is then annotated in sentence-by-sentence mode.

Each sentence is automatically split into words. A split sentence is presented in Figure 2. The user may also override the word split, for example to divide a word into a stem and a suffix. DiaDef may be configured to serve a variety of annotation tasks. The "configuration" option allows one to manage the languages of tagged documents as well as to configure annotation levels. Annotation levels may be freely ordered, added, deleted or edited. Editing of an

1. ▶ ✏ Thet ⚡ var ⚡ en ⚡ timæ ⚡ en ⚡ værliz ⚡ man ⚡ oc ⚡ han ⚡ haffde ⚡ en ⚡ dotter ✎

2. ▶ ✏ Han ⚡ fech ⚡ then ⚡ hugh ⚡ At ⚡ han ⚡ vildhe ⚡ sigh ⚡ i ⚡ closter ⚡ giffue ✎

FIGURE 1   Sentence splitting in DiaDef

	1.	Thet	var	en	timæ		en	værliz	man
Lexeme		There	was	one	time		a	worldly	man
POS					N				N
ART					EN			EN	ADJ-ST
REF					NON-SPEC			NEW	SPEC
Anchor									
Grammar					SG M NO-END			SG M NO-END	
Syntax					ADV			SBJ	
Semantics					INANIM COUNT CONCR			ANIM COUNT CONCR P-OR	

FIGURE 2   An example of an annotated sentence in DiaDef

annotation level consists in defining admissible values of respective tags. The DiaDef tool is thus very flexible, as it enables non-restricted editing and adding of tags on different levels of annotation, so that the information entered is well-suited for the objectives of the project at hand.

Words are annotated at eight levels: Lexeme (where the closest English lexical equivalent is given), POS (Parts of Speech), ART (article), REF (reference), Anchor (related "anchor" word), Grammar, Syntax, and Semantics. The annotation levels are presented in Table 20 together with the tags within these levels.

As indicated in Figure 2, each utterance is presented in the form of a table in DiaDef, where each lexeme appears as a separate column, and the abovementioned levels of tags appear as rows in the table. To facilitate and simplify the statistics generated in DiaDef, almost all of the information is annotated on the noun of the NP. We also occasionally tag possessive pronouns, but generally it is the noun that carries the full information. All of the tag annotation levels (all except for *Lexeme*, *Anchor* and *Add info*, which do not operate on tags) have a multiple-choice structure, i.e., several tags may be marked within one level, as long as the tags are not mutually exclusive. Clicking on the row of a given

SOURCES, METHODS AND TOOLS

TABLE 20   The annotation tags defined for the present project

No.	Annotation levels	Tags
1.	Lexeme (English translation)	–
2.	POS (Part of speech)	N (noun), PRON (pronoun), ART (article), NUM (numeral), P (preposition), V (verb)
3.	ART (articles, lack of articles, other elements)	BN (bare noun), BN-PL (plural bare noun), -IN (postposed definite article), EN (indefinite article), DEN (preposed definite article), DEM (demonstrative), ADJ-ST (strong adjective), ADJ-WK (weak adjective), REL (relative clause), NUM (numeral), POSS (possessive), Poss-refl (reflexive possessive pronoun), Poss-gen (genitive), Poss-pro (possessive pronoun)
4.	REF (type of discourse reference)	DIR-A (direct anaphora), INDIR-A (indirect anaphora), U (unique reference), G (generic reference), NEW (new referent), SPEC (specific reference), NON-SPEC (non-specific reference), NON-REF (non-referential)
5.	Anchor (of the discourse reference)	–
6.	Grammar	SG (singular), PL (plural), NOM (nominative case), ACC (accusative case), DAT (dative case), GEN (genitive case),

TABLE 20 The annotation tags defined for the present project (*cont.*)

No.	Annotation levels	Tags
7.	Syntax	OBL (oblique case), NO-END (no case ending), M (masculine gender), F (feminine gender), N (neuter gender) SBJ (subject), OBJ (object), ADV (adverbial), MOD (modifier), NEG (includes negation), P-OBJ (prepositional object), PRED (predicative)
8.	Semantics	ANIM (animate), INANIM (inanimate), COUNT (countable), MASS (mass NP), ABSTR (abstract), CONCR (concrete), P-OR (possessor), P-UM (possessum)
9.	Add info (additional information)	–

level highlights the tags that one can choose from. Simple keyboard shortcuts displayed in brackets are assigned to the tags, which facilitates the tagging process.

The first annotation level, called *Lexeme*, is a free write-in row where we enter the English translation of each lexeme. The second level defines the part of speech (POS) of a given lexeme. Since in this project we deal exclusively with nominal phrases, the vast majority of lexemes are tagged as N (noun) or PRON (pronoun). The third level is the article level (ART), where we annotate information about the types of articles (or the lack thereof) that appear in an NP. On this level we include not exclusively articles, but also other elements that appear with articles or in their place (e.g., possessive pronouns, adjectives, numerals) or elements that may have some influence on the articles used in an NP (e.g., a following relative clause). On the fourth level, REF, we tag

SOURCES, METHODS AND TOOLS   89

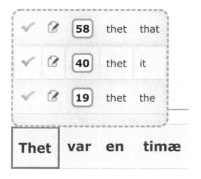

FIGURE 3
Automatically generated tagging suggestions in DiaDef

the discourse reference type, i.e., whether the referent is new (specific or non-specific), unique, generic, anaphoric (direct or indirect), or non-referential. The fifth level is called *Anchor*, and enables us to mark in the previous discourse the referent in which the reference of a given noun is anchored. The sixth level covers grammatical information, i.e., the number, case and gender of a given noun. On the seventh level information about syntactic roles is entered. The eighth level pertains to semantic information. Three pairs of mutually exclusive features are defined here, i.e., animate–inanimate, countable–mass, and abstract–concrete, as well as the role in a possessive construction, i.e., possessor–possessum. Next, there is an additional annotation level where we tag the types of indirect anaphora in a more detailed way. The last level is again a free write-in option where in the course of the tagging process we enter any additional information, such as notes on problematic cases.

The corpus texts were tagged in DiaDef manually by the authors with the help of a master's degree student who assisted in the project for six months. The texts were tagged primarily from February 2017 to February 2018, although after that period the tagged texts were continually checked and corrected, and minor changes were also frequently made when necessary.

3.3.3 *Automatically Generated Suggestions*

To improve tagging efficiency, the system suggests hints whenever possible, i.e., when a word has already been tagged or when the tagging could be deduced automatically. Tag suggestions appear in a "cloud" above the word (Figure 3).

Figure 3 presents tag suggestions for the word *thet* 'that'. The suggestions come from previous annotations of the word. The user can accept the set of suggestions by clicking the 'check' symbol in the leftmost column.

TABLE 21 Overall numbers of annotated words in the DiaDef system

Language	Word count
Danish	15,788
Icelandic	20,308
Norwegian	989[a]
Swedish	14,533
Total	51,618

a   As it was difficult to obtain a comparable corpus of Norwegian texts, these annotated texts were not analyzed further.

3.3.4 Collected Data

The DiaDef system for Scandinavian languages has been in active use since early 2017. The current (as of 30 September 2019) counts of annotated words in four languages from the database are presented in Table 21.

The collected data have been used to compute various statistics.

3.3.5 Statistics Generator

The DiaDef tool has a Statistics Module, which is used to compute on demand statistics based on the data collected in the system. The module has two key functionalities: searching for words or phrases which meet specified criteria, and computing various statistics regarding those words. There are several functions that can be invoked from the Statistics Module, i.e., specific word form search, collocation search and proportional statistics.

Using the specific word form search option, the user can search for a specific word form with a single tag or various combinations of tags. The user can specify criteria for word search using the search window illustrated in Figure 4.

In this case the system will search for words tagged as nouns (N) in the singular (SG). The system enables preliminary sorting of the data by language and period (by using the filter panel at the top of the page), and it generates lists of cases displayed in larger context with direct links to the edition of a given case, as shown in Figure 5. By clicking on the "Edit" icon, the user is redirected to sentence edit mode, where the word in question is automatically highlighted. This feature greatly facilitates the control and correction of individual tags and examples within these tags. For instance, by searching for all occurrences of the dative case we can browse through the lists of words and correct possible mistakes.

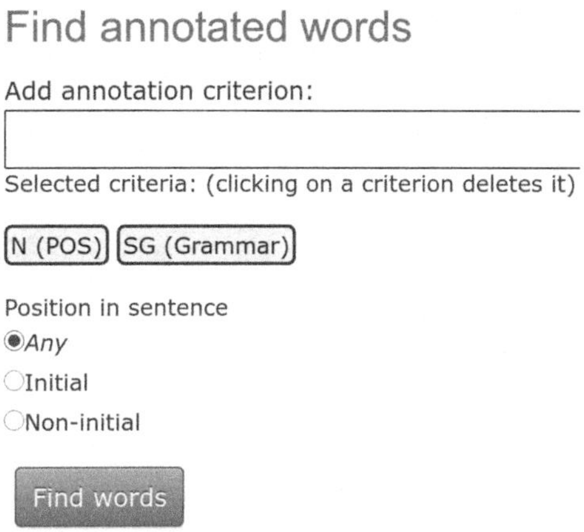

Find annotated words

Add annotation criterion:

Selected criteria: (clicking on a criterion deletes it)

[N (POS)] [SG (Grammar)]

Position in sentence
● *Any*
○ Initial
○ Non-initial

[Find words]

FIGURE 4
The search window for simple statistics in DiaDef

No.	Document	Language	Epoque	Word	Context
1	DA_ErL.doc	da	classical	bonden	Takær **bonden** sinæ dottær man i flet til sich
2	DA_ErL.doc	da	classical	dottær	Takær bonden sinæ **dottær** man i flet til sich
3	DA_ErL.doc	da	classical	man	Takær bonden sinæ dottær **man** i flet til sich

FIGURE 5 An example of simple statistics generated in DiaDef—the dative case in Old Swedish

Using collocation search the user can also search for multiple words which appear together in a single sentence. These are referred to in the system as collocations. An example of a collocation search is given in Figure 6.

In this case the user is searching for sentences which contain both a noun and an article. It is possible to search for collocations of a maximum of five words. The number of criteria for each word is limited only by the number of tags available in the system. Results of collocations search are presented in the same way as in specific word forms search.

The last option is the proportional statistics search. This kind of search is based on the word form search, although it takes two sets of criteria: main search criteria and additional specific criteria. The system first takes the main search criteria and counts the number of words that meet those criteria. It then appends the additional specific criteria to the main criteria list and counts how many words meet all these criteria. Lastly, it computes the ratio of the number of words meeting all the criteria to the number of words meeting only the main criteria. For instance, we can search for the number of animate (ANIM) and singular (SG) referents within the main search of NPs with a postposed definite article (-IN). The result will be presented as in Figure 7. Note that the results can be refined with the use of filtering to a specified language, epoch and documents.

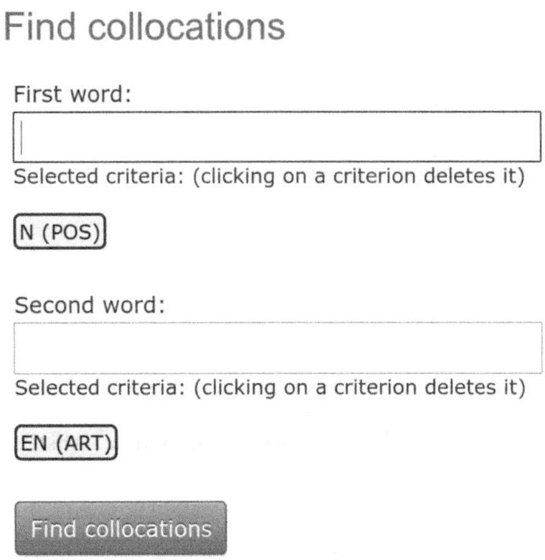

Find collocations

First word:

[   ]

Selected criteria: (clicking on a criterion deletes it)

[N (POS)]

Second word:

[   ]

Selected criteria: (clicking on a criterion deletes it)

[EN (ART)]

[Find collocations]

FIGURE 6
An example of collocation statistics search in DiaDef

Proportional statistics

Narrow by:

Language	Epoque
☐ Any	☑ Any
☑ Swedish	☐ middle
☑ Danish	☐ old
☐ Norwegian	☐ classical
☑ Icelandic	
☐ Modern Swedish	

Number of words tagged as: *Noun*, . Position in sentence: *Any*
1176

Number of words more specifically tagged as: *Noun*, *singular*, . Position in sentence: *Any*
494 (42.01%)

FIGURE 7
An example of proportional statistics generated in DiaDef—animate singular referents within referents with postposed definite article

3.3.6 *Regression Analysis*

With the use of data collected in DiaDef, a set of statistics regarding the usage of articles was computed. The methodology of this analysis was the following. The problem of choosing the correct article was treated as multi-class classification in the set of all words tagged as nouns in the DiaDef system. The three classes (i.e., possible article choices) were:

1. -IN (the incipient definite article)
2. EN (the incipient indefinite article)
3. BN (bare nouns)

SOURCES, METHODS AND TOOLS   93

The independent variables were tags assigned to the nouns at the following levels: case, number, gender, function, animacy, countability, concrete and anaphora. The aim of the analysis was to measure the impact of these tags on the choice of article.

The analysis was performed using Vowpal Wabbit software, which is capable of performing efficient multi-regression for the needs of classification. It can also be used to output information about the relative impact of features on the choice of class. In this scenario, the features are the tags assigned to words, and the class, as mentioned above, is the choice of the article.

3.4   Annotation Issues

Anyone who has worked with authentic diachronic data will appreciate that even the best tool will not always help resolve all problems. Even though great care was taken to include only self-contained text fragments in the corpus, at times we had to struggle with the classification of a given form and its use. In this section we briefly present the most important issues that arose and how they were dealt with. The choices made were to some extent arbitrary, however, we strove to remain consistent in making similar choices in similar circumstances.

We encountered relatively few problems with tags concerning the form of the noun, such as information on number or gender. There are a number of excellent dictionaries available which may be consulted (e.g., the Swedish dictionaries at spraakbanken.gu.se), often the form of other constituents of the NP revealed the correct gender or number. However, tagging case was more of a challenge, since in the period studied the case system in Danish and Swedish is dismantled and by Period III can no longer be tagged. We have therefore introduced the tag NO-END to mark such nouns that had no ending, but had the system been viable, would have them.

The fact that the case system underwent such significant changes between 1200 and 1550 in both Danish and Swedish has consequences for the annotation of the corpus. While it is possible to annotate each NP for case in Icelandic in all three periods, the annotation presents more of a challenge in Danish as early as Period I, and in Swedish in both Period II and III. Apart from the tags NOM, ACC, DAT and GEN for distinct case forms, we also used OBL to annotate forms that were not unequivocally accusative, dative or genitive (most such forms were found among feminine nouns, but also quite a few among masculine nouns, such as *bondi* 'yeoman'). A certain degree of syncretism is a natural part of any inflectional system. However, we encountered problems when dealing with certain nouns in Danish, and later in Swedish, which always appeared without endings, irrespective of their function in the clause. The lack of ending should not be confused with zero ending, which was a part of the paradigm in all languages studied. The focus of our study is the rise of definiteness and not the decline of case. For that reason, some nouns which had no case ending were still annotated with a given case if they were modified by adjectives whose form unequivocally displayed a case ending, even if, strictly speaking, the noun itself did not show case inflection at all, as in (118).

(118)   oc   ropaþo   mz   högh-o   **röst**   sighiande
        and   called   with high-OBL voice   saying
        'and called with a high voice saying' (SV_HML, Period II)

It is important to bear in mind that the tag NO-END was limited only to cases in which there was no declined form of the noun available; it was not used where a zero-ending contrasted with other forms, as in (119).

(119)   Ok   ginstan   wiste   diäfwl-en   at   thät war   sand-ir   **gudh**
        and   immediately knew   devil-DEF   that it   was   true-NOM   god
        som   präst-in   fördhe
        which   priest-DEF   carried
        'And the devil knew immediately that it was the true God which the priest carried' (SV_Järt, Period II)

In (119) above the noun is in the expected form, with a zero ending signifying nominative case (which is also visible on the adjective), and contrasting with *gudh-s* in the genitive and *gudh-i* in the dative (the accusative being syncretic with the nominative).

However, in a number of examples in Period II in both Danish and Swedish the nouns appeared without the expected endings, e.g., the genitive -s (the expected forms after the preposition *til* 'to' are *bords* 'table's', *lands* 'land's').

(120)   Nu   tha   the   sama   quinna-n   thiänte til   **bordh** sin-om
        now   that DEF   same   woman-DEF   served   to   table   her.REFL-DAT
        herra   vm   middaghin
        master.OBL   about   dinner
        'Now that the same woman served her master at the table at dinnertime.' (SV_Järt, Period II)

(121) *The toko hona in j thera skip oc førdho hona mz*
they took her in in their ship and led her with
*sik   til **land***
themselves to land
'They lifted her (out of the water) onboard their ship and carried her with them to the land.' (SV_ST, Period II)

In such cases the tag NO-END was used, to demonstrate that the syntactic position would call for the genitive ending, had the case system been intact.

While the annotation of formal features did cause some problems, it was the annotation of the function of a given NP that proved to be challenging, since at times it required making arbitrary choices. The functions could be tagged as: direct anaphor DIR-A, indirect anaphor INDIR-A, larger situation use (unique reference) U. A rule of thumb was that if an NP included a noun which had a co-referring NP with an identical lexeme in the preceding text, it was tagged as direct anaphor; if there was no connection between the NP and any other element (nominal or verbal) in the text it was tagged as larger situation use; all uses that could be considered anchored in the text were tagged as indirect anaphora. Any element that could serve as an anchor was linked via the Anchor tag with the indirect anaphor.

As it turned out, this rule of thumb worked well. Nevertheless, in several cases the choices were not easy to make. In (122) an example from Danish is presented. The noun marked in bold, *haff-it* 'sea-DEF', is definite and could be definite for a number of reasons. It could be treated as anaphora, since 'sea' is mentioned earlier in the text, albeit by a different term, *mær-it* 'sea-DEF'.[6] The question remains, which anaphora is it? Is it a direct one, since obviously the same referent is presented by both NPs? Or indirect, anchored in the situation of traveling on a sailing ship? Or perhaps 'locally' unique, connected with the area in which the scene takes place? It could even be considered unique in the sense of Hawkins' larger situation use, if we assume that for the people of the 15th century the world consisted of one large piece of land, one large reservoir of water and the skies. In this interpretation 'the sea' would receive definite marking just as 'the heaven' does.

---

6   There were two terms which described large reservoir of water in Old Swedish, *hav* and the obsolete *mær*, which could be used synonymously.

(122) *Tha the vpa **mær-it** como saghdho the som hænne førsho*
when they upon sea-DEF came said they who her led
at hon skulde theras vilgha giøra ælla the vildo hænne i
that she should their will do or they will her in
***haff-it** casta*
sea-DEF throw
'As they came out to sea, those who had kidnapped her said that she must abide by their will or they will throw her into the sea.' (DA_ST, Period II)

In fact, the referent is presented as definite at the beginning of the story; the text opens with the passage in (123) below.

(123) *budho sinum thiænarum at the skuldo hænne mæth skip ofvir*
asked their servants that they should her with ship over
***mær-it** føra*
sea-DEF take
'(They) asked their servants that they should take her by ship over the sea.' (DA_ST, Period II)

Mærit 'sea-DEF' is used in definite form from the first mention; the referent may be considered anchored in the phrase *mæth skip* 'by ship' and in this sense constitute an indirect anaphoric use.

In this particular case we opted for indirect anaphora. Even though the referent has been mentioned previously, the choice of a different lexeme suggests different qualities of the referent. It is also anchored in the situation of sea voyage presented in the text.

The choices that had to be made naturally imply that the quantitative results could be slightly different, had different choices been made. This is inevitable in any diachronic study. Therefore, we have also examined the data qualitatively and inspected each example separately. In this section it is the most troublesome examples that are of greatest interest and provide greatest insight (see Chapter 5).

3.5 Summary

In this chapter, we have presented our corpus, or rather a collection of three sub-corpora, comprising Danish, Icelandic and Swedish texts from 1200–1550. 1200 corresponds roughly to the beginnings of literacy based on the Roman script rather than the runic alphabet futhark. The date marks the beginning of the so-called 'old' period in Danish, Swedish and Icelandic language history. 1550 is a discretionary date concluding the 'old' period, which coincides with a number of important social events, such as the divorce from the Catholic church, the introduction of print and the establishment of the national states. It is customary to subdivide the 1200–1550 period into older (or classical) and younger with, again, a discretionary date 1350, which coincides with the Black Death plague, which had a catastrophic effect on the population of the Scandinavian countries and profound results for their languages. We have additionally subdivided the younger period into two, 1350–1450 and 1450–1550, in order to study the ongoing linguistic change more precisely. In the book, we refer to these periods as Period I (1200–1350), Period II (1350–1450) and Period III (1450–1550) respectively.

From the extant corpora of texts, we have chosen whole texts or longer passages representing all prosaic genres of the time, i.e., legal, religious and profane prose. The total amount of tokens is about 280,000, from which we have annotated over 9000 NPs, ca. 3000 for each language in the sample.

For annotation, a programme called DiaDef was used, which is a manual tagging system allowing multi-level tagging and adding both new tags and new tagging levels. The tool also includes a statistics generator which can be used to obtain a number of statistical data, in particular proportional statistics, which were utilized to a great extent in the present study. It further allows export of data to other statistics generators, so that other types of analysis can be conducted. For the present study, we have used this function to perform regression analysis.

We have also discussed some issues arising when annotating historical texts, concerning both the form of a given noun, in particular the annotation of case, and its function, in particular the indirect anaphora as opposed to the direct anaphora, on the one hand, and the larger situation use, on the other. The case system is weakened or dismantled in Danish and Swedish within the period studied, which has consequences for the categorization of a given form. Also, the limited context does not always allow unequivocal categorization of the NP function and it is the decision of the annotator which function is chosen. The decisions made have consequences for the statistical analysis presented in the following chapter and the most troublesome examples are discussed at length in Chapter 5.

CHAPTER 4

The Diachrony of (In)definiteness—A Quantitative Study

4.1 Introduction

In this chapter we present the results obtained from the annotated corpus. We will discuss the 'profile' of a defNP and an indefNP in all languages and periods chosen for the study. We aim to establish a connection between the grammaticalizing category of definiteness and other syntactic categories such as number, gender and case, and semantic categories such as animacy.

4.2 General Data

We begin by presenting an overview of the data. In Chapter 3 we described the corpus built for the purposes of the project and the tool employed to annotate the texts and harvest data. As mentioned there, there are some discrepancies in terms of size between the three languages studied, the Icelandic part of the corpus being the longest. We aimed to analyse ca. 3000 NPs in each language; however, we also wished to study longer narrative passages and to do so *in extenso*. Tables 22 and 23 present the total percentages of definite and indefinite NPs in each language and period respectively. We will begin by discussing the overall results for defNPs.

In discussing these results, we should keep in mind that the texts in Period I represent two genres: legal prose and religious prose. As BNs are notoriously favoured in legal prose (even in modern times; see Gunnarsson 1982) this may be reflected in the results, even though we selected passages of high narrativity to avoid this as far as possible (see Chapter 3).

Percentage-wise there are more definite nouns in the Swedish part of the corpus than in either Danish or Icelandic, and the difference between Swedish and the other two languages is most clearly visible in Period II. Each language exhibits different results and developments in each of the three periods studied: in Danish we observe a gradual but constant rise in the frequency of the definite form, with the numbers from Period I doubling in Period II and again in Period III, resulting in triple the value from Period I in Period III. Icelandic exhibits more uniform results in all three periods, but again with the highest-

TABLE 22 The definite nouns in the corpus—an overview

Language	Words	Nouns	-IN		Nouns	-IN		Nouns	-IN		Nouns	-IN	
					Period I			Period II			Period III		
Danish	15,788	2,900	349	12.03%	1,097	67	6.11%	1,016	139	13.68%	787	143	18.17%
Swedish	14,533	2,922	495	16.94%	1,194	94	7.87%	1,093	294	26.90%	635	107	16.85%
Icelandic	20,308	3,221	330	10.25%	1,536	157	10.22%	1,037	91	8.78%	648	82	12.65%

TABLE 23 Indefinite nouns in the corpus—an overview

Language	Words	Nouns	EN		Nouns	EN		Nouns	EN		Nouns	EN	
					Period I			Period II			Period III		
Danish	15,788	2,900	147	5.07%	1,097	16	1.46%	1,016	78	7.68%	787	53	6.73%
Swedish	14,533	2,922	143	4.89%	1,194	24	2.01%	1,093	70	6.40%	635	49	7.72%
Icelandic	20,308	3,221	42	1.30%	1,536	14	0.91%	1,037	21	2.03%	648	7	1.08%

percentage in Period III. Finally, Swedish begins with similar results to Danish in Period I, but peaks in Period II to reach a lower percentage of definites in Period III.

The variation in Icelandic is, at least superficially, marginal, and the results in all three periods are quite similar. A fact often noted in the literature on Icelandic is how little the language seems to have changed (with respect to morphology and syntax) between 1200 and modern times (e.g., Friðriksson 2008). This would perhaps mean that the definite article in Icelandic is already well-developed in Period I, while in Danish and Swedish it seems to be a form intermediate between the original demonstrative and the target definite article. We will return to this hypothesis by the end of this chapter.

The very high percentage for Swedish in Period II also calls for closer inspection. It may be a result of the dominant genre of the period (religious prose) with many definite abstract nouns, such as *högfärdh-in* 'pride-DEF' (Skrzypek 2012:146–151). The tendency to mark abstract nouns as definite is present in Modern Swedish as well (e.g., *Kärleken är blind*, lit. 'The love is blind'; Perridon 1989:174). Interestingly, Danish and Swedish have similar values in both Period I and Period III, the significant difference between them being found in Period II. In modern Danish and Swedish defNPs differ in terms of their internal structure in the presence of modifiers—in Swedish the definite suffix is used with modifiers (see section 2.4.1 on double definiteness), while Danish uses the pre-adjectival definite article only (see also Chapter 1 on NPs in North Germanic). This does not, however, account for the differences found in the periods studied, as double definiteness has not yet become fully established. In the Swedish corpus the incipient definite article is combined with the preposed definite article (i.e., in a double definiteness structure) only in 1.06 %, 12.59 % and 16.82 % of uses of defNPs in the three periods respectively. Further, we even find some examples of double definiteness structure in Danish as well (in 5.76 % of defNP uses, only in Period II). The difference in frequencies of -IN in Period II is thus most probably connected to the type of texts and referents that they include.

Where the grammaticalizing indefinite article is concerned, the division between Continental (Danish and Swedish) and Insular (Icelandic) languages is very pronounced. While Danish and Swedish return very similar results—the overall percentage of NPs with EN is similar in both languages, and the trend across periods also indicates similarities, with lower frequencies in Period I and higher in Periods II and III—the results for Icelandic are lower in Period I and remain lower, which may be an indication of the fact that the grammaticalization of the indefinite article does not take place in the timeframe of our study. Indeed, Icelandic has not developed the indefinite article (so far), although there seem to have been some article-like uses of the numeral EN in its history, beyond Period III as defined here (see Kliś 2019).

We must bear in mind that EN signifies both a pure numeral and the incipient indefinite article (see Chapter 2, grammaticalization of the indefinite article). Even though there is no indefinite article in Icelandic we naturally find the numeral EN, and such results and examples will be reported here. The general results presented in this section indicate that as early as the 1200s Icelandic differed from Danish and Swedish, and that differences between them persist until 1550. The definite article seems to have been well-developed as early as Period I in Icelandic. The indefinite article does not grammaticalize at all. Although Danish and Swedish also exhibit some mutual differences, they follow roughly the same path from article-less languages to languages with both definite and indefinite articles.

It would naturally be interesting to examine how the results in Tables 22 and 23 compare with modern data. It is unfortunately not feasible to obtain data from large corpora including frequencies of suffixed definite articles in the Nordic languages without conducting an in-depth study. It is, however, possible to compare the frequencies of indefinite articles in present-day Swedish, Danish and Icelandic with our historical data. For Danish we use the data available from KorpusDK, particularly from *Korpus 2000* with 30 million tokens.[1] In that corpus the relative frequency of indefinite articles (*en/et*) per 1000 tokens is 25.61. In Old Danish, as indicated in Table 23, the relative frequency is much lower, with 9.31 indefinite articles per 1000 words. For Swedish we use the data available from one of the Språkbanken's corpora, the PAROLE corpus, which includes over 24 million tokens.[2] The relative frequency of the indefinite articles (*en/ett*) in that corpus is 18.05 per 1000 tokens. In our Old Swedish material, the frequency is substantially lower and is very close to the frequency of indefinite articles in Old Danish, at 9.84 per 1000 tokens. Note that the relative frequencies in present-day Danish and Swedish differ greatly from each other, indicating that Danish uses indefinite articles more frequently than Swedish. For the Icelandic data we use The Tagged Icelandic Corpus (MÍM), which has 25 million tokens.[3] Since present-day Icelandic does not have an indefinite article, the lexeme *einn* 'one' occurs in frequency lists as a numeral or as a pronoun (e.g., *I met one girl*). *Einn* as a pronoun has a relative frequency of 0.48 per 1000 tokens, while the frequency of *einn* as a numeral is 1.48 per 1000 tokens. If these two are taken together, the frequency amounts to 1.96 per 1000 tokens, which is very close to the results for the Old Icelandic data, in which the frequency of the numeral *einn* is 2.07 per 1000 tokens. In sum, as expected, Icelandic does not reveal any substantial differences in the frequency of the numeral one. Old Swedish and Old Danish, on the other hand, differ from their present-day counterparts in that the frequency of indefinite articles has doubled in Swedish and almost tripled in Danish.

In the following sections we will study the correlations between the occurrence of either -IN or EN and major grammatical categories of the noun, such as number, case and gender, and semantic categories such as animacy, and finally between the occurrence of the incipient articles and syntactic roles.

4.3 Definiteness and Number

Modern North Germanic languages have all developed definite articles which may be used in both singular and plural NPs. The indefinite article, on the other hand (in all languages apart from Icelandic, which has not grammaticalized the

---

[1] Source: https://ordnet.dk/korpusdk; *Korpus 2000*; 30 million tokens; accessed: 18/11/2019.
[2] Source: https://spraakbanken.gu.se/korp/#?lang=en&stats_reduce=word&cqp=%5B%5D&corpus=parole; *PAROLE*; 24,303,096 tokens; accessed: 18/11/2019.
[3] Source: http://www.malfong.is/index.php?lang=en&pg=mim; 25 million tokens; accessed: 18/11/2019.

TABLE 24 Singular and plural nouns in the corpus (total frequencies)

N	Number	Period I		Period II		Period III	
Danish	SG	921	83.96%	809	79.63%	651	82.72%
	PL	176	16.04%	207	20.37%	136	17.28%
	Total	1,097	100.00%	1,016	100.00%	787	100.00%
Swedish	SG	938	78.56%	891	81.52%	516	81.26%
	PL	256	21.44%	202	18.48%	119	18.74%
	Total	1,194	100.00%	1,093	100.00%	635	100.00%
Icelandic	SG	1182	76.95%	740	71.36%	488	75.31%
	PL	354	23.05%	297	28.64%	160	24.69%
	Total	1,536	100.00%	1,037	100.00%	648	100.00%

indefinite at all), has grammaticalized only in the singular, unlike in languages such as Spanish where plural indefinites are also morphologically marked.

The lack of a plural indefinite article is a natural consequence of the fact that the article's etymology is the numeral 'one', by definition difficult to combine with a plural noun. The numeral needs to be fully grammaticalized in the indefinite article function to be used with plural referents.

We would expect the overall proportions between the numbers to remain constant in each language, irrespective of the period chosen. The results presented in Table 24 confirm these expectations, revealing that the percentage of singular nouns among all nouns oscillates around 80% and that of plural nouns around 20% in all languages in our study, in all periods. The Icelandic data exhibit a certain difference from the other languages, in that the percentage of plural nouns is on average higher. In general, considering the whole dataset, 78.91% of all noun phrases in the corpora are singular, while 21.09% are plural.

The percentages for the suffixed definite article -IN (see Table 25) are slightly higher for SG for all languages in all periods, and slightly lower for PL for all languages and in all periods, in comparison with the overall results. This is hardly surprising, since the modern North Germanic languages allow bare plurals, and the use of the definite article with plural referents is subject to the additional criterion of inclusiveness, or in Hawkins' terms, totality. As Hawkins discusses at length, the felicitous use of the definite article with plural count nouns and mass nouns requires that the speaker refer to the totality of the objects, e.g., *the tables* is equivalent to ***all the tables*** and *the water* to ***all the water*** in the relevant shared set. "If the speaker refers to less than this totality […] the hearer

TABLE 25   Singular and plural nouns with -IN

-IN	Number	Period I		Period II		Period III	
Danish	SG	63	94.03%	120	86.33%	134	93.71%
	PL	4	5.97%	19	13.67%	9	6.29%
	Total	67	100.00%	139	100.00%	143	100.00%
Swedish	SG	90	95.74%	266	90.48%	97	90.65%
	PL	4	4.26%	28	9.52%	10	9.35%
	Total	94	100.00%	294	100.00%	107	100.00%
Icelandic	SG	129	82.17%	79	86.81%	78	95.12%
	PL	28	17.83%	12	13.19%	4	4.88%
	Total	157	100.00%	91	100.00%	82	100.00%

objects" (Hawkins 1978:159). Thus, the use of the definite article with plurals is motivated by other factors than referent identifiability.

We can further note that -IN is least likely to be used with a plural referent in Period I in both Danish and Swedish, but also in Period III in Icelandic. The use of plural definites is highest in Period II in both Danish and Swedish and in Period I in Icelandic. We do not find EN with plural referents; as mentioned above the plural indefinite article has not developed at all in North Germanic.

Finally, we should note that there is at least one reason why we would not expect definite NPs to contain significantly different percentages of singular and plural nouns than those found in the overall data. It has been noted in the literature that number distinctions may be limited to nouns high in the animacy hierarchy or that there may be splits lower in the hierarchy (Smith-Stark 1974, Corbett 2000). Considering the plurality markings on the noun, Corbett cites English as an example of such a split, where abstract inanimates such as *friendliness* are unlikely to appear in the plural, as opposed to concrete inanimates such as *table* (Corbett 2000:66). A similar split applies in North Germanic, where more abstract inanimates often lack plural forms (e.g., *vänlighet* 'friendliness'). However, in contrast to English, these abstract inanimates easily take a definite form, e.g., *vänligheten* 'the friendliness'. In other words, the fact that there are abstract nouns in the corpus would influence the results in a language such as English, where these do not appear in the plural and do not (usually) take the definite article. In North Germanic abstract nouns take the definite article as concrete ones do, hence the higher percentage for singular definites in our results. We will return to the animacy hierarchy in section 4.7.

4.4 Definiteness and Gender

In all of the languages studied here the category of gender had three values in the studied periods, identical with those of Proto-Indo-European: masculine, feminine and neuter. In the Continental languages Danish and Swedish (and in some varieties of Norwegian Bokmål) the category has since been reduced to two values only: the so-called *utrum*, which came about through coalescence of the former masculine and feminine, and *neutrum*, which is a continuation of the original neuter gender. This change did not begin until the 16th century and was first noticeable in legal and official prose, while religious prose, being more conservative in this aspect, maintained the masculine–feminine distinction longer than other genres (Davidson 1990). Some Swedish dialects have retained the tripartite gender and even in standard language it is not impossible to use the pronoun *hon* 'she' with inanimate referent, but this use is restricted to a handful of nouns, e.g., *klocka* 'clock' in *Vad är klockan? Hon är tre*. 'What time is it? (lit. How much is the clock) She is three'. The process of gender reduction most likely originated in the pronominal paradigm (ibid.). Since the evolution of gender marking is of later date than the formation of the articles and falls well beyond the scope of the present work, we will not delve into the process further; however, we shall highlight some of the important interdependencies between the categories of gender and definiteness, in particular with reference to their exponents.

Gender is an inherent quality of the noun, which needs to be learned and usually cannot be deduced from the form of the noun (although in some languages there may exist quite reliable ways of 'guessing' the word's gender based on its form, e.g., the ending -*a* in Polish almost infallibly signals feminine gender). However, for other nominals it is an inflectional category. Both demonstratives and the numeral 'one', i.e., the etymological sources of articles, are inflected for gender. In this sense they may become exponents of this category, similarly as they are exponents of number and case.

The diachrony of gender reduction in North Germanic is as yet understudied. Davidson (1990) studies the development in Swedish, but the study is limited to the process of change in the pronominal paradigm only, i.e., the replacement of the original pronouns *han* 'he' and *hon* 'she', originally used as anaphoric pronouns for all nouns irrespective of their animacy (in Modern Swedish their use is limited to human referents), by the pronoun *den* 'it.UTR', in analogy to *det* 'it.N', used as an anaphoric pronoun for nouns of neuter gender.

Davidson does not research other pronouns or agreement phenomena, which means that the picture of gender reduction is not fully clear. However,

TABLE 26 The inflectional paradigm of the demonstrative *hinn* 'yon' in the singular

Hinn	M	F	N
NOM	hinn	hin	hit
ACC	hin	hina	hit
DAT	hinum	hinni	hinu
GEN	hins	hinnar	hins

TABLE 27 The inflectional paradigm of the numeral *enn* 'one'

Enn	M	F	N
NOM	enn	en	ett
ACC	enn	ena	ett
DAT	enom	enne	enom
GEN	ens	enna	ens

considering the forms relevant to our study, we may observe that the masculine and feminine distinction relied on case distinctions (the paradigms differ in each case) and that the masculine and feminine forms in the nominative were more similar to each other than either of them was to the neuter *det* or *ett*. Evidently, there were formal grounds for gender reduction, such as the similarity of masculine and feminine forms in the demonstrative paradigm and the loss of case, which in turn led to fewer distinctions between masculine and feminine words. It should be noted, however, that despite these formal premises, the process of gender system reduction may have been facilitated by semantic similarities between masculine and feminine classes, i.e., the higher proportion of nouns denoting animate, and in particular, human referents than in the neuter gender. Animacy seems to be the driving force of many changes in nominal categories in North Germanic.

The results for all of the NPs in the corpus (see Table 28) reveal that nouns of the masculine gender constitute on average 48% of all nouns, while the feminine and the neuter genders constitute on average around 25% each. Although it is natural that some genders may form larger classes, with more constituents

TABLE 28 The proportions of all genders in the corpus

N	Gender	Period I		Period II		Period III	
Danish	M	502	45.76%	514	50.59%	380	48.28%
	F	297	27.07%	247	24.31%	242	30.75%
	N	298	27.16%	255	25.10%	165	20.97%
	Total	1,097	100.00%	1,016	100.00%	787	100.00%
Swedish	M	520	43.55%	520	47.58%	263	41.42%
	F	341	28.56%	320	29.28%	174	27.40%
	N	333	27.89%	253	23.14%	198	31.18%
	Total	1,194	100.00%	1,093	100.00%	635	100.00%
Icelandic	M	744	48.44%	525	50.62%	355	54.78%
	F	371	24.15%	256	24.69%	136	20.99%
	N	421	27.41%	256	24.69%	157	24.23%
	Total	1,536	100.00%	1,037	100.00%	648	100.00%

than others, the results do not necessarily indicate that this is the case in North Germanic. The results reported are the token and not the type frequencies; thus, out of all of the nouns in the corpus ca. 48% are masculine. However, it is possible that this number is a result of the fact that some high-frequency nouns (like 'king', 'bishop', 'knight', 'god') are masculine. In fact, the data available would suggest that it was the feminine nouns that constituted the largest group when type and not token is considered, at least in Swedish (Davidson 1990:88–89). On the other hand, earlier researchers on gender in Swedish report intuitions that it is the masculine gender that is the most frequent (Tegnér 1962 [1892]:135, Andersson 1979:44); since the authors do not quote any quantitative studies, we may conclude that their impression was formed by the abundance of masculine referents in the texts. Davidson claims further that concrete nouns are more often masculine, and abstract ones feminine (Davidson 1990:89), which may also explain some differences between genres in terms of the frequency of masculine and feminine nouns. Our observation is that the masculine nouns found in the texts denote humans more often than the feminine nouns do.

4.4.1 *Results by Gender*
In the following we report the results regarding definite and indefinite nominal phrases for each gender separately, beginning with the masculine gender. In the following tables we compare the frequency of the given gender among

THE DIACHRONY OF (IN)DEFINITENESS—A QUANTITATIVE STUDY 107

TABLE 29   Definiteness and the masculine gender

Masculine	Context	Period I		Period II		Period III	
Danish	M / N	502 / 1,097	45.76%	514 / 1,016	50.59%	380 / 787	48.28%
	M / -IN	43 / 67	64.18%	77 / 139	55.40%	87 / 143	60.84%
Swedish	M / N	520 / 1,194	43.55%	520 / 1,093	47.58%	263 / 635	41.42%
	M / -IN	57 / 94	60.64%	158 / 294	53.74%	46 / 107	42.99%
Icelandic	M / N	744 / 1,536	48.44%	525 / 1,037	50.62%	355 / 648	54.78%
	M / -IN	60 / 157	38.22%	42 / 91	46.15%	48 / 82	58.54%

TABLE 30   Indefiniteness and the masculine gender

Masculine	Context	Period I		Period II		Period III	
Danish	M / N	502 / 1,097	45.76%	514 / 1,016	50.59%	380 / 787	48.28%
	M / EN	5 / 16	31.25%	38 / 78	48.72%	29 / 53	54.72%
Swedish	M / N	520 / 1,194	43.55%	520 / 1,093	47.58%	263 / 635	41.42%
	M / EN	11 / 24	45.83%	40 / 70	57.14%	24 / 49	48.98%
Icelandic	M / N	744 / 1,536	48.44%	525 / 1,037	50.62%	355 / 648	54.78%
	M / EN	8 / 14	57.14%	12 / 21	57.14%	5 / 7	71.43%

all of the nouns in the dataset (N) and among the nouns in definite (-IN) or indefinite (EN) form.

Masculine nouns (see Table 29) are better represented in definite NPs in both Danish and Swedish throughout the three periods, albeit in Swedish in Period III the values are similar. In Period I in both Danish and Swedish the proportion of definite masculine nouns is higher by ca. 40% than the overall proportion of masculine nouns. In Period II the difference is around 10% for both languages. In Period III Danish and Swedish diverge; in Danish the frequency of definite masculine nouns is 27% higher than the overall proportion, while in Swedish it is higher by only 4.5%. In Icelandic the values are quite similar throughout the three periods.

Similarly, masculine nouns constitute a large proportion of the indefinite NPs (see Table 30), especially in Icelandic in all three periods, but on the whole the results do not form a uniform pattern. The Icelandic results can be explained by the fact that EN, if not used purely as a numeral, was used as a presentative marker introducing salient new referents.

TABLE 31   Definiteness and the feminine gender

Feminine	Context	Period I		Period II		Period III	
Danish	F / N	297 / 1,097	27.07%	247 / 1,016	24.31%	242 / 787	30.75%
	F / -IN	10 / 67	14.93%	25 / 139	17.99%	23 / 143	16.08%
Swedish	F / N	341 / 1,194	28.56%	320 / 1,093	29.28%	174 / 635	27.40%
	F / -IN	19 / 94	20.21%	83 / 294	28.23%	32 / 107	29.91%
Icelandic	F / N	371 / 1,536	24.15%	256 / 1,037	24.69%	136 / 648	20.99%
	F / -IN	44 / 157	28.03%	23 / 91	25.27%	19 / 82	23.17%

(124)   *Grím-ur   hét   **einn bónd-i,**   mikils hátt-ar*
Grim-NOM was.called EN yeoman-NOM very important-NOM
og   vel   fjáreigand-i.
and well wealthy-NOM
'Grim was called a yeoman, important and rich.' (IS_Jart, Period I)

The noun most frequently used in this construction was *maðr* 'man', a masculine noun.

The results for the feminine gender (see Table 31) are quite different from those for masculine nouns. The feminine nouns are heavily under-represented in defNPs in Danish in all periods. In Period I and III the proportion of feminine definite nouns is smaller by almost 50% than the overall proportion of feminine nouns, and in Period II the difference is ca. 25%. In Swedish feminine defNPs are strongly under-represented only in Period I, where the difference between the results for N and -IN amounts to 28%. In Periods II and III the results are similar. In Icelandic, on the other hand, feminine nouns are better represented in definite nominal phrases throughout all of the periods.

In the case of the frequency of feminine nouns in indefinite nominal phrases (see Table 32), none of the languages exhibits any clear patterns. In Danish in Periods I and II the proportions are very close, while in Period III feminine indefinite NPs are strongly under-represented, i.e., there is a difference of 20% between the results for N and EN. In Swedish feminine indefinite NPs are very strongly represented in the first period, but heavily under-represented in the following periods. We observe a reverse tendency in Icelandic, where feminine indefinite NPs are under-represented in Period I, but in Periods II and III the proportion is higher by 36% than the proportion of feminine nouns overall. However, the overall number of instances of EN is very low in Icelandic so the results are not statistically significant.

TABLE 32   Indefiniteness and the feminine gender

Feminine	Context	Period I		Period II		Period III	
Danish	F / N	297 / 1,097	27.07%	247 / 1,016	24.31%	242 / 787	30.75%
	F / EN	4 / 16	25.00%	20 / 78	25.64%	13 / 53	24.53%
Swedish	F / N	341 / 1,194	28.56%	320 / 1,093	29.28%	174 / 635	27.40%
	F / EN	9 / 24	37.50%	17 / 70	24.29%	8 / 49	16.33%
Icelandic	F / N	371 / 1,536	24.15%	256 / 1,037	24.69%	136 / 648	20.99%
	F / EN	3 / 14	21.43%	6 / 21	28.57%	2 / 7	28.57%

TABLE 33   Definiteness and the neuter gender

Neuter	Context	Period I		Period II		Period III	
Danish	Ne / N	298 / 1,097	27.16%	255 / 1,016	25.10%	165 / 787	20.97%
	Ne / -IN	14 / 67	20.90%	38 / 139	27.34%	33 / 143	23.08%
Swedish	Ne / N	333 / 1,194	27.89%	253 / 1,093	23.14%	198 / 635	31.18%
	Ne / -IN	17 / 94	18.09%	54 / 294	18.37%	29 / 107	27.10%
Icelandic	Ne / N	421 / 1,536	27.41%	256 / 1,037	24.69%	157 / 648	24.23%
	Ne / -IN	51 / 157	32.48%	26 / 91	28.57%	14 / 82	17.07%

The neuter gender is in general under-represented in definite NPs compared with all NPs (see Table 33); the results are very similar to those for the feminine. Even though in Danish in Periods II and III and in Icelandic in Periods I and II neuter definite NPs are better represented, the differences here are not substantial, being no higher than 20%.

Again, in the case of indefinite NPs no clear patterns are revealed (see Table 34). In the Icelandic data neuter NPs with an indefinite article, or in many cases a numeral, are heavily under-represented. In the Danish and Swedish data there are no considerable differences between the proportions, with two exceptions: in Danish in Period I the proportion of neuter indefinite NPs is ca. 60% higher than the overall proportion, while in Swedish in the same period the proportion of neuter indefinite NPs is ca. 55% lower than the overall proportion.

Overall, the results indicate that, as expected, definite and indefinite expression in the periods studied is not essentially linked to grammatical gender, but rather to the type of referents that are expressed through nouns with a partic-

TABLE 34 Indefiniteness and the neuter gender

Neuter	Context	Period I		Period II		Period III	
Danish	Ne / N	298 / 1,097	27.16%	255 / 1,016	25.10%	165 / 787	20.97%
	Ne / EN	7 / 16	43.75%	19 / 78	24.36%	11 / 53	20.75%
Swedish	Ne / N	333 / 1,194	27.89%	253 / 1,093	23.14%	198 / 635	31.18%
	Ne / EN	3 / 24	12.50%	12 / 70	17.14%	17 / 49	34.69%
Icelandic	Ne / N	421 / 1,536	27.41%	256 / 1,037	24.69%	157 / 648	24.23%
	Ne / EN	2 / 14	14.29%	1 / 21	4.76%	0 / 7	0.00%

ular gender. If there are pragmatic factors at play, and the definite form is used primarily with important discourse referents before it is used with all semantically definite referents, this would explain the difference between the definite marking of masculine nouns, on the one hand, and feminine and neuter nouns, on the other. The masculine class includes many animate, human nouns, which are very often sentence subjects and/or topics. The neuter class includes very few animate and next to no human nouns, and nouns from this class typically appear in sentences as objects (or prepositional objects). This would explain why there are proportionally more masculine nouns among the definites than there are neuters, assuming that the definite article is strongly connected with the role of subject or topic, at least at the early stages of grammaticalization. Another category which correlates, more strongly, with subjecthood and topicality is case, which will be discussed in the next section.

4.5 Definiteness and Case

During the period of article grammaticalization other grammatical categories undergo changes as well. The most spectacular is the decline of case in the Continental North Germanic languages, Danish and Swedish (and in Norwegian, which is not studied here). The reduction of case proceeds for more than 200 years (see Norde 1997, Skrzypek 2005, Delsing 2014) and partly overlaps with the rise of the definite and indefinite articles.

The two processes—the decline of case and the development of definiteness—have taken place in other Indo-European languages in the course of their history, for example, in some Germanic languages like English and Dutch, in the Romance languages French, Spanish and Italian, and in two Slavic languages, Bulgarian and Macedonian. At the same time the case system is more or less intact in Icelandic and Faroese and reduced but still present in German, all three languages having developed definite articles. The case system is preserved in most Slavic languages (apart from Bulgarian and Macedonian), while no definite or indefinite articles have developed in these languages (though see Dvorak 2019 on possible early stages of definite article grammaticalization in Czech). In other words, it does not seem that there is a straightforward interdependency between loss of case and rise of definiteness. In fact, diachronic research into the loss of dative case in Swedish suggests that the rise of the definite article in that language had a temporary conserving effect on the case system (Skrzypek 2005). It is also to be noted that the case distinctions preserved in German are found mainly on determiners, including definite and indefinite articles, while the noun paradigms exhibit little inflection (Harbert 2006). In this sense, the two categories of case and definiteness interact, in that they are encoded together on the same formative (see also Lyons C. 1999:199).

In languages beyond Indo-European other types of interdependencies may be observed. One is the restriction of certain case markers to definite noun phrases. For example, the accusative case may be marked morphologically only on definite objects, as in Turkish (see Lyons C. 1999:201 and references therein).

The reduction of case was not a process with a uniform history in all North Germanic languages. Firstly, it has not taken place at all in the Insular languages Icelandic and Faroese. Secondly, it seems to have originated in Danish and spread from the southern boundaries of Scandinavia to the north, with Danish at the fore of the change and Swedish and Norwegian following later on. Although it has long been claimed that a major force behind case reduction was language contact with Low German, it has since been demonstrated that while such contact could in fact have been a catalyst of the change, the change was initiated before the contact ever took place (see especially Ringgaard 1986, Norde 1997, Skrzypek 2005).

The loss of case is best documented in Swedish sources, since in Danish the system becomes undermined before the first texts are written. In Norwegian the loss of case comes so late that it cannot be studied in actual texts, since at the time of case reduction Norwegian was no longer the written standard in Norway and there are hardly any extant Norwegian texts (Delsing 2014:27). The reduction comprised two major phases: the first was the reduction of case endings resulting in growing syncretism of forms (paradigmatic change), while the second consisted of a limited use of marked cases in certain constructions, which instead favoured unmarked forms with zero endings, such as the accusative and (later) the nominative (syntagmatic change; see Delsing 2014:28). Although the paradigmatic change was the first stage of the decline of

TABLE 35   Example declination of weak nouns: *bondi* 'yeoman' and *kirkja* 'church'[a]

	bondi	bondi-DEF	kirkja	kirkja-DEF
NOM	bondi	bondin	kirkja	kirkjan
ACC	bonda	bondan	kirkju	kirkjuna
DAT	bonda	bondanom	kirkju	kirkjunni
GEN	bonda	bondans	kirkju	kirkjunnar
English	*yeoman*	*the yeoman*	*church*	*the church*

a Bare nouns with weak endings such as *bond-a* and *kirkj-u* in Table 35 are annotated as oblique case (OBL) in the corpus, the leftmost column in Table 35 lists the cases as they apply to the definite-marked forms of these nouns.

the case system in Danish and Swedish, the syntagmatic changes partly coincided with it; in Danish from 1200 onwards, in Swedish from ca. 1300 and later.

It should be noted here that the rise of the definite article had, to some extent, a petrifying effect on case. Because the definite article retained its own case inflection after it was cliticized onto the noun, in some instances the case of the noun would be clarified. This is clearly discernible with weak masculine nouns such as *bondi* 'yeoman' (forms from Old Swedish) or most feminine nouns, such as *kirkja* 'church' (forms from Modern Icelandic), as presented in Table 35.

Table 36 presents an overview of the frequencies of all of the noun case forms in the corpus.

The results illustrate a number of important facts. Firstly, we observe that case reduction in Danish is of very early date. Only ca. 13% of nouns in Period II and ca. 9% in Period III could be tagged with any certainty as NOM, ACC, DAT or GEN, the majority of them representing the genitive, the case of which a remnant (the so-called s-genitive) is found in Modern Danish (and Modern Swedish); see in particular Norde (1997). Over 86% and 90% of nouns in Periods II and III respectively were tagged as NO-END, as there was no ending and no other information to indicate their case form.

The Swedish results are similar to those for Danish, but it is clear that the case reduction is of later date. Periods I and II exhibit very similar results, but a slump occurs in Period III, where over 80% of the nouns could be tagged only as NO-END. The fact that there was such a difference in the time of case reduction between Danish and Swedish has been noted in the literature; see in particular Ringgaard (1986).

TABLE 36 Proportions of cases in the corpus

N	Case	Period I		Period II		Period III	
Danish	NOM	281	25.62%	5	0.49%	0	0.00%
	ACC	421	38.38%	27	2.66%	0	0.00%
	DAT	59	5.38%	3	0.30%	0	0.00%
	GEN	89	8.11%	48	4.72%	59	7.50%
	OBL	128	11.67%	54	5.31%	12	1.52%
	No ending	119	10.85%	879	86.52%	716	90.98%
	Total	*1,097*	*100.00%*	*1,016*	*100.00%*	*787*	*100.00%*
Swedish	NOM	315	26.38%	284	25.98%	13	2.05%
	ACC	388	32.50%	429	39.25%	15	2.36%
	DAT	180	15.07%	171	15.65%	37	5.83%
	GEN	153	12.81%	98	8.97%	49	7.72%
	OBL	76	6.37%	56	5.12%	5	0.79%
	No ending	82	6.87%	55	5.03%	516	81.26%
	Total	*1,194*	*100.00%*	*1,093*	*100.00%*	*635*	*100.00%*
Icelandic	NOM	454	29.56%	288	27.77%	181	27.93%
	ACC	423	27.54%	345	33.27%	212	32.72%
	DAT	348	22.66%	245	23.63%	124	19.14%
	GEN	205	13.35%	108	10.41%	95	14.66%
	OBL	103	6.71%	50	4.82%	35	5.40%
	No ending	3	0.19%	1	0.10%	1	0.15%
	Total	*1,536*	*100.00%*	*1,037*	*100.00%*	*648*	*100.00%*

The Icelandic case system, on the other hand, remains intact; the nouns annotated as NO-END are indeclinable words, e.g., *frændsemi* 'relationship, kinship', and constitute about 0.15% of all nouns. The proportions between all cases remain the same in all three periods, which may be understood in terms of the original cases retaining their functions, but any interpretation of the results would need a more in-depth study. Finally recall that the Danish and Swedish case systems are reduced through two types of change: the growing syncretism of forms and the loss of case marking.

4.5.1 *Case and the Definite Article*
Even though there is no compelling evidence for interdependencies between the loss of case and the emergence of definiteness marking, there are enough tendencies to assume that there will be some degree of correspondence be-

tween the two processes. Not least because grammatical cases often overlap with particular functions, such as subject or object, which in turn differ with respect to definiteness (see 4.6). One should, however, proceed with caution positing a simple scenario, in which the dwindling case system makes way for definiteness marking, as the North Germanic languages differ among themselves with respect to the category of case (see in particular Barðdal 2001 and 2009).

In this section, we will examine the case forms that appear earliest as definites, without considering roles in sentences, which will be the topic of the next section. Table 37 illustrates the distribution of all of the suffixed definite forms (-IN) in the corpus between the case forms. The results are not separated into SG and PL.

The results presented in Table 37 are to be analysed in the context of the overall results in Table 36 (section 4.5). We noted that nouns that were unequivocally NOM are found in Danish in Period I (25.62% of all nouns), but they are virtually non-existent in Periods II and III. We therefore cannot expect to find any defNPs in the nominative in Periods II and III, because we have no endings to tell us that that is the case. Similarly, the lower frequency of NOM in Swedish in Period III is not to be understood as implying the fact that nouns in NOM no longer appear as definite, but rather that the NOM ending is now lost on virtually all nouns. They appear instead in the results for nouns without any case endings.

We observe that the distribution of -IN between cases is quite consistent throughout the three periods in Icelandic, with lower results for GEN and DAT, but similar values for NOM and ACC. The grammatical roles of subject and object, which are strongly associated with these cases, will be discussed in the following section. Firstly, we compare the frequencies for all nouns and for those tagged as -IN only for each case separately, beginning with the nominative (see Table 38).

Compared with its overall frequency, the nominative is preferred in defNPs in Danish in Period I and in Swedish in both Period I and II, especially in the latter. It seems that while the overall frequency of the nominative remains unchanged in Swedish between Period I and II, the grammaticalizing definite article comes to be strongly associated with the nominative, and most likely with the function of subject (see section 4.6).

In Icelandic the values for all NPs and for defNPs are similar in Period I, but we observe a clear drop in the value for defNPs in Period II, something we would not expect in a language with a stable case system and relatively well-developed definite article. It seems therefore that even though the definite article may seem well-developed in Icelandic (at least in comparison with

TABLE 37   Proportions of cases among definite NPs

-IN	Case	Period I		Period II		Period III	
Danish	NOM	28	41.79%	0	0.00%	0	0.00%
	ACC	25	37.31%	7	5.04%	0	0.00%
	DAT	1	1.49%	2	1.44%	0	0.00%
	GEN	12	17.91%	4	2.88%	3	2.10%
	OBL	0	0.00%	1	0.72%	0	0.00%
	No ending	1	1.49%	125	89.93%	140	97.90%
	Total	*67*	*100.00%*	*139*	*100.00%*	*143*	*100.00%*
Swedish	NOM	31	32.98%	134	45.58%	6	5.61%
	ACC	37	39.36%	102	34.69%	11	10.28%
	DAT	14	14.89%	33	11.22%	13	12.15%
	GEN	9	9.57%	25	8.50%	14	13.08%
	OBL	3	3.20%	0	0.00%	1	0.93%
	No ending	0	0.00%	0	0.00%	62	57.94%
	Total	*94*	*100.00%*	*294*	*100.00%*	*107*	*100.00%*
Icelandic	NOM	48	30.57%	15	16.48%	16	19.51%
	ACC	51	32.48%	43	47.25%	35	42.68%
	DAT	43	27.39%	22	24.18%	16	19.51%
	GEN	15	9.55%	11	12.09%	13	15.85%
	OBL	0	0.00%	0	0.00%	2	2.44%
	No ending	0	0.00%	0	0.00%	0	0.00%
	Total	*157*	*100.00%*	*91*	*100.00%*	*82*	*100.00%*

TABLE 38   The nominative and definiteness

NOM	Context	Period I		Period II		Period III	
Danish	NOM / N	281 / 1,097	25.62%	5 / 1,016	0.49%	0 / 787	0.00%
	NOM / -IN	28 / 67	41.79%	0 / 139	0.00%	0 / 143	0.00%
Swedish	NOM / N	315 / 1,194	26.38%	284 / 1,093	25.98%	13 / 635	2.05%
	NOM / -IN	31 / 94	32.98%	134 / 294	45.58%	6 / 107	5.61%
Icelandic	NOM / N	454 / 1,536	29.56%	288 / 1,037	27.77%	181 / 648	27.93%
	NOM / -IN	48 / 157	30.57%	15 / 91	16.48%	16 / 82	19.51%

TABLE 39 The accusative and definiteness

ACC	Context	Period I		Period II		Period III	
Danish	ACC / N	421 / 1,097	38.38%	27 / 1,016	2.66%	0 / 787	0.00%
	ACC / -IN	25 / 67	37.31%	7 / 139	5.04%	0 / 143	0.00%
Swedish	ACC / N	388 / 1,194	32.50%	429 / 1,093	39.25%	15 / 635	2.36%
	ACC / -IN	37 / 94	39.36%	102 / 294	34.69%	11 / 107	10.28%
Icelandic	ACC / N	423 / 1,536	27.54%	345 / 1,037	33.27%	212 / 648	32.72%
	ACC / -IN	51 / 157	32.48%	43 / 91	47.25%	35 / 82	42.68%

Danish and Swedish), there are still some changes in its functions, which may be reflected in the proportions between the cases.

Interestingly enough, and in contrast to the results for the nominative, the results for the accusative (see Table 39) are similar for all NPs and for defNPs. This indicates that there was no preference for this case in definite contexts, but neither was it disfavoured. A significant difference in proportions is found in Icelandic in Period II (which was also the time when the values for NOM in defNPs dropped significantly below the values for all NPs) and Period III, as well as in Swedish in Period III. The latter difference can be explained by the fact that while the accusative was on the whole lost (the ending either reduced or coalesced with the ending for some other case) in the bare noun, it was retained in the definite form (the double inflection). Consider a neutral noun *land* 'country'. Originally, its paradigm consisted of three distinct forms: *land* (NOM/ACC), *landi* (DAT), *lands* (GEN). With the reduction of the case system the dative form was lost. However, even after that happened, the definite dative form could be found as *land-i-n-o* 'country-DAT-DEF-DAT'. With the accusative case, this effect is almost entirely limited to the plural forms, as the accusative and the nominative have coalesced at an earlier stage in most paradigms.

Definite NPs in the dative (see Table 40) are slightly preferred in Icelandic in Period I and in Swedish in Period III, but on the whole the values are similar for all NPs and for defNPs. As in the case of the accusative, the higher results in Swedish are again due to the preservation of the dative form in the definite, which is a result of the double inflection of the noun.

Similar to the results regarding the dative case, there is no clear preference for the genitive case in definite NPs (see Table 41), except in Danish in Period I and in Swedish in Period III. However, while we could explain the higher values for dative and accusative defNPs by double inflection, the situation is less straightforward with the genitive. It is a case whose formal representation is

TABLE 40 The dative and definiteness

DAT	Context	Period I		Period II		Period III	
Danish	DAT / N	59 / 1,097	5.38%	3 / 1,016	0.30%	0 / 787	0.00%
	DAT / -IN	1 / 67	1.49%	2 / 139	1.44%	0 / 143	0.00%
Swedish	DAT / N	180 / 1,194	15.07%	171 / 1,039	15.65%	37 / 635	5.83%
	DAT / -IN	14 / 94	14.89%	33 / 294	11.22%	13 / 107	12.15%
Icelandic	DAT / N	348 / 1,536	22.66%	245 / 1,037	23.63%	124 / 648	19.14%
	DAT / -IN	43 / 157	27.39%	22 / 91	24.18%	16 / 82	19.51%

TABLE 41 The genitive and definiteness

GEN	Context	Period I		Period II		Period III	
Danish	GEN / N	89 / 1,097	8.11%	48 / 1,016	4.72%	59 / 787	7.50%
	GEN / -IN	12 / 67	17.91%	4 / 139	2.88%	3 / 143	2.10%
Swedish	GEN / N	153 / 1,194	12.81%	98 / 1,093	8.97%	49 / 635	7.72%
	GEN / -IN	9 / 94	9.57%	25 / 294	8.50%	14 / 107	13.08%
Icelandic	GEN / N	205 / 1,536	13.35%	108 / 1,037	10.41%	95 / 648	14.66%
	GEN / -IN	15 / 157	9.55%	11 / 91	12.09%	13 / 82	15.85%

preserved until today, in the so-called s-genitive, a phrasal marker used with possessor NPs (see Norde 1997 for a historical description and Börjars & Harries 2008 for a modern discussion). It is important to remember, though, that while one of the original genitive endings was preserved and spread to all nouns, the use of the s-form was gradually limited to possessor NPs and no longer appeared in NPs governed by prepositions or verbs. The higher values in Swedish in Period III are mostly due to possessor NPs. As a recent study on present-day Swedish indicates, the s-genitive strongly prefers definite NPs and proper names, disfavouring indefinite NPs (Piotrowska 2020). This development towards explicitly definite possessor-NPs in the s-genitive is already discernible in Old Swedish and Old Danish, especially in Periods II and III, when we observe a surge of definite possessor NPs with the s-ending (Piotrowska, in press).

Of the four cases present in Period I in all three languages, only the nominative exhibits a correlation with definiteness. Percentage-wise the nominative accounts for a greater proportion among definite NPs than among the overall number of nouns in Period I, in both Danish and Swedish. This correlation gradually weakens as the original case endings are lost and the definite article grammaticalized.

4.5.2 Case and the Indefinite Article

Table 42 gives the distribution of all indefinite forms (EN) in the corpus between the case forms. The results include only singular NPs, as there are no plural NPs in the corpus where EN would be used.

As was the case with the results in Table 37 (section 4.5.1), the results in the tables above reflect not only the use of definite or indefinite NPs in each case, but the fate of the cases as well. In the case of indefinite NPs (EN) presented in Table 42, we note that the case reduction proceeds fastest in Danish, and that by Period III only two noun forms are found in the texts: those in the genitive (or some remnant thereof) and those with no ending. We can further note that the grammaticalization of the indefinite article seems to have progressed furthest in Danish. As early as Period I indefNPs appear in ACC, as objects, which is the typical context for an indefinite NP, as it usually carries new information. The results for NOM, i.e., subjects, are considerably lower.

In Icelandic, on the other hand, the highest values are for NOM, in both Period I and III. This is understandable, since the most typical use of EN in Icelandic prose is to introduce new and salient referents, typically in some variant of the following sentence:

(125) **Ein jungfrú** er út í Myklagarð-i er heitir Ríkilað
 EN maiden is out in Myklagarð-DAT which is.called Ríkilað.NOM
 'There is a maiden out in Myklagarð who is called Ríkilað.' (IS_Jarl, Period III)

It is to be noted that the EN in these NPs is not really an indefinite article (which, as we have mentioned before, has not grammaticalized in Icelandic at all), but the original numeral 'one', used in a presentative function (see section 2.3), which is the first stage of the indefinite article's grammaticalization. Comparing the percentages in Table 42, it is also important to keep in mind that the Icelandic texts in the corpus have a relatively low frequency of EN, with 40 instances against 142 and 146 in Swedish and Danish respectively.

Swedish also exhibits some unexpected developments. The already high values for nominative indefNPs in Period I rise even further in Period II, reaching a peak of 42%, only to drop to ca. 2% in Period III. The explanation is to be found in the history of the indefinite article in Swedish, which, like in other languages, begins with a presentative function, although, more specifically lim-

TABLE 42 Proportions of cases among indefinite NPs

EN	Case	Period I		Period II		Period III	
Danish	NOM	2	12.50%	2	2.56%	0	0.00%
	ACC	9	56.25%	4	5.13%	0	0.00%
	DAT	0	0.00%	0	0.00%	0	0.00%
	GEN	0	0.00%	1	1.28%	3	5.66%
	OBL	3	18.75%	1	1.28%	0	0.00%
	No ending	2	12.50%	70	89.74%	50	94.34%
	Total	*16*	*100.00%*	*78*	*100.00%*	*53*	*100.00%*
Swedish	NOM	8	33.33%	30	42.86%	1	2.04%
	ACC	11	45.83%	27	38.57%	3	6.12%
	DAT	1	4.16%	9	12.86%	0	0.00%
	GEN	1	4.16%	2	2.86%	0	0.00%
	OBL	3	12.50%	2	2.86%	0	0.00%
	No ending	0	0.00%	0	0.00%	45	91.84%
	Total	*24*	*100.00%*	*70*	*100.00%*	*49*	*100.00%*
Icelandic	NOM	9	64.29%	6	28.57%	4	57.14%
	ACC	0	0.00%	13	61.90%	1	14.29%
	DAT	5	35.71%	2	9.52%	2	28.57%
	GEN	0	0.00%	0	0.00%	0	0.00%
	OBL	0	0.00%	0	0.00%	0	0.00%
	No ending	0	0.00%	0	0.00%	0	0.00%
	Total	*14*	*100.00%*	*21*	*100.00%*	*7*	*100.00%*

ited to sentence-initial subjects (see Skrzypek 2012, 2013). A classic example is quoted in (126).

(126)   **En diäkne** war j   enom stadh som   heet   montepessolanus
        EN deacon was in EN   city   which was.called Montepessolanus
        'There was a deacon in a city called Montepessolanus.' (SV_Jart, Period II)

This presentative construction, familiar from the Icelandic sagas among others, is not found in Modern Swedish, where indefinite subjects are instead placed further from the beginning of the sentence. The tendency to place certain other elements, typically adverbials, in the initial position when the subject is indefinite begins in Old Swedish in Period II; see (127).

(127) *I Room war **een keysare** han hafdhe en-a dyghdhelik-a oc*
In Rome was EN emperor he had EN-ACC virtuous-ACC and
gudhlik-a keysarinn-o
godly-ACC empress-ACC
'There was an emperor in Rome who had a virtuous and godly wife.'
(SV_ST, Period II)

There are also relatively high values for EN with the dative case, especially in Icelandic. At first, we considered the possibility of some correlation with animacy; however, the frequent uses of the dative turned out to be mainly locative phrases, as in (128).

(128) *Sá eg þá bræður, Helga og Gunnar, í **hell-i ein-um***
Saw I them brothers, Helgi and Gunnar, in cave-DAT en-DAT
norður með á-nni.
north with river-DEF.DAT
'I saw these brothers, Helgi and Gunnar, in a cave north downstream.'
(IS_Gun, Period II)

It seems that the high values for the dative case in Icelandic are the result of its use in prepositional phrases rather than any connection with the animacy of the referent.

4.6 Definiteness, Subjecthood and Objecthood

Having examined the interactions between definiteness and case we now turn to syntactic roles, primarily those of subject and object. We have decided to treat them separately from case, even if we expect the results for NOM and subject, and for ACC and object, to be largely similar. In the timeframe of our study oblique subjects can occasionally be found in both Danish and Swedish (with the decline of the case system, they gradually disappear) and in Icelandic (where they are preserved until modern times).

(129) *Sýnist **dróttning-u** nú sem er, at þeir gerðust nú*
seemed queen-DEF.DAT now which is, that they made.REFL now
mann-vænligir
man-attractive
'The queen found them attractive.' (IS_Ge, Period I)

TABLE 43   The main syntactic functions of NPs in the corpus

N	Syntactic roles	Period I		Period II		Period III	
Danish	subject	246 / 1,097	22.42%	209 / 1,016	20.57%	156 / 787	19.82%
	object	305 / 1,097	27.80%	326 / 1,016	32.09%	214 / 787	27.19%
Swedish	subject	297 / 1,194	24.87%	255 / 1,093	23.33%	103 / 635	16.22%
	object	363 / 1,194	30.40%	285 / 1,093	26.08%	190 / 635	29.92%
Icelandic	subject	354 / 1,536	23.04%	226 / 1,037	21.79%	157 / 648	24.23%
	object	418 / 1,536	27.21%	279 / 1,037	26.90%	182 / 648	28.09%

(130)   en þó grunaði **kóng**   hvað konu   hún mundi vera
        and yet suspected king.ACC what woman she may be
        'And yet the king suspected what kind of a woman she may be.' (IS_Vil, Period III)

We found 22 oblique subjects in our material (in all languages, but they are solely restricted to Period I), and thus conclude that subjects are overwhelmingly nominative, while objects may appear as accusative, dative or genitive phrases. See also Maling (2002) and Skrzypek (2005) for overviews of object marking in Old Icelandic and Old Swedish respectively.

As presented in Table 43, the proportions remain relatively stable in all three periods in Danish and Icelandic, while the Swedish results reveal more fluctuation in terms of the percentage of subjects, with somewhat lower results in Period III. This variation seems to be the result of a higher percentage of pronominal subjects in the Swedish texts from this period, compared with texts both in other languages and from other periods.

4.6.1   *Syntactic Functions and Definiteness*

Syntactic roles and definiteness exhibit a number of interdependencies, and languages seem to pattern differently with respect to how subject or object role may affect definite marking or its absence. The best recognized interdependencies are differential case marking in objects and definite object marking (for an overview and typology see Lyons C. 1999:200–205). In languages exhibiting such interdependencies we find that objects differ in case marking depending on whether or not they are definite.

It has further been noted that subjects may remain unmarked for definiteness, even if they are definite, as long as they are located clause-initially, as this position creates a so-called definiteness effect. As subjects tend to be topics (a cross-linguistic tendency; Lyons C. 1999:230), this interaction between syntactic role and definiteness marking seems to be secondary.

North Germanic does not demonstrate differential case marking, but it has been claimed that at the onset of definite article grammaticalization only objects that were definite and not clause-initial (and therefore not subject to a definiteness effect) were marked for definiteness. All elements that could be considered definite due to their position in the clause remained unmarked. Such a view is advocated in Leiss (2000, 2007) and in Abraham (2007). In her discussion of the Old Icelandic data, Leiss quotes an example of possible underspecification of the object in one of the most famous excerpts from *Heimskringla* (ca. 1225), quoted here as (131).

(131) *þá   verþr   hann varr   viþ **griþung-enn** ok   reið   til ok*
      then became he   aware of   ox-DEF   and   rode   to and
      *vill   drepa hann **griþungr** snýr í móti   ok   kom   konungr*
      wants   kill   him   ox   turns towards and came king
      *lagi á   hann ok   skar ór   spjót-it   **griþungr** stakk*
      stab on   him and   cut out lance-DEF   ox   stuck
      horn-onom   í   síþo hest-inum   svá at   hann fell
      horn-DEF.DAT.PL   in side horse-DEF.DAT   so that he   fell
      þegar   flatr ok   svá konungr þá   hljóp   konungr á   føtr
      immediately   flat and so king   then jumped   king   on feet
      *ok   vill   bregða sverði **griðungr** stakk þá   horn-unum*
      and wants   draw   sword ox   stuck then horn-DEF.DAT.PL
      fyrir brjóst honum svá at   á   kafi   stóð   þá   komu at
      for   breast him   so that on depth   stood   then came to
      *konung-s menn drópu **griþung-enn**.*
      king-GEN men   killed ox-DEF
      'He observed at last that it was the bull, and rode up to it to kill it. The bull turned round suddenly, and the king struck him with his spear; but it tore itself out of the wound. The bull now struck his horn in the side of the horse, so that he instantly fell flat on the earth with the king. The king sprang up, and was drawing his sword, when the bull struck his horns right into the king's breast. The king's men then came up and killed the bull.' (Heimskringla, cf. Nygaard 1905:47, Møller 1945:36, Heusler 1950:125, Leiss 2000:38–39; translation by Samuel Laing, London 1844)

Admittedly, the example exhibits exactly the predicted distribution: definite marking appears only with the object and not with the subject, despite the latter being anaphoric. However, Leiss does not provide any more examples or indeed statistical data to support this hypothesis. In our Icelandic corpus we found only 16 instances of NPs that are objects, are direct anaphors (thus identifiable) and appear as BNs. Nine of these involve the noun *konung* 'king', three *biskop* 'bishop' and one *abot* 'prior'. The reason for their bare form may have nothing to do with their syntactic function, since they represent Hawkins' 'larger situation use', and in a limited context, of one country or one parish, are unique. We find a number of anomalies and inconsistencies similar to those reported in Leiss (2000), where the referent is presented as a BN when it is a subject, but as a definite if it is an object, as in (132).

(132)   *Um kveld-it,   er **konungr** kom   heim   ok   hafði setzt í*
        In   evening-DEF, as king   came   home   and   had   sat   in
        *hásœti sitt, þá   gengr dróttning fyrir   **konung-inn** ok   leiðir*
        throne his, then went queen   before king-DEF   and lead
        *svein-ana   með sér ok   segir **konung-i** allt, sem   við   nemr*
        boy-DEF.PL   wih her and says king-DAT all, which before named
        ok   hverju hon hafði keypt   við   ambátt-ina   ok   biðr
        and which she had bought from servant.woman-DEF and asks
        ***konung** hrinda   af sér reiði.*
        king   dismiss of self anger
        'In the evening, when the king had come home and sat in his throne, the queen came before him leading the boys and told the king all that was told here before about how she had bought the boys from the servant-woman and she asked the king to hold his anger.' (IS_Ge, Period I)

In example (133) there does not seem to exist a clear connection between either syntactic function or case and definiteness marking or the lack thereof.

(133)   *En tima þœr   iohannes prœdicaþe fik han se   en   ungan suen*
        en time there Johannes preached got he   see EN   young boy
        *vœnan   ok þo   vildan iohannes fik **biskop-e**   suen-en ii*
        beautiful and though wild Johannes got bishop-DAT boy-DEF in
        hand [...] Iohannes kom   atar tel staþ-en   ok   sporþe at
        hand   Johannes came back to town-DEF and asked about
        *suen-en-om **biscop-en** sagþe hanom vm   suen-en som*
        boy-DEF-DAT bishop-DEF said him   about boy-DEF which

> *sant var Johannes gaf **biskop**   skuld for vangømo*
> true was Johannes gave bishop.DAT guilt for negligence
> 'One time as Johannes was preaching, he saw a young boy, beautiful but wild. Johannes gave a/the bishop charge of the boy. [...] Johannes returned to the town and asked about the boy. The bishop told him the truth. Johannes blamed the bishop for negligence.' (SV_Bur, Period I)

Leiss' idea of a definite article appearing first in NPs used as clause-internal objects (since this syntactic context does not create a definiteness effect) but later with subjects (as this context does create a definiteness effect rendering the article superfluous) does not find support in the data, as presented in Figures 8–10. The definite is used to mark subjects in Period I, and this seems to be its main domain, particularly in Danish texts, in which there are more definite subjects than there are definite objects in all three periods. In Swedish the proportions are more equal in Period I and Period III, but there are almost thrice as many definite subjects than there are definite objects in Period II. Icelandic exhibits quite diverse results: in Period I there are more definite subjects than objects, but that proportion is reversed in Period III.

In Table 44, we compare the overall number of subjects in the corpus with the number of definite subjects. The proportion is arrived at through proportional statistics with the query: out of all of the nouns marked as -IN, how many are subjects?

In both Danish and Swedish, defNPs appear in the role of subject more frequently than NPs do generally. It seems that the incipient definite article favours the role of subject. No comparable discrepancies were found in Icelandic; even if the proportions for all NPs and defNPs are not identical, they are quite similar and consistent throughout all three periods.

It should be noted that definite marking (-IN) is used despite the fact that the context is considered to be definite already (by virtue of the topicality of the subject and the overwhelmingly most frequent initial position of the subject). So -IN, even at the onset of grammaticalization, is not reserved for unclear cases (typically objects), but rather develops first in contexts that are prototypically definite. Therefore, we may talk of morphologization of the category of definiteness, i.e., acquisition of a morphological exponent.

In Table 45 we compare the overall number of subjects in the corpus with the number of subjects marked with the indefinite article (EN).

The surprisingly high percentage of indefinite subjects in Icelandic in Period I and III is an illustration of the fact that EN could be used as a presentative marker in Icelandic, although without progressing further on the grammaticalization scale. Its use was reserved for introducing salient discourse referents.

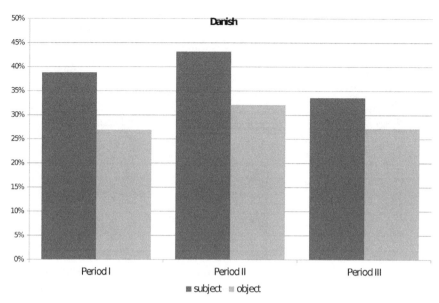

FIGURE 8   Proportions of definite subjects and objects in Danish

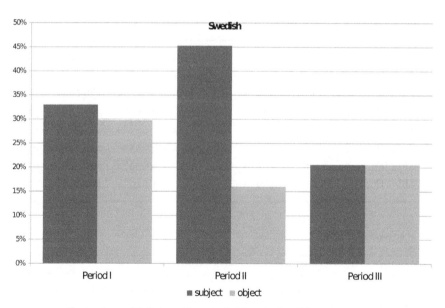

FIGURE 9   Proportions of definite subjects and objects in Swedish

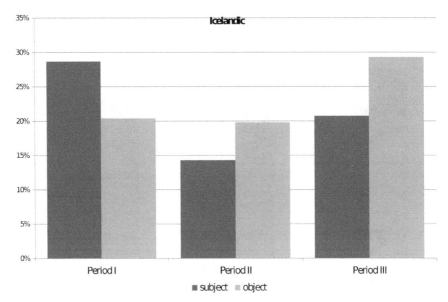

FIGURE 10   Proportions of definite subjects and objects in Icelandic

TABLE 44   Definite subjects in the corpus

Subject	Context	Period I		Period II		Period III	
Danish	SBJ / N	246 / 1,097	22.42%	209 / 1,016	20.57%	156 / 787	19.82%
	SBJ / -IN	26 / 67	38.81%	60 / 139	43.17%	48 / 143	33.57%
Swedish	SBJ / N	297 / 1,194	24.87%	255 / 1,093	23.33%	103 / 635	16.22%
	SBJ / -IN	31 / 94	32.98%	134 / 294	45.58%	22 / 107	20.56%
Icelandic	SBJ / N	354 / 1,536	23.04%	226 / 1,037	21.79%	157 / 648	24.23%
	SBJ / -IN	45 / 157	28.66%	13 / 91	14.29%	16 / 82	19.51%

TABLE 45   Indefinite subjects in the corpus

Subject	Context	Period I		Period II		Period III	
Danish	SBJ / N	246 / 1,097	22.42%	209 / 1,016	20.57%	156 / 787	19.82%
	SBJ / EN	3 / 16	18.75%	15 / 78	19.23%	12 / 53	22.64%
Swedish	SBJ / N	297 / 1,194	24.87%	255 / 1,093	23.33%	103 / 635	16.22%
	SBJ / EN	19 / 24	41.67%	25 / 70	35.71%	9 / 49	18.37%
Icelandic	SBJ / N	354 / 1,536	23.04%	226 / 1,037	21.79%	157 / 648	24.23%
	SBJ / EN	7 / 14	50.00%	3 / 21	14.29%	5 / 7	57.14%

TABLE 46 Definite objects in the corpus

Object	Context	Period I		Period II		Period III	
Danish	OBJ / N	305 / 1,097	27.80%	326 / 1,016	32.09%	214 / 787	27.19%
	OBJ / -IN	18 / 67	26.87%	33 / 139	23.74%	22 / 143	15.38%
Swedish	OBJ / N	363 / 1,194	30.40%	285 / 1,093	26.08%	190 / 635	29.92%
	OBJ / -IN	28 / 94	29.79%	49 / 294	16.66%	22 / 107	20.56%
Icelandic	OBJ / N	418 / 1,536	27.21%	279 / 1,037	26.90%	182 / 648	28.09%
	OBJ / -IN	32 / 157	20.38%	18 / 91	19.78%	24 / 82	29.27%

(134) *Kona   ein fór   of morgun snemma að kanna fjöru því að*
      woman EN went of morning early   to search shore for that
      búandi   hennar var eigi heima. Sér   hún síðan örkn mikið liggja
      husband her   was not home sees she then seal large lie
      á steini skammt frá   sér.
      on stone close   from her.
      'There was a woman who went out early one morning in search of her husband who was not at home. She saw a large seal lying on a stone not far from her.' (IS_Jart, Period I)

The story, the introduction of which is given in (134), continues with a description of the woman's actions and her slaying of the seal. It may be noted that the woman is consistently referred to pronominally (she, her, hers, etc.) and the seal appears in the definite form of *selr* 'seal', a part of its full name, *örkn-selr* (*örkn* is most likely related to Latin *orca*). We may further note that EN could be either pre- or postposed (see also section 5.6 on the rise of the indefinite article in Icelandic for more discussion on the position of the indefinite article).

As we noted in Table 44, the definite seems to favour subjects at the onset of grammaticalization. The results presented in Table 46 regarding the object role are inconclusive. In many cases the definite neither favours nor disfavours the role of object, since the values for all NPs and for defNPs are similar, especially for Danish and Swedish in Period I and Icelandic in Period III. Otherwise, definite objects are considerably under-represented in comparison with the overall proportion of objects in the corpus.

In modern North Germanic new discourse referents are mainly introduced as objects (unless some presentative structures are used to introduce them as subjects). We would therefore expect the percentage of indefNPs among

TABLE 47   Indefinite objects in the corpus

Object	Context	Period I		Period II		Period III	
Danish	OBJ / N	305 / 1,097	27.80%	326 / 1,016	32.09%	214 / 787	27.19%
	OBJ / EN	5 / 16	31.25%	40 / 78	51.28%	13 / 53	24.53%
Swedish	OBJ / N	363 / 1,194	30.40%	285 / 1,093	26.08%	190 / 635	29.92%
	OBJ / EN	7 / 24	29.17%	18 / 70	25.71%	19 / 49	38.78%
Icelandic	OBJ / N	418 / 1,536	27.21%	279 / 1,037	26.90%	182 / 648	28.09%
	OBJ / EN	0 / 14	0.00%	6 / 21	28.57%	1 / 7	14.29%

objects to be higher than among the total number of NPs. This prediction is borne out to some extent (see Table 47) and there is a clear preference for indefNPs as objects in Danish in Period II and Swedish in Period III. Again, these results suggest that the developments in Danish precede those in Swedish, with the grammaticalization of the indefinite article already being more advanced in Danish than in Swedish in Period II.

Interestingly, no indefinite objects marked with EN were found in Icelandic in Period I, although they appear in later texts, as in (135).

(135)   Og   að enduðum gjöfum lét jarl fram bera   eina hörpu.
        And to final   gifts   let jarl forth bring EN   harp
        'And for the final gift the jarl let bring forth a harp.' (IS_Vig, Period II)

The results presented above indicate quite clearly that the incipient definite article is more likely to appear with subjects. The indefinite article favours subjects in Swedish, too, but no such preference was found in either Danish or Icelandic. With objects, there is a more pronounced preference for indefNPs than for defNPs. Article usage seems to have followed the given–new dichotomy associated with subject and object roles rather than being connected with the syntactic roles as such.

4.7   Definiteness and Animacy

Let us now consider the interactions between the animacy of an NP and definiteness. Animacy has been shown to play a significant role in the placing and marking of NPs (Dahl and Fraurud 1996, Yamamoto 1999). Animacy is also connected to the notion of topicality and saliency of information, which is also

TABLE 48 Animate and inanimate NPs in the corpus

N	Animacy	Period I		Period II		Period III	
Danish	animate	463	42.21%	464	45.67%	330	41.93%
	inanimate	634	57.79%	552	54.33%	457	58.07%
	Total	*1,097*	*100.00%*	*1,016*	*100.00%*	*787*	*100.00%*
Swedish	animate	567	47.49%	421	38.52%	188	29.61%
	inanimate	627	52.51%	672	61.48%	447	70.39%
	Total	*1,194*	*100.00%*	*1,093*	*100.00%*	*635*	*100.00%*
Icelandic	animate	601	39.13%	394	37.99%	267	41.20%
	inanimate	935	60.87%	643	62.01%	381	58.80%
	Total	*1,536*	*100.00%*	*1,037*	*100.00%*	*648*	*100.00%*

strongly linked to definiteness. Language is anthropocentric in nature, which results in the centralization and singling out of animate and human referents as the most salient.

As with singulars and plurals, we would expect the relative frequencies of animates and inanimates to remain constant for each language, although more variation may be expected than in the case of number, since the character of the text (e.g., the presence of many human referents) may skew the results.

The overall results for all nouns in the corpus (Table 48) reveal that animate nouns constitute ca. 40% of all nouns, and the percentage is similar in all periods for Danish and Icelandic. Swedish exhibits more variation between the periods studied; however, on the whole, there are ca. 40% of animates among all nouns in the Swedish corpus as well, with different distributions in each period.

In both Danish and Swedish, animate NPs predominate among the defNPs (see Table 49). The proportions change first in Period III. However, the dominance of animate NPs is not absolute, and inanimate definites constitute ca. 40% of all definites in Danish and Swedish as early as in Period I. Icelandic, on the other hand, exhibits a clear dominance of inanimate NPs among the definite NPs.

The data for indefinite NPs presented in Table 50 indicate a dominance of inanimates in Period I in all three languages; in both Danish and Icelandic the values in Period III are similar to the overall results reported in Table 48. Surprisingly, while the Swedish results for Period I and Period III are very similar, there is a different picture in Period II. However, we believe that this is a conse-

TABLE 49 Animate and inanimate definite NPs (-IN) in the corpus

-IN	Animacy	Period I		Period II		Period III	
Danish	animate	38	56.72%	84	60.43%	66	46.15%
	inanimate	29	43.28%	55	39.57%	77	53.85%
	Total	67	100.00%	139	100.00%	143	100.00%
Swedish	animate	61	64.89%	168	57.14%	36	33.64%
	inanimate	33	35.11%	126	42.86%	71	66.36%
	Total	94	100.00%	294	100.00%	107	100.00%
Icelandic	animate	57	36.31%	23	25.27%	15	18.52%
	inanimate	100	63.69%	68	74.73%	66	81.48%
	Total	157	100.00%	91	100.00%	82	100.00%

TABLE 50 Animate and inanimate indefinite NPs (EN) in the corpus

EN	Animacy	Period I		Period II		Period III	
Danish	animate	3	18.75%	32	41.03%	29	54.72%
	inanimate	13	81.25%	46	58.97%	24	45.28%
	Total	16	100.00%	78	100.00%	53	100.00%
Swedish	animate	8	33.33%	37	52.86%	16	32.65%
	inanimate	16	66.67%	33	47.14%	33	67.35%
	Total	24	100.00%	70	100.00%	49	100.00%
Icelandic	animate	3	21.43%	5	23.81%	4	57.14%
	inanimate	11	78.57%	16	76.19%	3	42.86%
	Total	14	100.00%	21	100.00%	7	100.00%

quence of the fact that the majority of the texts included in the material from Period II are shorter (in particular Jart and HML, which are collections of short morality tales) than the texts in other periods. Therefore, there are more characters to be introduced, and this is done by means of EN. The preference for animate referents is also a result of the fact that these morality tales always feature humans as the main characters.

The percentage of animates among definite NPs (-IN) is higher than the corresponding percentage of animates among all NPs in the corpus, as presented in Table 51. While the latter is consistently around 40% in all languages and in all periods, we note some variation within the defNPs in both Danish and

TABLE 51 Animate NPs in definite form—a comparison with all nouns

Animate NPs	Context	Period I		Period II		Period III	
Danish	ANIM / N	463 / 1,097	42.21%	464 / 1,016	45.67%	330 / 787	41.93%
	ANIM / -IN	38 / 67	56.72%	84 / 139	60.43%	66 / 143	46.15%
Swedish	ANIM / N	567 / 1,194	47.49%	421 / 1,093	38.52%	188 / 635	29.61%
	ANIM / -IN	61 / 94	64.89%	168 / 294	57.14%	36 / 107	33.64%
Icelandic	ANIM / N	601 / 1,536	39.13%	394 / 1,037	37.99%	267 / 648	41.20%
	ANIM / -IN	57 / 157	36.31%	23 / 91	25.27%	15 / 82	18.52%

TABLE 52 Animate NPs in indefinite form—a comparison with all nouns

Animate NPs	Context	Period I		Period II		Period III	
Danish	ANIM / N	463 / 1,097	42.21%	464 / 1,016	45.67%	330 / 787	41.93%
	ANIM / EN	3 / 16	18.75%	32 / 78	41.03%	29 / 53	54.72%
Swedish	ANIM / N	567 / 1,194	47.49%	421 / 1,093	38.52%	188 / 635	29.61%
	ANIM / EN	8 / 24	33.33%	37 / 70	52.86%	16 / 49	32.65%
Icelandic	ANIM / N	601 / 1,536	39.13%	394 / 1,037	37.99%	267 / 648	41.20%
	ANIM / EN	3 / 14	21.43%	5 / 21	23.81%	4 / 7	57.14%

Swedish. In Icelandic the proportions seem to be very similar for all NPs and defNPs in Period I, but in both Period II and III fewer defNPs are animate, while the percentage of animates among all NPs remains at the same level. An explanation of this may be the genre and type of the texts, as well as the kind of discourse referents which appear in them.

Comparing the proportions of animates in indefinite NPs and in all NPs in the corpus (Table 52), we observe that the results are quite varied. Indefinite animate NPs are strongly under-represented in Period I in all languages, but this changes in Period II, when in Danish the results are very similar, and in Swedish animate indefinite NPs are over-represented (as mentioned above, the reason for this is most likely the text type). In Period III the percentage of animate indefinite NPs is considerably higher, in all of the languages, than the corresponding percentage for all NPs.

We have already considered (in section 4.3) the animacy hierarchy (Silverstein 1976, Comrie 1981) with respect to number marking, which is often lacking with abstract inanimates in North Germanic. The hierarchy is often cited in discussions of different patterns of morphological marking of grammatical categories, perhaps none more so than definiteness. C. Lyons (1999) is particularly critical of the explanatory power of such a hierarchy; he considers it rather an expression of 'some real cross-language generalizations' (Lyons C. 1999:215) which reflects a variation in salience, or prominence, between different types of referents, where human referents would intuitively be the most salient ones (ibid.).

The animacy hierarchy is motivated functionally, as for example most subjects tend to be more animate and definite than objects. C. Lyons points out that this leads to compensating morphological marking if the situation deviates from the stereotypical one and the object is more animate and definite than the subject (Lyons C. 1999:214). This insight is also the foundation of Leiss' idea that definite marking originated in the object position, to mark objects that were definite, before such marking appeared on subjects, which were definite by virtue of their initial position in the clause (Leiss 2000, 2007). As already noted in section 4.6, this hypothesis is not borne out in the material of this study, which clearly demonstrates a preference for animate subjects (in the nominative) to be marked as definite before objects.

4.8 Definiteness and Type of Reference

So far, we have considered the interactions between definiteness and other grammatical phenomena. In the remaining part of the chapter, we address a different interdependency, namely that between definiteness and type of reference.

In Chapter 2 we discussed the meaning of definiteness and the uses of the definite article, noting that they are not isomorphic, but that article languages can use articles to different extents, depending on the context. We discussed a typology of definite article uses as presented by Hawkins (1978) and noted some overlaps between certain uses and certain articles, in languages with more than one definite article (see also Schwarz F. 2009). All of these observations were synchronic; however, they are even more relevant diachronically. North Germanic originally had no definite (or indefinite) article, while modern North Germanic languages do. In the course of article grammaticalization we expect different article uses to be available for the incipient definite article, but not all simultaneously. We therefore turn to an analysis of the occurrence of -IN in each of the three uses: direct anaphora, indirect anaphora and larger situation use. As we did with grammatical categories above, we take each use of the definite article separately and discuss its representation in the corpus.

TABLE 53   Expressions of direct anaphora in the corpus

Direct anaphora	Forms	Period I		Period II		Period III	
Danish	BN	98 / 241	40.66%	44 / 251	17.53%	17 / 194	8.76%
	-IN	31 / 241	12.86%	87 / 251	34.66%	74 / 194	38.14%
	DEN	19 / 241	7.88%	34 / 251	13.55%	25 / 194	12.89%
	DEM	15 / 241	6.22%	32 / 251	12.75%	25 / 194	12.89%
Swedish	BN	88 / 263	33.46%	0 / 305	0.00%	1 / 124	0.81%
	-IN	52 / 263	19.77%	218 / 305	71.48%	57 / 124	45.97%
	DEN	10 / 263	3.80%	33 / 305	10.82%	24 / 124	19.36%
	DEM	18 / 263	6.84%	23 / 305	7.54%	27 / 124	21.77%
Icelandic	BN	81 / 314	25.80%	51 / 177	28.81%	46 / 127	36.22%
	-IN	86 / 314	27.39%	42 / 177	23.73%	47 / 127	37.01%
	DEN	41 / 314	13.06%	9 / 177	5.08%	5 / 127	3.94%
	DEM	44 / 314	14.01%	45 / 177	25.42%	9 / 127	7.09%

We follow the proposed grammaticalization chain (see Chapter 2), beginning with direct anaphora.

The expressions considered here include bare nouns (BN), the incipient definite article annotated with -IN, and two types of other determiners: the annotation DEN refers to the proximal demonstrative *sá* 'this', while DEM refers to other determiners, such as *thenne* 'that'.

The results presented in Table 53 reveal a common tendency in Danish and Swedish to avoid BNs in direct anaphoric uses as the grammaticalization of the definite article progresses. In Period I we find BNs as direct anaphors in about one-third of all Swedish examples and over 40% of the Danish ones. As early as Period II they vanish in Swedish, while in Danish they constitute ca. 19% of all direct anaphors. The Icelandic results, on the other hand, exhibit some variation between Period I and III; surprisingly the percentage of BNs increases with time.

(136)   Þess er getið eitt sinn að   kóng-ur   var   á   skóg farinn með
        it   is told   EN time   that king-NOM was on forest gone   with
        hirð sinni sem oftar
        court his   as often
        'It is told that once the king was gone to the woods with his court, as he often did.' (IS_Vil, Period III)

In (136), the discourse referent *kóng-ur* 'king-NOM' was introduced as *Ríkharður kongur* two lines earlier, so it is neither new nor unique. Notably, the direct anaphors in Icelandic that appear as BNs are almost exclusively NPs including the noun *konungr* 'king' (in Period I also *drottning* 'queen'). Even though it is always a specific referent, introduced early on in the story, the noun appears bare, as if it were used to refer uniquely.

The BNs used as direct anaphors in Danish and Swedish are less frequent and sometimes not necessarily anaphors at all. Consider the example in (137) from Swedish, Period III.

(137) **thetta mäkta skipp-ed** [...] *steg thän dristog-a man-en oc*
 this mighty ship-DEF rose DEF bold-WK man-DEF and
 *strängh-e riddar-en Jason till **skip**-s mz mangha ädel-a*
 strong-WK knight-DEF Jason to ship-GEN with many noble-PL
 oc fri-burn-e män aff tessalia
 and free-born-PL men of Thessalia
 'This mighty ship [...] the bold and strong knight Jason came onboard [= to the ship] with many noble and free-born men of Thessalia.'
 (SV_Did, Period III)

The expression *till skips*, although it may refer anaphorically to the previously mentioned ship in the phrase 'this mighty ship', may also be non-referential, a use of BNs similar to the modern pseudo-incorporation in Danish and Swedish (Asudeh and Mikkelsen 2000). In Periods II and III in Danish and Swedish the incipient definite article (-IN) is used in the majority of direct anaphors.

It is important to note that Swedish (and also Norwegian) developed so-called double definiteness in NPs in which the head noun is accompanied by an adjective; see example (138a). The proximal demonstrative *sá* 'this' grammaticalized in Swedish into a free preposed definite article, *den/det/de* 'the' (its form depending on the gender and number of the head noun). Double definiteness did not develop in Danish or Icelandic (with the exception of poetry and older texts, where the preposed *hinn* occasionally appears). In Danish only the preposed article DEN occurs in an NP with an adjective, blocking the suffixed article, while in Icelandic only the suffixed article occurs. In all languages the adjective appears in its weak form in definite NPs.

Swedish
(138) a. *det stor-a hus-et*
 DEF big-WK house-DEF

Danish
    b. *det stor-e hus*
       DEF big-WK house

Icelandic
    c. *stór-a hús-ið*
       big-WK house-DEF
       'the big house'

It is thus possible, in our corpus, that both demonstratives DEN and DEM co-occur within the same NP with the suffixed definite article -IN (for DEN see examples (139–141) and (143), from DEM example (142)). In Old Swedish determiners co-occur with -IN relatively frequently in comparison with the other two languages, out of all NPs with the suffixed article -IN, 15.7 % co-occur with demonstratives, as in examples (139–143).

(139) *þön sami ætt-in*
     DEF same family-DEF
     'the same family' (SV_OgL, Period I)

(140) *Vm ena nat war **thän riddar-in** j enom stadh näst the*
     on EN night was DEF knight-DEF.NOM in EN town next DEF
     ***quinn-onne** som diäfwl-en war j*
     woman-DEF.ACC which devil-DEF was in
     'One night the knight was in a town near the place where the possessed woman stayed.' (SV_Jart, Period II)

(141) *Nu litin tima ther äpte tha doo **thän sami riddarin**.*
     now little time there after then died DEF same knight-DEF
     ther nu sagdhi-s aff
     which now told-REFL of
     'A short time afterwards the same knight of which we spoke here died.' (SV_Jart, Period II)

(142) *Jak seer thz thässa vng-a **gran-en** haffwer swa mykith op*
     I see that this young-WK spruce-DEF has so much up
     wäxt thz hon fortagher the stor-o at wäxa
     grown that she deprives DEF large-WK to grow
     'I see that this young spruce has grown so much that it does not allow the large one to continue growing'. (SV_SVM, Period II)

(143) *oc wndradho alle hwat gudh-i täkti-s framdelis göra*
and wondered all what god-DAT thought-REFL henceforth do
mz **the *klene*** *iomffrw-n-ne*
with DEF delicate maiden-DEF-DAT
'And all wondered what God would do henceforth do with the delicate maiden.' (SV_Linc, Period III)

In Danish the co-occurrence is very rare; only 4% of NPs with -IN co-occur with demonstratives, as in examples (144–145).[4] Interestingly, the only examples of this type of double definiteness are found within one Danish text, *Sjælens trost*, which might be heavily influenced by the Swedish text, as both were translated from the same German source text around the same time. This is consistent with the fact that, under the periods studied, double definiteness was developing in Swedish but not in Danish (see also section 2.4.1.1 on double definiteness).

(144) *Tha com oc **thæn ful-r** mordhar-in løbande oc grep*
then came also DEF vile-ST murderer-DEF running and seized
***the** ædhl-a quinn-ona i har-it*
DEF noble-WK woman-DEF in hair-DEF
'Then the vile murderer came running and grabbed the noble woman by the hair.' (DA_ST, Period II)

(145) *oc drikkir hon af **the** yrte-ne tha faar hon bot*
and drinks she of DEF herb-DEF then receives she cure
'And if she drinks the herb she will be cured.' (DA_ST, Period II)

In Icelandic there are even fewer examples of the co-occurrence: only 2.4% of all instances of -IN co-occur with demonstratives. The example (146) is the only one in the Icelandic corpus where the distal demonstrative *sá* co-occurs with the suffixed article.

(146) *og hafi **sá** okkar hring-inn sem betur veitir*
and had that our ring-DEF.NOM which better knows
'And one which knows better will have this ring of ours.' (IS_Vil, Period III)

---

4 Note that in example (144) the adjective 'vile' appears in its strong form; compare to example (275) in section 6.1from the same text in Swedish where the corresponding adjective is in a weak form.

TABLE 54 Expressions of indirect anaphora in the corpus

Indirect anaphora	Forms	Period I		Period II		Period III	
Danish	BN	59 / 243	24.28%	13 / 230	5.65%	11 / 215	5.12%
	-IN	19 / 243	7.82%	26 / 230	11.30%	44 / 215	20.47%
	DEN	15 / 243	6.17%	13 / 230	5.65%	9 / 215	4.19%
	DEM	6 / 243	2.47%	4 / 230	1.74%	3 / 215	1.40%
	POSS-PRO	50 / 243	20.58%	84 / 230	36.52%	51 / 215	23.27%
	POSS-REFL	28 / 243	11.52%	30 / 230	13.04%	29 / 215	13.49%
	POSS-GEN	25 / 243	10.29%	28 / 230	12.17%	47 / 215	21.86%
Swedish	BN	102 / 291	35.05%	20 / 208	9.62%	12 / 130	9.23%
	-IN	26 / 291	8.93%	38 / 208	18.27%	14 / 130	10.77%
	DEN	12 / 291	4.12%	9 / 208	4.33%	7 / 130	5.38%
	DEM	12 / 291	4.12%	12 / 208	5.77%	9 / 130	6.92%
	POSS-PRO	30 / 291	10.31%	47 / 208	22.60%	30 / 130	23.08%
	POSS-REFL	13 / 291	4.47%	45 / 208	21.63%	21 / 130	16.15%
	POSS-GEN	61 / 291	20.96%	21 / 208	10.10%	28 / 130	21.54%
Icelandic	BN	25 / 166	15.06%	39 / 193	20.21%	19 / 76	25.00%
	-IN	30 / 166	18.07%	35 / 193	18.13%	11 / 76	14.47%
	DEN	9 / 166	5.42%	8 / 193	4.15%	6 / 76	7.89%
	DEM	5 / 166	3.01%	8 / 193	4.15%	5 / 76	6.58%
	POSS-PRO	32 / 166	19.28%	2 / 193	1.04%	14 / 76	18.42%
	POSS-REFL	19 / 166	11.45%	33 / 193	17.10%	11 / 76	14.47%
	POSS-GEN	18 / 166	10.84%	22 / 193	11.40%	6 / 76	7.89%

In the case of indirect anaphora, as presented in Table 54, the picture becomes more complicated, as there is an abundance of forms with which the incipient definite article competes in this context. Apart from BNs and demonstratives, we also find possessives in the form of genitival NPs (tagged as POSS-GEN) or pronouns, both regular (POSS-PRO) and reflexive (POSS-REFL). The results for -IN are inconclusive. While in Danish the proportion of -IN in indirect anaphors consistently grows over the periods, it fluctuates in Swedish and even declines in Icelandic. As expected, possessives are used very frequently in the context of indirect anaphora. In Swedish and Danish regular possessive pronouns are especially frequent: they constitute on average 27% of indirect anaphors in Danish and 19% in Swedish. In Icelandic possessive pronouns are not used quite as often in indirect anaphors, appearing in only ca. 13% of exam-

TABLE 55 Expressions of larger situation use in the corpus

Unique reference	Forms	Period I		Period II		Period III	
Danish	BN	49 / 65	75.38%	56 / 115	48.70%	70 / 112	62.50%
	-IN	4 / 65	6.15%	9 / 115	7.83%	20 / 112	17.86%
	DEN	2 / 65	3.08%	13 / 115	11.30%	10 / 112	8.93%
	DEM	0 / 65	0.00%	2 / 115	1.74%	2 / 112	1.79%
Swedish	BN	85 / 109	77.98%	63 / 107	58.88%	16 / 26	61.54%
	-IN	5 / 109	4.59%	14 / 107	13.08%	6 / 26	23.08%
	DEN	0 / 109	0.00%	3 / 107	2.80%	1 / 26	3.85%
	DEM	0 / 109	0.00%	0 / 107	0.00%	0 / 26	0.00%
Icelandic	BN	17 / 28	60.71%	8 / 19	42.11%	2 / 4	50.00%
	-IN	0 / 28	0.00%	4 / 19	21.05%	2 / 4	50.00%
	DEN	0 / 28	0.00%	1 / 19	5.26%	0 / 4	0.00%
	DEM	1 / 28	3.57%	0 / 19	0.00%	0 / 4	0.00%

ples. Reflexive possessive pronouns are at least equally frequent as -IN in this context in all languages. The genitive is quite frequently used in Swedish (17.5% of all indirect anaphors on average), and almost as frequently in Danish (14.8% on average). Icelandic does not make such a frequent use of the genitive as the other languages (it accounts for only 10% of examples). Overall, possessives are used much more frequently indirect anaphors in Swedish and Danish than in Icelandic.

In the case of larger situation use, as presented in Table 55, there is a persistent high frequency of BNs for all languages and all periods. The proportion of -IN in unique reference, even though not very high, exhibits steady growth over the three periods. Here it is important to note that the results for Icelandic are of lower statistical significance, as there are fewer examples of unique reference than in the other two languages. In the Icelandic corpus unique referents occur only in 1.6% of all NPs (51 examples), compared with 8.3% (242 examples) and 10.1% (292 examples) for the Swedish and Danish corpora respectively. This disparity is due to the presence of religious texts in the Swedish and Danish corpora, but not in the Icelandic corpus.

4.9 All Factors—A Refined Analysis

In this chapter we have examined the interdependencies between definiteness (and indefiniteness) and a number of factors, such as case, number, gender and animacy. Each of these factors was discussed individually. We noted that some values favoured the definite article early on, e.g., nominative case, subject function, masculine gender and animacy, while others disfavoured the definite article, e.g., neuter gender and inanimacy. Even from these individual analyses we obtain a picture of an NP that is most likely to be definite in Period I in all languages in the sample, as well as a picture of an NP that is least likely to be marked with -IN in that period. We can also discern how the factors change over time.

In this section we will study the data more globally. In particular, we present statistics revealing the influence of particular values on the choice of NP form between defNP, indefNP and BN. This influence is presented as a weight: factors favouring selection of a particular NP form have positive values, while those disfavouring selection of the form have negative values. In the case of positive values, the higher the values for a given factor, the stronger is its explanatory power. Apart from the weight, we also present the relative score, that is, we order the values from the most favourable to a given form to the least favourable. A relative score of +100 means that if the factor (e.g., nominative case) is present, the form will always be chosen, while a relative score of –100 means that the presence of the factor excludes the possibility of using the form; for example, number_plural excludes indefNP.

The calculated weights come from applying a regression algorithm on all gathered data. The aim of the algorithm is to produce a mathematical function that will take all properties of a word (case, singularity, anaphora ...) as input and return the definiteness of this word. Theoretically, this function could be applied to any word with known properties and the definiteness of the word would be automatically calculated. This function, however, would not always return correct values due the fact that not all linguistic phenomena can be modelled accurately and globally for all words. Therefore, the construction and evaluation of such a function was not the primary goal of the research. The function was, indeed, constructed, but for the purpose of retrieving the weight values it applies to different linguistic properties of words. These weights reflect the impact of each individual property on the definiteness of the word. The relative score of a feature is calculated as the percentage of the weight of this feature compared to the weight of the feature which has the strongest impact on the definiteness (i.e., has the highest weight).

Further research plans include examining the impact of pairs or sets of features (like masculine + direct anaphora) on the definiteness of the word. Such calculations require modifications of the regression algorithm.

4.9.1 *The Definite Article*

Factors favouring the use of -IN in Danish in Period I are genitive case, masculine gender, and the function of direct anaphora. -IN is disfavoured by both subjects and objects, but less so by subjects; the relative score for objects is almost twice as high as for subjects. Animacy and feminine and neuter gender have similar relative scores. Factors clearly disfavouring the use of -IN are abstractness of the noun and the oblique or no-ending form of the noun.

In Swedish the factors most favourable to the selection of -IN in Period I are the function of direct anaphora, masculine gender and singular number. Animate nouns are more favoured than inanimate, while nominative case is the least favourable of the four basic cases. Plural number and abstractness of the noun strongly disfavour the use of -IN. Only one factor favours the selection of -IN in Icelandic in Period I, namely the function of direct anaphora. Of those that disfavour it the least, the most notable are subject function and nominative case; masculine gender appears surprisingly low on this scale. The use of -IN is, surprisingly, more favoured with inanimate referents than with animate ones.

We may conclude that direct anaphora is a common factor favouring the selection of -IN in Period I in all three languages. Danish and Swedish produce similar results with respect to subject function and masculine gender, but differ in how they treat animate and inanimate nouns.

In Period II in Danish, accusative case and direct anaphora are the strongest variables favouring the incipient definite article (-IN). Dative case and neuter gender also favour -IN, while, surprisingly, the masculine gender is resistant to the occurrence of -IN in all three languages in this period. Factors that strongly disfavour -IN are again the abstractness of the NP, as well as mass nouns and plural number.

In Swedish direct anaphora remains the strongest predictor for -IN, followed by the function of subject and genitive case. Plural and abstract nouns remain strong 'repellents' of -IN, together with the oblique case and no-ending forms of the noun. Animacy is not a strong predictor for either Swedish or Danish, but in both languages animate nouns have a higher relative score than inanimate ones. In Icelandic, similarly to Danish, direct anaphora and accusative case are the strongest variables favouring -IN. Among the factors that strongly disfavour -IN are oblique case, mass and abstract nouns, and plural number. Again, inanimate nouns are higher on the scale than animate nouns, in contrast to the other two languages.

TABLE 56 Variables influencing the selection of the definite article (-IN) in Period I

Danish			Swedish			Icelandic		
Feature name	Weight	Relative score	Feature name	Weight	Relative score	Feature name	Weight	Relative score
case_gen	+0.0955	20.62	anaphora_dir-a	+0.1222	19.52	anaphora_dir-a	+0.2616	30.85
anaphora_dir-a	+0.0869	18.77	gender_m	+0.0304	4.85	case_nom	−0.0290	−3.42
gender_m	+0.0528	11.41	number_sg	+0.0287	4.59	function_sbj	−0.0420	−4.95
function_sbj	−0.0434	−9.37	case_acc	−0.0056	−0.89	gender_f	−0.0465	−5.48
function_obj	−0.0773	−16.68	animacy_anim	−0.0446	−7.13	case_gen	−0.0533	−6.28
countability_count	−0.0843	−18.19	concrete_concr	−0.0478	−7.64	case_acc	−0.0563	−6.64
case_acc	−0.0914	−19.74	case_gen	−0.0710	−11.34	gender_n	−0.0661	−7.80
case_nom	−0.0974	−21.03	case_dat	−0.0816	−13.03	concrete_concr	−0.0700	−8.26
concrete_concr	−0.1139	−24.59	function_sbj	−0.0941	−15.03	number_sg	−0.0900	−10.61
number_sg	−0.1160	−25.05	countability_mass	−0.1312	−20.97	animacy_inanim	−0.0934	−11.02
animacy_inanim	−0.1299	−28.05	gender_f	−0.1463	−23.38	number_pl	−0.0941	−11.10
animacy_anim	−0.1528	−33.00	case_nom	−0.1466	−23.42	countability_count	−0.1015	−11.96
case_dat	−0.1804	−38.96	animacy_inanim	−0.1953	−31.21	case_dat	−0.1059	−12.49
countability_mass	−0.1819	−39.27	function_obj	−0.2120	−33.87	animacy_anim	−0.1660	−19.57
gender_f	−0.1953	−42.17	countability_count	−0.2125	−33.96	countability_mass	−0.1759	−20.73
gender_n	−0.1980	−42.76	case_obl	−0.2569	−41.05	gender_m	−0.2542	−29.97
number_pl	−0.2300	−49.66	gender_n	−0.3457	−55.24	concrete_abstr	−0.3005	−35.43
concrete_abstr	−0.3131	−67.61	case_no-end	−0.4288	−68.51	case_obl	−0.8482	−100.00
case_obl	−0.3803	−82.10	number_pl	−0.4326	−69.11	—	—	—
case_no-end	−0.4631	−100.00	concrete_abstr	−0.4843	−77.39	—	—	—

TABLE 57   Variables influencing the selection of the definite article (-IN) in Period II

Danish			Swedish			Icelandic		
Feature name	Weight	Relative score	Feature name	Weight	Relative score	Feature name	Weight	Relative score
case_acc	+0.2537	39.16	anaphora_dir-a	+0.3730	60.29	anaphora_dir-a	+0.3065	55.31
anaphora_dir-a	+0.1884	29.07	function_sbj	+0.2418	39.09	case_acc	+0.1254	22.63
case_dat	+0.1215	18.75	case_gen	+0.1272	20.57	number_sg	+0.0067	1.21
gender_n	+0.1083	16.72	concrete_concr	+0.0474	7.66	case_no-end	+0.0000	0.00
function_sbj	+0.0773	11.93	case_acc	+0.0417	6.74	case_dat	−0.0562	−10.14
concrete_concr	+0.0325	5.01	case_dat	+0.0294	4.75	gender_n	−0.0610	−11.01
countability_count	−0.0398	−6.14	number_sg	+0.0221	3.57	animacy_inanim	−0.0667	−12.05
case_gen	−0.0414	−6.39	number_pl	+0.0114	1.84	countability_count	−0.0776	−14.01
case_nom	−0.0831	−12.83	countability_count	+0.0102	1.65	concrete_concr	−0.0973	−17.57
animacy_anim	−0.0997	−15.39	function_mod	−0.0082	−1.32	case_gen	−0.1060	−19.13
case_no-end	−0.1012	−15.62	case_nom	−0.0110	−1.78	gender_f	−0.1525	−27.52
function_obj	−0.1164	−17.96	gender_n	−0.0428	−6.92	function_sbj	−0.1623	−29.29
animacy_inanim	−0.1181	−18.23	animacy_anim	−0.0518	−8.37	function_obj	−0.1632	−29.45
gender_m	−0.1518	−23.43	gender_m	−0.0784	−12.67	case_nom	−0.2050	−37.00
number_sg	−0.1672	−25.81	animacy_inanim	−0.1045	−16.90	gender_m	−0.2148	−38.76
gender_f	−0.2249	−34.72	countability_mass	−0.1237	−19.99	concrete_abstr	−0.2457	−44.34
case_obl	−0.2340	−36.12	gender_f	−0.1362	−22.03	number_pl	−0.2567	−46.33
countability_mass	−0.2640	−40.75	number_pl	−0.2490	−40.25	animacy_anim	−0.2692	−48.58
number_pl	−0.2759	−42.59	function_obj	−0.2506	−40.52	countability_mass	−0.2876	−51.91
anaphora_other	−0.3022	−46.65	concrete_abstr	−0.3760	−60.79	case_obl	−0.5541	−100.00
concrete_abstr	−0.3043	−46.97	case_no-end	−0.5468	−88.40	—	—	—
—	—	—	case_obl	−0.6186	−100.00	—	—	—

142   CHAPTER 4

TABLE 58 Variables influencing the selection of the definite article (-IN) in Period III

Danish			Swedish			Icelandic		
Feature name	Weight	Relative score	Feature name	Weight	Relative score	Feature name	Weight	Relative score
anaphora_dir-a	+0.1746	30.40	case_acc	+0.2447	65.47	anaphora_dir-a	+0.3930	84.92
number_sg	+0.0943	16.43	anaphora_dir-a	+0.2004	53.61	animacy_inanim	+0.1592	34.41
function_sbj	+0.0882	15.35	case_dat	+0.1180	31.57	number_sg	+0.0076	1.65
gender_m	−0.0119	−2.08	case_gen	+0.0507	13.58	gender_f	−0.0111	−2.40
concrete_concr	−0.0315	−5.49	function_sbj	+0.0248	6.64	case_acc	−0.0376	−8.12
animacy_inanim	−0.0660	−11.50	number_sg	+0.0116	3.11	gender_m	−0.0430	−9.30
case_no-end	−0.0734	−12.78	function_obj	−0.0037	−0.99	countability_count	−0.0489	−10.57
countability_count	−0.0750	−13.05	gender_m	−0.0080	−2.13	function_sbj	−0.0590	−12.75
gender_n	−0.1671	−29.09	case_nom	−0.0529	−14.15	concrete_concr	−0.0822	−17.76
countability_mass	−0.2161	−37.63	concrete_concr	−0.0686	−18.36	case_dat	−0.0887	−19.16
gender_f	−0.2239	−38.98	countability_count	−0.0815	−21.82	case_nom	−0.0906	−19.57
animacy_anim	−0.2297	−40.00	animacy_inanim	−0.0973	−26.04	case_gen	−0.0933	−20.16
case_obl	−0.2996	−52.17	gender_f	−0.1084	−29.01	function_obj	−0.1069	−23.10
function_obj	−0.3062	−53.33	animacy_anim	−0.1390	−37.20	case_no-end	−0.1259	−27.21
case_gen	−0.3750	−65.31	case_obl	−0.1519	−40.65	concrete_abstr	−0.1495	−32.31
concrete_abstr	−0.4978	−86.68	countability_mass	−0.1678	−44.91	countability_mass	−0.2090	−45.16
number_pl	−0.5414	−94.28	gender_n	−0.1756	−46.99	gender_n	−0.2259	−48.81
—	—	—	concrete_abstr	−0.2336	−62.52	case_obl	−0.2688	−58.09
—	—	—	number_pl	−0.3361	−89.94	number_pl	−0.4529	−97.87
—	—	—	case_no-end	−0.3737	−100.00	animacy_anim	−0.4628	−100.00

Direct anaphora, singular number and subject function remain the strongest predictors of definiteness in Period III. Inanimacy is no longer a strong repellent for -IN, and inanimates 'climb up' the scale. The decline of the case system in Swedish is visible in the results, even though the oblique cases rank highly with respect to how strongly they favour the appearance of -IN, the nominative is classed very low. In Danish the cases have disappeared as an explanatory factor, apart from genitive and oblique forms or no ending forms. Interestingly, in the Icelandic texts in the corpus the definite article has a strong preference for inanimate nouns, while animate nouns are strongly disfavoured.

4.9.2 *The Indefinite Article*

Only in Icelandic do we find factors favouring the selection of EN in Period I, all related to case. The disfavouring factors include plural (as we would expect) and mass values, as well as abstract nouns. Surprisingly, the genitive case in Danish and the object function in Icelandic also strongly disfavour the occurrence of the indefinite article in Period I.

In the second period, only in Danish are there more factors favouring the indefinite article. It is the nominative case and countable nouns that are preferred by EN. In Swedish the function of subject has the highest relative score; this is most likely due to the frequency of the presentative construction. The factors that are the strongest repellents of EN include the plural, as well as direct anaphora and mass and abstract nouns. The results for all languages are quite uniform in Period II.

In the third period, in Danish EN is preferred in the function of adverbial and in singular NPs. In Swedish it is preferred in the function of predicative, albeit the relative score is not very high. As in the previous periods EN is strongly disfavoured with plural and mass NPs, as well as with direct anaphora.

4.9.3 *The Definite Article vs. Bare Nouns—Classification Tree Analysis*

Lastly, to ascertain which independent variables have the greatest influence on the presence of the definite article in our dataset on a larger scale, we perform a classification tree analysis. Since we have already presented detailed results for each language and period in sections 4.9.1 and 4.9.2, here we aim to present more global results, treating all three languages together. Further, the classification trees for different languages did not vary to a significant degree, thus we deem that displaying one figure per period is a good enough generalization. The classification tree analysis tests each independent variable separately and chooses the variable that has the greatest association with the response. The algorithm then splits the data into subsets or classes, which can be visu-

THE DIACHRONY OF (IN)DEFINITENESS—A QUANTITATIVE STUDY   145

TABLE 59 Variables influencing the selection of the indefinite article (EN) in Period I

	Danish			Swedish			Icelandic	
Feature name	Weight	Relative score	Feature name	Weight	Relative score	Feature name	Weight	Relative score
case_acc	−0.0419	−10.52	number_sg	−0.0265	−6.29	case_nom	+0.0626	15.31
gender_n	−0.0664	−16.67	case_acc	−0.0314	−7.45	case_dat	+0.0181	4.42
countability_count	−0.0668	−16.77	animacy_inanim	−0.0479	−11.35	case_no-end	+0.0000	0.00
function_sbj	−0.0766	−19.24	case_obl	−0.0732	−17.36	function_sbj	−0.0162	−3.97
function_obj	−0.0877	−22.02	function_sbj	−0.0757	−17.96	number_sg	−0.0495	−12.11
concrete_concr	−0.0931	−23.37	countability_count	−0.0784	−18.58	gender_m	−0.0887	−21.70
case_dat	−0.1012	−25.42	concrete_concr	−0.1000	−23.71	gender_f	−0.0974	−23.84
number_sg	−0.1039	−26.08	function_obj	−0.1064	−25.24	animacy_inanim	−0.1074	−26.29
case_obl	−0.1104	−27.72	gender_m	−0.1275	−30.23	concrete_concr	−0.1148	−28.08
animacy_inanim	−0.1277	−32.06	gender_f	−0.1439	−34.11	countability_count	−0.1351	−33.07
case_no-end	−0.1366	−34.29	case_dat	−0.1675	−39.72	case_acc	−0.2226	−54.48
gender_m	−0.1471	−36.95	function_mod	−0.1922	−45.57	case_gen	−0.2275	−55.66
case_nom	−0.1628	−40.88	animacy_anim	−0.2113	−50.11	countability_mass	−0.2348	−57.46
gender_f	−0.1804	−45.31	case_no-end	−0.2173	−51.51	animacy_anim	−0.2393	−58.55
concrete_abstr	−0.1812	−45.50	case_gen	−0.2194	−52.02	gender_n	−0.2455	−60.08
animacy_anim	−0.2164	−54.33	case_nom	−0.2418	−57.33	case_obl	−0.2498	−61.13
countability_mass	−0.2359	−59.23	gender_n	−0.2554	−60.56	number_pl	−0.3194	−78.16
case_gen	−0.3959	−99.42	concrete_abstr	−0.2703	−64.09	function_obj	−0.3297	−80.67
number_pl	−0.3983	−100.00	number_pl	−0.3825	−90.69	concrete_abstr	−0.4087	−100.00
—	—	—	countability_mass	−0.4217	−100.00	—	—	—

TABLE 60 Variables influencing the selection of the indefinite article (EN) in Period II

Danish			Swedish			Icelandic		
Feature name	Weight	Relative score	Feature name	Weight	Relative score	Feature name	Weight	Relative score
case_nom	+0.1356	20.09	function_sbj	−0.0072	−1.37	case_no-end	+0.0000	0.00
countability_count	+0.0526	7.79	case_nom	−0.0407	−7.77	case_acc	−0.0045	−1.08
function_obj	+0.0360	5.34	countability_count	−0.0456	−8.70	number_sg	−0.0227	−5.49
function_adv	+0.0161	2.39	concrete_concr	−0.0478	−9.13	function_p-obj	−0.0292	−7.07
case_dat	+0.0000	0.00	function_pred	−0.0525	−10.03	gender_m	−0.0563	−13.64
function_pred	−0.0377	−5.59	gender_m	−0.0686	−13.10	animacy_inanim	−0.0635	−15.39
concrete_concr	−0.0432	−6.41	case_dat	−0.0785	−14.99	countability_count	−0.0703	−17.02
anaphora_other	−0.0493	−7.31	case_acc	−0.0792	−15.12	concrete_concr	−0.0722	−17.48
animacy_inanim	−0.0540	−8.00	anaphora_other	−0.0830	−15.85	case_nom	−0.0897	−21.72
number_sg	−0.0598	−8.86	animacy_anim	−0.0867	−16.55	gender_f	−0.0952	−23.06
gender_m	−0.0879	−13.02	function_obj	−0.0984	−18.78	function_adv	−0.0961	−23.28
gender_f	−0.0972	−14.40	concrete_abstr	−0.1037	−19.80	case_dat	−0.1041	−25.22
function_sbj	−0.1039	−15.40	case_gen	−0.1134	−21.64	function_obj	−0.1322	−32.02
concrete_abstr	−0.1087	−16.11	number_sg	−0.1291	−24.65	function_sbj	−0.1577	−38.19
case_acc	−0.1369	−20.29	function_adv	−0.1308	−24.96	anaphora_other	−0.1983	−48.02
case_no-end	−0.1571	−23.28	case_obl	−0.1327	−25.34	animacy_anim	−0.2313	−56.03
gender_n	−0.1751	−25.95	gender_f	−0.1404	−26.80	function_mod	−0.2371	−57.41
function_mod	−0.1875	−27.78	animacy_inanim	−0.1414	−27.00	case_obl	−0.2434	−58.95
animacy_anim	−0.1875	−27.79	gender_n	−0.1719	−32.81	countability_mass	−0.2870	−69.51
case_obl	−0.1995	−29.56	function_p-obj	−0.2411	−46.02	case_gen	−0.3111	−75.34
case_gen	−0.3766	−55.81	function_mod	−0.2697	−51.49	gender_n	−0.3297	−79.86
function_p-obj	−0.4045	−59.94	case_no-end	−0.2964	−56.59	function_pred	−0.3307	−80.10
countability_mass	−0.5327	−78.93	countability_mass	−0.3295	−62.90	concrete_abstr	−0.3798	−91.98

TABLE 60 Variables influencing the selection of the indefinite article (EN) in Period II (*cont.*)

	Danish		Swedish			Icelandic		
Feature name	Weight	Relative score	Feature name	Weight	Relative score	Feature name	Weight	Relative score
anaphora_dir-a	−0.5524	−81.85	anaphora_dir-a	−0.4052	−77.35	anaphora_dir-a	−0.3820	−92.51
number_pl	−0.6749	−100.00	number_pl	−0.5238	−100.00	number_pl	−0.4129	−100.00

TABLE 61 Variables influencing the selection of the indefinite article (EN) in Period III

Danish			Swedish			Icelandic		
Feature name	Weight	Relative score	Feature name	Weight	Relative score	Feature name	Weight	Relative score
function_adv	+0.3088	76.06	function_pred	+0.0727	11.85	function_sbj	+0.0021	0.46
number_sg	+0.0503	12.39	number_sg	−0.0045	−0.73	case_no-end	+0.0000	0.00
gender_n	−0.0276	−6.80	function_adv	−0.0141	−2.30	function_adv	−0.0084	−1.90
anaphora_other	−0.0315	−7.75	case_nom	−0.0225	−3.68	gender_m	−0.0281	−6.36
countability_count	−0.0781	−19.23	countability_count	−0.0302	−4.93	case_dat	−0.0343	−7.75
case_no-end	−0.0806	−19.84	gender_f	−0.0336	−5.48	case_nom	−0.0478	−10.80
gender_f	−0.0835	−20.56	anaphora_other	−0.0433	−7.06	animacy_anim	−0.0536	−12.10
animacy_anim	−0.0870	−21.44	function_obj	−0.0466	−7.60	number_sg	−0.0664	−14.99
function_pred	−0.0888	−21.87	case_acc	−0.0657	−10.72	concrete_concr	−0.0832	−18.78
gender_m	−0.1171	−28.84	concrete_concr	−0.0988	−16.11	countability_count	−0.0955	−21.57
concrete_concr	−0.1172	−28.88	gender_m	−0.0998	−16.28	gender_f	−0.1172	−26.46
concrete_abstr	−0.1471	−36.23	case_no-end	−0.1015	−16.55	concrete_abstr	−0.1193	−26.93
function_obj	−0.1546	−38.07	animacy_inanim	−0.1091	−17.80	anaphora_other	−0.1701	−38.41
function_p-obj	−0.1546	−38.09	gender_n	−0.1157	−18.86	case_acc	−0.1784	−40.28
case_obl	−0.1603	−39.48	function_sbj	−0.1275	−20.79	case_obl	−0.2010	−45.38
animacy_inanim	−0.1787	−44.01	concrete_abstr	−0.1367	−22.29	function_mod	−0.2032	−45.87
function_sbj	−0.1936	−47.68	animacy_anim	−0.1400	−22.83	animacy_inanim	−0.2112	−47.68
case_gen	−0.2123	−52.29	function_mod	−0.1513	−24.68	function_obj	−0.2664	−60.15
function_mod	−0.2418	−59.55	case_obl	−0.1940	−31.64	case_gen	−0.2679	−60.49
anaphora_dir-a	−0.3163	−77.91	function_p-obj	−0.2282	−37.22	function_pred	−0.2774	−62.64
countability_mass	−0.3640	−89.66	countability_mass	−0.3404	−55.51	gender_n	−0.2901	−65.51
number_pl	−0.4060	−100.00	anaphora_dir-a	−0.3828	−62.43	function_p-obj	−0.2978	−67.23
—	—	—	case_gen	−0.4094	−66.77	countability_mass	−0.3232	−72.99

TABLE 61 Variables influencing the selection of the indefinite article (EN) in Period III (*cont.*)

	Danish		Swedish			Icelandic		
Feature name	Weight	Relative score	Feature name	Weight	Relative score	Feature name	Weight	Relative score
—	—	—	number_pl	−0.5356	−87.35	anaphora_dir-a	−0.3585	−80.95
—	—	—	case_dat	−0.6132	−100.00	number_pl	−0.4429	−100.00

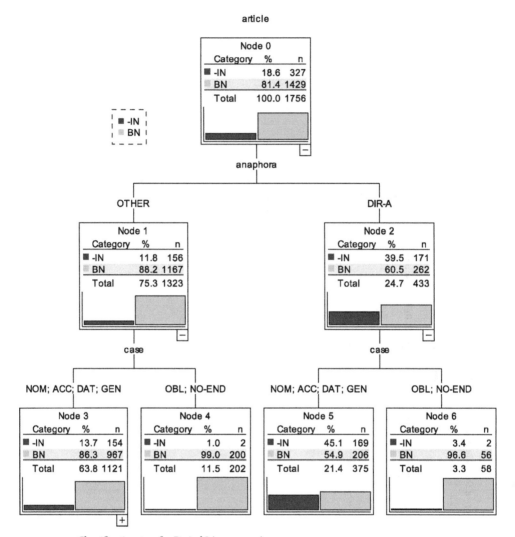

FIGURE 11 Classification tree for Period I (1200–1350)

alised in the form of 'trees' with several 'branches' and 'leaves' (i.e., nodes). For each period, the trees presented below compare instances of the definite article (-IN) and bare nouns (BN).

In Period I there are overwhelmingly more bare nouns than definite NPs (see Fig. 9). Thus, even though the analysis finds statistically significant splits, bare nouns dominate at every node. In the first split, we observe that direct anaphora is associated with a higher proportion of definite NPs (Node 2). Out of all direct anaphors, NPs in the nominative, accusative, dative and genitive are much more likely to be definite (Node 5) than NPs in the oblique case or

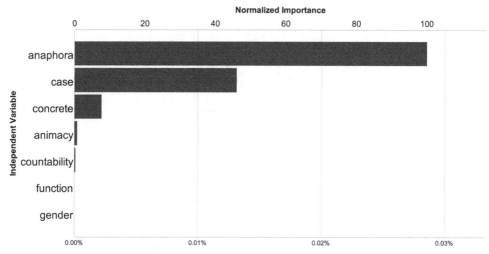

FIGURE 12   The importance of each independent variable in Period I

those with no ending (Node 6).[5] On the left side of the graph, we observe a similar tendency; namely that, if -IN is used in other types of reference than direct anaphora, it appears almost exclusively in the nominative, accusative, dative and genitive.

The tree analysis also provides us with an assessment of the impact of individual predictors on the model. In Figure 10, the importance of the predictors in Period I is presented. The most important predictor, anaphora, has the highest relative value of importance (100%), and the others are displayed as percentages of that value. The second most influential predictor of the definite article in Period I is case, while the remaining variables are virtually irrelevant.

Unfortunately, due to the large imbalance in the numbers of definite NPs and bare nouns, the model presented in Figure 9 does not offer an improvement in accuracy. Whether or not the independent variables are included, the model predicts 81.4% of cases correctly, which is the exact number of BNs in the model. Thus, a model predicting that all cases will be BNs would also be correct in 81.4% of cases.

In the second period, definite NPs are more frequent in the material, resulting in a more balanced classification (see Fig. 11). The first split is yet again deter-

---

[5]   The four examples with -IN and OBL/NO-END listed in Nodes 4 and 6 are instances of weak nouns in which the ending is not a proper case ending even with a definite article, but rather a non-nominative case ending, as in *pripiung af bono* 'a third of the property' (SV_AVL, Period I).

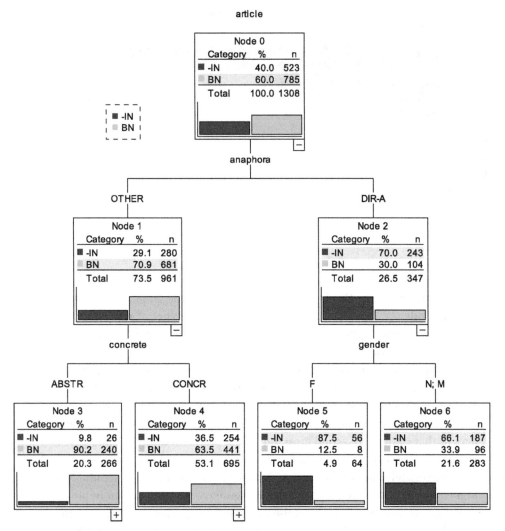

FIGURE 13 Classification tree for Period II (1350–1450)

mined by the presence of direct anaphoric reference. Definite NPs are much more frequent in direct anaphora than bare nouns (Node 2). Within direct anaphora, the second split in our tree is determined, quite surprisingly, by gender. Thus, the definite article is most likely to occur in Period II in feminine NPs that are used anaphorically (Node 5). An explanation of this unfortunately cannot be found in correlation with case, as one reviewer suggests, since feminine accusatives or datives are in no way more frequently marked with -IN in this period than masculine or neuter nouns. The selection of feminine gender as significant in Node 5 is of little importance for overall results (compare

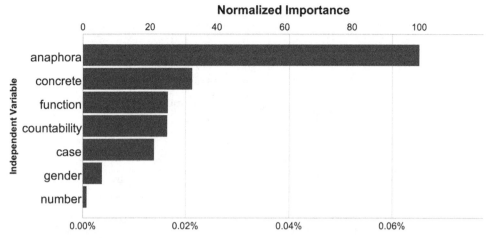

FIGURE 14   The importance of each independent variable in Period II

with Table 57 which illustrates that feminine gender is not higher in its relative score than other genders for either of the languages, and with Figure 12 below which will reveal that the weight of the factor of gender is not particularly large). In this case, the classification tree seems to be overfitting the data, namely feminine nouns are not particularly frequent in the corpus, but it so happens that they are unusually frequent in Swedish texts from Period II (relative to other languages and periods). Thus, even though feminine gender is overall not a strong factor in predicting whether the definite article will be used, it is selected as significant in Figure 11 due to an unusual high frequency of feminine nouns in Swedish texts from this period. Further, within reference other than direct anaphora (Node 1) the incipient definite article occurs more frequently with concrete rather than abstract nouns (Nodes 3 and 4), although bare nouns dominate here in both categories.

Figure 12 reveals that anaphora is again the most important predictor of -IN. Such variables as concreteness of the NP, syntactic function, countability and case are also relevant for the model, as is gender, albeit to a smaller degree.

As regards the goodness-of-fit of the model, if the algorithm assigned the type of the NP trivially, guessing that all cases are BNs, it would be correct in 60% of cases. That is our baseline model. The tree classification for Period II offers some improvement over the baseline model, as its accuracy is measured at 71.6%. This means that the inclusion of the independent variables has a positive impact on the model.

In Period III (see Fig. 13), anaphoric reference determines the first split, which results in almost identical subsets to those determined for Period II. Within direct anaphora, case is the predictor that resolves the second split.

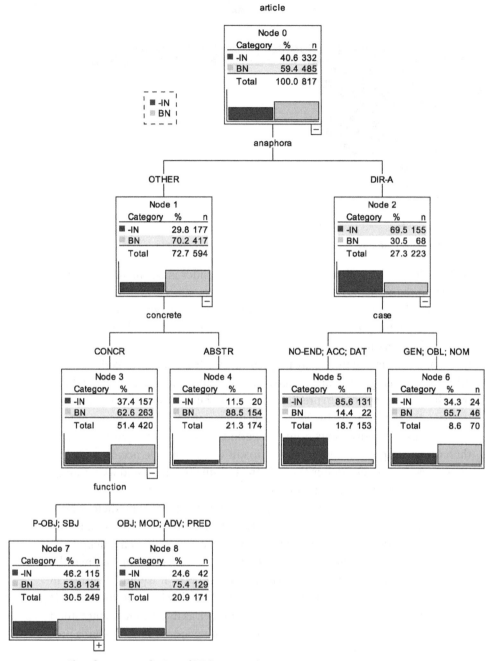

FIGURE 15 Classification tree for Period III (1450–1550)

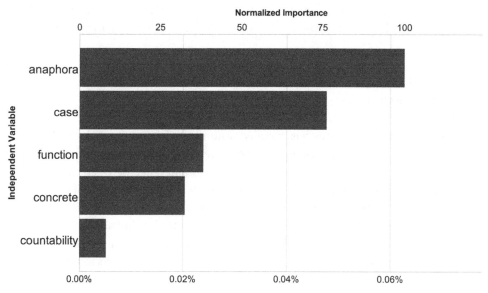

FIGURE 16   The importance of each independent variable in Period III

Here, definite NPs are used more frequently with nouns in the accusative or dative or nouns with no ending (Node 5), while bare nouns are used more often with nouns in the genitive, oblique or nominative case (Node 6). On the left side of the tree, if there is no direct anaphoric reference, definite NPs are more likely to occur with concrete than abstract nouns (Nodes 3 and 4). Among non-anaphoric, concrete NPs, the definite article occurs more frequently in the subject or prepositional object position (Node 7) than it does with other syntactic roles.

Anaphoric reference remains the most important predictor, closely followed by case (see Fig. 14). The syntactic function and concreteness of the NP are also relevant variables. The accuracy of the baseline model is 59.4% (i.e., the number of BNs in this period). The classification tree offers a significant improvement over the baseline, as it predicts 74.4% of the cases correctly. Of the three models presented in this section, the model for Period III is the most accurate.

Overall, the results of the classification tree analysis confirm our previous findings, presented in section 4.9.1, that direct anaphora is the strongest predictor for definite NPs throughout all of the studied periods. The other predictors that were selected as significant, such as case, function and concreteness, were also ranked relatively high for each language, as we indicated in section 4.9.1. It is, however, important to bear in mind that the classification tree analysis presented here compares definite NPs with bare nouns only. Thus, animacy, for instance, may not be a highly ranked predictor when -IN is compared with BNs. However, this does not mean that animacy has no influence on the presence of -IN.

4.10   Summary

The qualitative analysis has revealed a number of facts about the incipient articles in Danish, Swedish and Icelandic, revealing different patterns in each language. As early as 1200 there is a palpable difference between the Continental and the Insular languages, despite many superficial similarities. On the whole, Icelandic is considered to be the language in which grammaticalization has proceeded furthest in Period I, judging by the stability and similarity of the results in the successive periods. Danish and Swedish, on the other hand, exhibit varied patterns, with many changes taking place from Period I to II and from Period II to III. In particular, a number of other changes taking place in Old Danish and Old Swedish at that time are reflected in the results, such as the decline of the case system, which took place in Danish a little earlier than in Swedish, but which is complete in both languages by the end of the studied period.

The data suggest that these developments were influenced by both semantic and syntactic properties of nouns, in particular animacy and subjecthood. Comparing the proportions of singular, animate subjects in all NPs and in defNPs we conclude that at the early stages of grammaticalization the definite form favours such referents over inanimate, mass or plural NPs in functions other than the subject. Also, the indefinite article, at its earliest stages of development, is associated with animate subjects, but it is less sensitive to animacy and case than the definite article. In fact, it seems that at the onset of indefinite article grammaticalization the development of the definite article is mirrored in the development of the indefinite, so that salient discourse referents are the first to receive regular article marking, but the factors which remain important for successive stages of definite article grammaticalization are not as significant with indefinite article grammaticalization.

The quantitative results confirm hypotheses advanced by, among others, De Mulder and Carlier (2011), that at the beginning of definite article grammaticalization pragmatic factors, in particular the salience of the discourse referent, play a significant role. The results also lend strength to the proposed model of grammaticalization of the indefinite article, revealing a surprising affinity of the incipient indefinite article with the subject function (in Danish and Swedish, Icelandic not having developed the indefinite article at all).

Despite their mutual differences, one variable has been demonstrated to greatly favour the definite article in all of the languages studied, namely direct anaphora. Annotating the texts for the types of use of articles was a formidable task, and one that we believe can be done more justice in a qualitative study of these contexts. This is the subject of Chapter 5.

CHAPTER 5

Grammaticalization Models Revisited—A Qualitative Analysis

5.1   Introductory Remarks

In the previous chapter we reported the results of a quantitative study of the rise of definite and indefinite articles in North Germanic. While the statistical data give us some picture of the grammaticalization processes—for instance, demonstrating that the grammaticalization of the definite article began with topicalized discourse referents—a qualitative analysis of the corpus is needed to elaborate on and clarify the picture. In the present chapter we will therefore return to the models of grammaticalizations of both articles which were presented in Chapter 1. We begin with a discussion of the model of grammaticalization of the definite article, and its limitations, with particular attention to the developments from one stage to the next, in particular the unclear path from direct to indirect anaphora as well as from indirect anaphora to larger situation use. We argue that these steps can be explained in terms of referent accessibility, and will give examples to support our claims. We then turn to the model of grammaticalization of the indefinite article and its applications. A proposal encompassing both models will be discussed in 5.5.

5.2   On Models of Grammaticalization

We have noted earlier that there remain unsatisfactory gaps in the proposed model of grammaticalization of the definite article (see section 1.1). For instance, it is still not entirely clear which uses of the definite article constitute the so-called bridging contexts (in the terminology of Heine 2002) between stage I and stage II of the grammaticalization (direct and indirect anaphoric use). In Chapter 4, we have noted that the proposed order of events seems to be confirmed in terms of the frequency of the incipient article; the form does appear earlier and with higher frequency as a marker of direct anaphoric reference, later as a marker of indirect anaphoric reference, and finally in larger situation use (see section 4.8). However, one of the purposes of the present chapter is to find examples which may illustrate the path from direct to indirect anaphor and from indirect anaphora to larger situation use.

Before we continue, we would like to make the following observations: even though the model of grammaticalization presents a chronological development, it is not unusual for different stages of grammaticalization to co-exist at the same time in a language's history. In a famous study of the grammaticalization of the future construction 'be going to', Fischer and Rosenbach (2000:3) demonstrate how all of the stages of grammaticalization are still present in modern English.

Etymologically, definite articles are derived from deictic elements, often demonstratives. It may happen that the original demonstrative lives on alongside its descendant—the definite article—although it may be more common that the two differ in form as well as in scope of use. In Icelandic the definite suffix *-inn* is found together with the demonstrative *hinn* from which it derives, and both may be used within the same NP; however, the two forms are quite distinct. In Danish and Swedish the demonstrative *hinn* is now lost.

Indefinite articles seem to stem universally from the numeral 'one'. Interestingly, very often the numeral and the indefinite article are both retained, sometimes with slight formal differences. In Danish and Swedish the numeral is typically stressed, while the indefinite article is unstressed unless contrast or emphasis is intended.

Irrespective of whether the original demonstrative is retained or lost after definite article grammaticalization has reached more advanced stages, the diachronic connection between the two must at some point come to a conclusion. We may imagine the process of grammaticalization as a gradual extension of the original demonstrative function, which may not be fully visible to users of the language. At some point in the process, however, the form comes to a turning point, from which it may continue as either a demonstrative or a definite article, but not as a form sharing some features of both. In other words, at some point we come to deal with a definite article, a form which may be used in certain contexts in which the use of the demonstrative is not grammatically correct.

The first purpose of a grammaticalization model is thus to establish this turning point in the form's development, after which the form will be categorized differently than it was before. From this point, the grammaticalization may also proceed even further. Because it is not always easy to decide when a given form has changed categorically, e.g., from a numeral into an indefinite article, in the text we refer to the grammaticalizing forms as *incipient* or *nascent* articles. The second purpose is to identify the successive stages of the process, some of which may be located chronologically before the turning point (e.g., the direct anaphoric use of the demonstrative) and some after the turning point (e.g., the use with unique referents). The grammaticalization model should also have a predictive value. It is much more interesting if the model, when applied to previously unstudied languages, indicates that they have gone through the same stages and in the same order.

In the following sections we will discuss the models proposed so far, evaluating them against the data from North Germanic. The empirical data gathered for the sake of the present project allows us greater insight into the process of article formation, and our intention is to incorporate it into the fine-grained models of article grammaticalization.

5.3   Grammaticalization of the Definite Article

5.3.1   *From Deixis to Direct Anaphora*

The model of grammaticalization adopted here assumes the definite article to derive from a deictic marker, typically a (distal) demonstrative pronoun, as is the case in North Germanic. In this model, the first step in article grammaticalization is the extension of the use of the demonstrative to point not only within a physical situation, but also within a text (anaphora). We have already noted that demonstratives are almost always allowed to be used anaphorically, including when a language has a grammaticalized definite article (in English, for example, *this* or *that* can be used to refer anaphorically, even though the definite article *the* is also available). However, some idiosyncrasies may exist as regards the anaphoric use of demonstratives, for example, a preference to be placed in postposition rather than in preposition, which is the case in Polish (a language without a definite article). Examples (147–148) illustrate the possible locations of the (proximal) demonstrative *ten* 'this' in deictic and anaphoric uses.

Deixis:

(147)   a. *Podaj mi tę   książk-ę.*
            pass me this.ACC.SG book-ACC.SG
            'Pass me this book.'

         b. *?Podaj mi książk-ę   tę.*
            pass me book-ACC.SG this.ACC.SG
            'Pass me this book.' (intended meaning)

Anaphora:

(148)   *Książka   ta   / ta   książka   ilustruje zmiany*
        book.NOM this.NOM.SG / this.NOM.SG book.NOM   depicts   changes

>   *jakie   zaszły   w polskim społeczeństwie.*
>   which took.place in Polish   society
>   'This book depicts changes which took place in Polish society.'

The Polish examples demonstrate that, while the preposed demonstrative may be used both deictically and anaphorically, the postposition of the demonstrative is allowed only in anaphoric use. Thus, even if the demonstrative cannot be said to be grammaticalizing into a definite article (yet?), its use as an anaphoric marker may be slightly different from its use as a deictic marker.

In the following section, we will investigate the direct anaphora, its markers, and the factors influencing the choice of marker, as well as at anaphoric chains, namely a number of different anaphors with the same antecedent. We will pay particular attention to the so-called Accessibility Marking Scale (Ariel 1988, 1994, 2014), which organizes the potential markers of direct anaphora on a scale, depending on the accessibility of the discourse referent.

5.3.1.1   Accessibility Marking Scale

By direct anaphora we understand a relation between two co-referring linguistic elements: an antecedent and an anaphor. While a typical antecedent is an indefinite NP and a typical anaphor is a pronoun or a definite NP, the form of the anaphor seems to be dependent first and foremost on the accessibility of the discourse referent—the more accessible the referent is, the less marking is necessary. For direct anaphors, referent accessibility, i.e., how easy it is to find a referent for an anaphor (via its antecedent), is influenced by a number of factors, such as the distance from the antecedent, the number of competitors for the role of antecedent, topicality, and reference frames (domains) relevant for the identification of the antecedent (Ariel 1988:65). The most accessible referents receive zero marking, while the least accessible ones need to be presented by means of full NPs, in Ariel's terminology *long definite descriptions*. Between these two extremes a number of possible structures are located, arranged in a hierarchy from most to least accessible in Ariel's Accessibility Marking Scale, as presented in (149).

> (149)   The Accessibility Marking Scale (Ariel 1988)
>   zero < reflexives < agreement markers < cliticized pronouns < unstressed pronouns < stressed pronouns < stressed pronouns + gesture < proximal demonstrative (+NP) < distal demonstrative (+NP) < proximal demonstrative (+NP) + modifier < distal demonstrative (+NP) + modifier < first name < last name < short definite description < long definite description < full name < full name + modifier

We may note that loss of accessibility is typically compensated for by choosing a fuller form for the anaphor, for example, a definite NP instead of a pronoun. We note further that a simple repetition of the same noun without any modifiers or determiners is not included in the marking scale. The model is thus applicable to an article language, where BNs are not allowed in direct anaphoric contexts. In a language with no grammaticalized definite article the definite descriptions need to include definite determiners other than the article; on the other hand, BNs must also be included in the scale, since it is perfectly natural to use a BN anaphorically in a language with no definite article.

(150)   *Samochód potrącił ojc-a   przechodzącego z*
        Car.NOM hit   father-ACC crossing   with
        córk-ą   na pas-ach.   Dziewczynk-ę odwiezio-no do
        daughter-INSTR on crossing-INSTR Girl-ACC   take-IMPERS to
        szpital-a.
        hospital-GEN
        'A car hit a father and a daughter who were crossing the street on a pedestrian crossing. The girl was taken to hospital.'

Historically, all article languages are derived from languages without grammaticalized articles; therefore, in a diachronic study BNs should also be considered as part of the Accessibility Marking Scale. For the sake of our study, we disregard pronominal NPs, since we wish to examine different forms of the noun in the anaphoric context. We therefore consider only the variation between BNs, NPs with a demonstrative, and definite NPs in direct anaphoric contexts. We propose a simplified accessibility marking hierarchy in the following form:

(151)   BN > NP + (adjectival) modifier > NP + demonstrative (+modifier) > short definite description > long definite description

We assume that among the referents referred to by means of a full NP, the most accessible referents will appear as BNs and the least accessible as long definite descriptions. Our accessibility marking hierarchy is based entirely on Ariel's, with BNs added and only full NPs included (i.e., those with nouns as heads and not pronouns).

We must stress that the extant texts on which our corpus is based already display a regular formal difference between the incipient definite article and the demonstrative from which it has developed (see also section 2.2.2). As early as 1200, the incipient definite article takes the form of a clitic, attached to an inflected form of the noun (and noun alone), while the demonstrative remains a free lexeme. We therefore differentiate between NPs of the type *thenne man* 'this man' and *mann-in* 'man-DEF' in the oldest texts, and even though we would not claim that the clitic is a definite article as early as 1200, we will treat NPs with -IN as definite descriptions.

5.3.1.2   Direct Anaphors in the Corpus

In the material we find that BNs do appear as direct anaphors, as in (152) where the noun *bo* 'estate' is consistently presented as a BN.

(152)   *Sitær konæ   i   bo   dör bonde   kallæ-s*
        Sits woman.NOM in estate.ACC dies husband.NOM call-REFL
        havandæ. varæ.   hon skal i   bo   sittia tyughu ukur.
        having   be.CONJ she shall in estate.ACC sit   twenty weeks
        þa   skal a   seæ æn hun ær havande. þa   skal bo
        then shall on see if she is having   then shall estate.ACC
        skiptæ
        divide
        'If a woman is in the estate and her husband dies and she is said to be pregnant she should remain in the estate for twenty weeks, then it will be seen whether she indeed is pregnant. Then, if she is found to be with child, the estate should be divided.' (SV_AVL, Period I)

The noun *bo* in example (152) is a common noun, used with a specific reference. In Modern Swedish the same noun would never appear as a BN in a direct anaphoric context.

For Period I, when the grammaticalization of the definite article has just began, we would expect to find BNs as anaphors. However, sometimes, when a BN is found in a direct anaphoric context, we find that there are some factors which may favour this NP type over others. Thus in (153), we find the BN *kóng-ur* 'king-NOM' used to refer anaphorically to King Rikardur, who has been presented earlier in the text.

(153)   *Ríkharður kóng-ur   hélt   mikla   skemmtun   á   að fara*
        Rikardur king-NOM held   great.ACC enjoyment.ACC on to travel
        á   skóg [...]. Þess   er getið eitt sinn að   kóng-ur   var á
        to forest.ACC this.GEN is said EN time that king-NOM was in
        skóg   far-inn.
        forest.ACC gone-PTCP
        'King Rikardur greatly enjoyed going to a forest [...]. This is said of one time when the king was travelling in a forest.' (IS_Vil, Period III; Piotrowska and Skrzypek 2020)

In this group of examples, we find mostly unique NPs (both more 'global' ones such as *konung* 'king', and more 'local' ones such as *höfding* 'chieftain') and kinship terms. It may be that their accessibility is strengthened by virtue of their relation to the utterance situation and therefore strong enough for no marking to be applied. We must note, however, that this use of BNs is found mainly in Period I and only occasionally later (see section 4.8).

The second group of direct anaphors consists of nouns with adjectival modifiers. These can be of two sorts: the strong form (the so-called indefinite adjective form) and the weak form (the so-called definite adjective form) (see also section 1.2). In modern North Germanic only, the weak form is allowed in definite NPs, while the strong form is combined with indefinite nouns. In the studied corpus such restrictions were not yet established, and strong adjective forms could be found in definite NPs (see especially Delsing 1994). In the material we found few instances of nouns with strong adjectival modifiers but no other determiners. The strong adjective form is found in (154) and (155); however, the latter is a clear example of an anaphoric adjective, meaning 'aforementioned'.

(154) *Tiughu aar boþo þøn saman barnløs. Ok baþo guþ giua*
twenty years lived they together childless. And prayed God give
sik **þæt barn** *hanom mate þiæna ok louaþo for* **oburit**
REFL that child him may serve and promised for unborn
barn *giua guþ-i þæt gærna tel þiænist*
child give God-DAT it gladly to service
'For twenty years they lived childless together and prayed to God to give them a child which may serve him and promised to give the unborn child gladly in God's service.' (SV_Bur, Period I)

(155) *og með umráði og samþykki kórs-brœðr-a*
and with consideration and approval cross-brother-GEN.PL
kaus hann **nú nefnd-an ábót-a** *til biskup-s*
appointed he now named-ACC abbot-ACC to bishop-GEN
'And by consideration and approval of the brothers he appointed the aforementioned abbot to bishop.' (IS_Arna, Period I)

In the entire corpus we have not found a single instance of direct anaphors consisting of just the noun and the adjectival modifier in the weak form (see also Pfaff 2019 who finds such combinations extremely rare in Old Norse). It seems that, since the anaphoric relation strongly resembles the deictic relation, it is unlikely that an adjectival modifier would suffice to make such a relation clear. The adjectives that we did find were mostly anaphoric ('aforementioned', 'said', etc.).

The next NP type is frequently used in direct anaphoric contexts. It consists of nouns with demonstratives, such as *denna* 'this here' (etymologically a compound of demonstrative *sá* 'this' and intensifying *-si*; Skrzypek 2012:64, though most likely no longer transparent in the texts quoted) and *den* 'this'. While the former often appears with noun alone (example 156), the latter is usually found with adjectival modifiers. NPs consisting of simple demonstrative and noun alone are more often found in Danish texts (see examples 156 and 157) and in Swedish texts translated from German; this structure is thus typically regarded as a result of German influence (Haskå 1972).

(156) *Hoss thæt closter   var haffu-er oc* **eth marke**   *var*
      by   this monastery.ACC was sea-NOM and EN market.NOM was
      thære hoos Huos **thet market**   *var eth huss*
      there by   By   that market.ACC was EN house.NOM
      'By this monastery, there was sea and a market was there. By this market, there was a house.' (DA_Mar, Period II)

Otherwise, the demonstrative is never used without an adjective in weak form and (in Swedish) without the clitic *-in*.

The compound *denne* is typically found with discourse referents that have been backgrounded for some time and are reinstated as topics.

(157) *Thet war en timæ* **en hellugh møø** *aff tyræ ther hob hafdæ*
      There was EN time EN holy   maid of Tyr who hope had
      til Vorherræ At   hun skulde syn   mødom   till tiæniste,
      to Our.Lord that she should her.REFL maidenhood to service
      oc til æræ hun var ey   en ælliuffue vinter gammell Hennis
      and to glory she was not yet eleven   winter old.   her
      fader var aff høgh slæct oc han var ridd-er-s   forman,
      father was of high family and he was knight-PL-GEN headman
      oc mester Hennis fader, oc hennis modær vare af enkyns folk
      and master her   father and her   mother were of kind folk
      slæct ther ethnici hetæ   oc the hafde **thennæ**
      family which heathen was.called and they had   this
      iomfruge til enugh dotter   och hun hedh   cristina
      maid   to only   daughter and she was.called cristina
      'There was one time a holy maid of Tyr who hoped to Our Lord that she should her maidenhood keep to service and glory, she was not

yet eleven winters old. Her father was of high family, he was knights' chief and master. Her father and her mother were of a heathen family and they had this maid as their only daughter, she was called Cristina.' (DA_Kerst, Period II)

Otherwise, we also find the compound *denne* when there is a risk of confusing two discourse referents. In (158) below there are two nuns described, Saint Catharine and another, who is jealous of Catherine and always trying to wrong the saint. When reintroduced in the text, the saint is presented by means of not only a demonstrative but also her full name.

(158) *Ther* **thenne heligh jomfrw sancta katherina** *saw oc*
       when this   holy   maid   saint   Catherine saw and
       fornam   thet. tha arbeydethe hwn ther om meth all øtmyghet
       understood that then worked   she on this with all humility
       och alle the thieneste oc kærlighet-z gærninghe. som   hwn
       and all the service and love-GEN deeds   which she
       kunne gøræ henne. at   hwn matthe mildgøræ hennes wredhe
       could make her   that she may   placate her   fury
       oc forbannethe affwyndh som   hwn till henne haffde
       and damned   jealousy which she to her   had.
       'When this holy maid Saint Catherine realized this [that the other nun hated her], she worked humbly to overcome her fury and jealousy by service and loving deeds.' (DA_Kat, Period III)

The marking of least accessible referents takes the form of definite descriptions. In Ariel's Accessibility Marking Scale two types of definite descriptions are included: short, with just the definite noun, and long, with some additional modifiers. We retain this distinction, but note that in our material we find that direct anaphors which are definite NPs are almost entirely of the short variety, as illustrated in Table 62.

In absolute numbers, there are more long definite descriptions used as direct anaphors in Swedish than in either Danish or Icelandic, with their highest concentration in Period II. On closer inspection, these long descriptions serve the purpose of differentiating between two discourse referents described by the same noun, e.g., *man* 'man'. The long definite description in (159) is used to avoid potential confusion of the competing referents. When there is no such risk the short definite description is used, in this case even despite the long distance between the two mentions of the same discourse referent.

TABLE 62 Short and long definite descriptions in direct anaphoric contexts

Type of description	Short definite descriptions as direct anaphors			Long definite descriptions as direct anaphors		
Period	1200–1350	1350–1450	1450–1550	1200–1350	1350–1450	1450–1550
Danish	31	83	74	0	4	0
Swedish	50	212	46	2	16	11
Icelandic	86	42	47	0	0	0

(159) *Thz war **en man** som pläghadhe hawa bistokka j sinom*
There was EN man who used.to have beehives in his.REFL
*gardh. **En annar man** kände hanum ok sagdhe wil-t   thu*
garden. EN other man knew him   and said   want-2SG you
at   thin bij   aldrigh bort-fliugha tha tak gud-z
that your bees.NOM never   away-fly   then take god-GEN
*likama ok   läg j en aff thinom bistokk-um   **Thän fawizske***
body   and place in EN of your   beehive-DAT.PL DEF stupid
***mann-in** giordhe som hanum war känt   ok gömde gud-z*
man-DEF did   as him   was known and hid   god-GEN
likama j   en-om stok
body   in EN-DAT hive
[12 *syntagms without mentioning either of the men*]
*Tha thän tim-in   kom at   **mann-in** wille sla   sina*
then this time-DEF came that man-DEF   want open his.REFL
stokk-a.   ok   taka honagh-in
hive-ACC.PL and take honey-DEF
'There was a man who used to have beehives in his garden. Another man knew him and said: If you want your bees to never fly away, then take God's body and place it in one of your beehives. The stupid man did as him was known and hid God's body in one of the hives. [...] Then the time came that the man wanted to open his hives and take the honey.' (SV_Jart, Period II)

One reviewer points out the adjective used in the long definite description may also be taken to be an epithet rather than a descriptive adjective, as it is evaluative (presents the speaker's attitude to the referent rather than describes the referent's qualities). Epithets are noun phrases that are treated as pronominal elements, i.e., the referent is so topical or salient that a pronoun could be used instead of the epithet, compare the following examples from English:

(160) *Hans* has called again. I don't want to hear anything anymore from **that idiot**.

(161) *Hans* has called again. I don't want to hear anything anymore from **him**.

In German, the strong definite article can be used. F. Schwarz gives these examples as *von dem Idioten* 'from the idiot' (without contraction of the preposition and the definite article) and gives the contracted form *vom Idioten* as incorrect (Schwarz F. 2009:31). However, the adjective 'stupid' can also be taken to be descriptive and in the example quoted above its addition clearly serves to differentiate between two referents.

Similarly, in a different Swedish text, there are two discourse referents that can only be told apart by their size, and are therefore referred to with long definite descriptions such as *den litla granen* 'the little spruce' and *den stora granen* 'the large spruce' (SV_SVM, Period II).

Based on the corpus data we may conclude that long definite descriptions are more likely to be used as direct anaphors when there are competing referents, but not necessarily due to the distance between the two mentions of the same discourse referent.

5.3.1.3   Interim Summary

The proposed Accessibility Marking Scale began with BNs for the most accessible discourse referents, and concluded with long definite descriptions for the least accessible ones.

(162) BN > NP + (adjectival) modifier > NP + demonstrative (+modifier) > short definite description > long definite description

The examples found in the corpus reveal that, while BNs are grammatical in direct anaphoric contexts in Period I in all languages (see also Chapter 4), their continued use as anaphors is only possible under 'extenuating circumstances', such as the discourse referent being not only familiar but also unique (as in example 153). Another important limitation on their use is that anaphoric BNs are restricted to neighbouring syntagms.

NPs with adjectival modifiers but without determiners were found sporadically in this context, usually with an anaphoric adjective ('aforementioned' etc.). There are also very few long definite descriptions amongst direct anaphors.

Among the factors influencing the choice of form, we find that the distance between the antecedent and the anaphor is important for the use of BNs as direct anaphors (if the distance is short, BNs are allowed) or definite descriptions and demonstratives (if the distance is more than one syntagm, either demonstratives or definite descriptions are used). The number of competing referents influences the choice between short (no competitors) and long (some competition) definite descriptions. The topicality of the discourse referent also plays a part, as we will illustrate in the next section.

5.3.1.4 Anaphoric Marking in Anaphoric Chains

We have noted that different NP types could be used in direct anaphoric contexts, the choice between them being partly determined by the age of the text (BNs were preferred in the oldest extant text, but then gradually abandoned in favour of the other NP types) and the accessibility of the discourse referent (according to the proposed scale). We have already presented examples of variation in direct anaphoric marking within one and the same text or even passage, in what are called anaphoric chains. We will now examine these more closely.

Anaphoric chains are sequences of anaphoric links between consecutive anaphors, which all share the same antecedent. It seems more accurate to speak of links rather than individual relations between the anaphors and the antecedent, mainly because the antecedent may change during a sequence of events described in the passage. Consider the following example:

(163)   Wash a bunch of *fresh spinach* well and then shred **it** finely. Sauté **it** in a little butter until **it** is wilted, drain ___ (*zero*), then put **a little** into each ramekin.
(Stirling and Huddleston 2002:1457)

We may note that with each action prescribed by the text, the referent *spinach* is different from what it was before that action took place: before it is sautéed it is shredded, after it is sautéed it wilts and so on. Therefore, we choose to consider such chains as sequences of links rather than collections of anaphors.

The fact that a variety of anaphoric markers may be applied within one anaphoric chain is not surprising—the choice of marker depends on a number of factors as discussed above, and these may differ for the same referent within one text passage. In the corpus, however, it is interesting to find that, even in texts which regularly use definite NPs in direct anaphoric contexts, BNs still occur in anaphoric chains. This fact has already been noted in a number of earlier publications (as well as in Chapter 4, section 4.6.1). In view of referent accessibility, we may conclude that there is hardly any difference between the direct anaphors in terms of distance or competing referents (see examples 132–133, section 4.6.1). Below we quote similar examples from three texts in the corpus. Seemingly, Icelandic (example 164) is most liberal in allowing BNs in direct anaphoric contexts alongside definite NPs, but we find similar variation within one passage in both Danish (example 165) and Swedish (example 166), although these are limited to Period I.

(164) *Loðhöttr hét   þræll sá,   er þar var fyrir stjórn annar-ra*
Loðhöttr was.called thrall that who was foreman   other-GEN
*þræl-a.   Þessi þræll var kvángaðr, ok   ól   kona hans **son***
thrall-GEN.PL that thrall was married   and bore wife his   son
*jafnframt því,   sem   dróttning varð léttari   Ok **þessi sveinn***
equally   this which queen   was birth.giving and this boy
var svá undarliga   fagr,   sem   þræls-kona-n   átti, at
was so wonderfully beautiful which thrall-wife-DEF had that
*dróttning þóttist ekki lýti   sjá á   **svein-i-n-um**,   ok*
queen   could no blemish see on boy-DAT-DEF-DAT and
*sýndist henni nú   **þessi sveinn** ástúðligri en   sínir   svein-ar.*
seemed her   now this boy   lovelier than her.REFL boy-PL
*Síðan ræðir dróttning til kaups um   **svein-a**   við*
then talks queen   to swap about boy-ACC.PL with
ambátt-ina.   En ambátt-inni   sýndist svá
bondswoman-DEF.ACC but bondswoman-DEF.DAT seemed so
*sem dróttning-u, at   henni þótti **sinn**   sonr tíguligri, en*
as queen-DAT   that her   liked her.REFL son better   but
þorði þó   eigi at synja   at kaupa við   dróttning-u um
dared though not to refuse to swap with queen-DAT about
*svein-a-n-a.   Ok   tekr   dróttning við **ambáttarsyn-i***
boy-ACC.PL-DEF-ACC and takes queen   by bondswomanson-DAT
*ok   lætr nafn gefa ok   kallar **svein-inn**   Leif.*
and lets name give and calls boy-DEF.ACC Leif
'Loðhöttr was called this thrall who was foreman over the other thralls. This thrall was married, and bore his wife a son at the same time as the queen gave birth. And this boy, that the thrall's wife had, was so marvellously beautiful that the queen could not see any blemish on the boy. It seemed to her now that this boy was lovelier than her own boys. Then the queen wants to swap the boys with the bondswoman. But to the bondswoman it seemed just like to the queen, that she liked her own son better, but she dared not refuse to swap the boys with the queen.

And so takes the queen the son of the bondswoman, and calls the boy Leif.' (IS_Ge, Period I)

(165) *Sak œngin skal af **byhd** stœfna num   man skilis*
suit none   shall of village sue   unless man separates
opinbarlika uiþœr kunu sinœ at   hionœ-lah   œn allœ andrœ
clearly   with wife his with marital-law and all other
sakœr stande u-sota   til   biskop kumbœr i þe   byhd [...] *um*
suits stand not-sued until bishop comes   to that village if
annœr man uarþœr sœktœpœr ok skiutœr   sik   undœn ok
other man is   accused and withdraws himself away   and
*uil   œi biskop-s   i **byhd** biþœ þa   skal han lœngre*
wants not bishop-GEN in village beg then shall he farther
um   land œftir ualkœs mœn skal huœr til loha takœ først af
about land after look.for men shall each to law take first of
***by**   sinum   i lahfasta man-na   eþ*
village their.REFL in lawful   men-GEN.PL oath
'A village shall not sue unless a man separates clearly from his wife of marital law, and all other suits are pending until a bishop comes to this village. [...] If another man is accused and withdraws himself, and does not want to beg the bishop in the village, then he shall be looked for [detained] farther away. Men shall each take to the law, first, men from the village in a lawful men's oath' (DA_SKL, Period I)

(166) *En tima þœr iohannes prœdicaþe fik han se en ungan suen*
EN time there Johannes preached got he see EN young boy
*vœnan   ok þo   vildan iohannes fik **biskop-e**   suen-en ii*
beautiful and though wild   Johannes got bishop-DAT boy-DEF in
hand [...] *Iohannes kom atar tel staþ-en   ok sporþe at*
hand   Johannes came back to town-DEF and asked about
*suen-en-om   **biscop-en**   sagþe hanom vm   suen-en som*
boy-DEF-DAT bishop-DEF said him   about boy-DEF which
*sant var Johannes gaf **biskop**   skuld for vangømo*
true was Johannes gave bishop.DAT guilt for negligence
'One time as Johannes was preaching, he saw a young boy, beautiful but wild. Johannes gave a/the bishop charge of the boy. [...] Johannes returned to the town and asked about the boy. The bishop told him the truth. Johannes blamed the bishop for negligence.' (SV_Bur, Period I; quoted after Skrzypek 2012:93–94)

In each of the three examples quoted above there is a BN anaphor in the anaphoric chain. In these passages the common denominator seems to be the topicality of the discourse referent. In the Icelandic example, first the son is put in focus, and referred to with demonstratives and definite NPs. Then the topic shifts to the queen (who, as a unique referent, is presented as a BN) and the mother, while the boy is backgrounded and appears as a BN. In the Danish example, the village is first in focus, as the place of the bishop's visit, but when it is referred to by means of a BN it is backgrounded in favour of the bishop, who is now in focus. Thus, even though the distance between the previous mention and the anaphor is significant, the discourse referent is a BN. Finally, in the Swedish example the bishop is only presented as a definite NP when it is topicalized (clause-initial subject); in other instances a BN is used.

5.3.1.5 From Deixis to Direct Anaphora—A Brief Summary

Variation in direct anaphoric marking, which is natural in all languages irrespective of whether or not they have grammaticalized articles, was also present in North Germanic texts written between 1200 and 1550. We have observed, however, that while BNs could be part of anaphoric chains in Period I, they gradually disappear in favour of definite NPs. We also find that the choice of anaphoric marking was determined by factors identified in previous research on referent accessibility, such as distance between the antecedent and the anaphor, the number of competitors for the role of antecedent, and the topicality of the discourse referent.

5.3.2 *From Direct Anaphora to Indirect Anaphora*

The first stage of definite article grammaticalization—the use of the demonstrative as an anaphoric marker—may be explained as an extension of situational deixis to textual deixis. It does not violate the original meaning of the grammaticalizing form, as its function is still to help the hearer identify a referent—a discourse referent—among other potential referents. Demonstratives can possibly be used to refer textually in any language, and the fact that they are used in this context does not necessarily mean that the grammaticalization of the demonstrative into an article is ongoing.

The second stage of definite article grammaticalization is the further extension of the original demonstrative to refer to entities newly introduced into the discourse, but connected with some entities or events mentioned earlier. This use is anaphoric and yet indirect, since the anaphor is not co-referential with any other NP in the previous text.

(167)   I bought *an interesting book* yesterday. **The author** is Nigerian.

The referent of the definite NP 'the author' must be retrieved indirectly via the previously mentioned referent 'an interesting book'. It is generally agreed that demonstratives cannot serve as indirect anaphoric markers (though see Charolles 1990, Kleiber 1990 and Apothéloz and Reichler-Béguelin 1999 for attempts to prove otherwise). De Mulder and Carlier argue that this shift in the use of the demonstrative is possible because the source of the definite article is not merely a demonstrative but a distal demonstrative and thus more vague, and it "can be understood as an invitation addressed to the hearer to mobilize previous knowledge in order to retrieve the referent" (De Mulder and Carlier 2011:530). In this way, the distal demonstrative can denote a referent that is not fully identifiable, appealing to specific knowledge shared by the speaker and the hearer (see also Himmelmann 2001:833).

We have already noted that the definite article in North Germanic is derived from a distal demonstrative, which is a marker located low on Ariel's Accessibility Marking Scale. Indirect anaphora is a case of even lower accessibility, since the referent is in fact new, though accessible through a different referent or event. However, we have also noted that, particularly in long anaphoric chains, the original discourse referent introduced at the beginning of the passage need not be (fully) identical to the discourse referent denoted by the last anaphoric expression in the chain (see example 163). Less spectacularly, subsequent mentions of the referent may furnish us with new information regarding its properties. There is a difference between direct anaphors that are (lexically) exact copies of their antecedents (example 168) and those that add new lexical information (example 169).

(168)   I came into *a room*. [...] **The room** was large.

(169)   This autumn *a new boy* started school with us. **The quiet newcomer** was the subject of gossip for a while.

While we might argue that although 'new boy' and 'newcomer' basically share the same semantic content, there is no indication of whether the new boy was quiet or rowdy or had any other qualities that are included in the anaphoric NP. We do not know that the newcomer is a male and so forth. In other words, new information may be incorporated in the co-referring definite NP, while some of the old information may be omitted. Similarly, a different term might be used to refer back to the antecedent, e.g., *a bookstore—the shop*.

In (170) we find an Icelandic example of this type, where the antecedent, *kjúklingar* 'goslings', is referred to anaphorically by means of the wider term *fugla-na* 'birds-DEF'.

(170) Síðan tók Grettir við **heim-gás-unum**. Þær voru fimm
then took Grettir by home-geese-DEF.DAT.PL there were five
tigir og með **kjúkling-ar margir**. Eigi leið langt áður honum
tens and with gosling-PL many not road far before him
þóttu þær heldur bágrækar en **kjúkling-ar** seinfærir.
seemed that rather unsteady and gosling-PL troublesome
Honum gerði mjög hermt við þessu því að hann var lítill
him made very vexed with these for that he was meagre
skapdeildar-maður Nokkuru síðar fundu föru-menn
temper-master some.time later found wayfaring-men
kjúkling-a dauða úti og heim-gæs væng-brotnar. Þetta
gosling-ACC.PL dead out and home-geese wing-broken that
var um haust-ið. Ásmundi líkaði stórilla og spurði hvort
was about autumn-DEF Asmund liked badly and asked if
Grettir hefði drepið **fugl-a-n-a**.
Grettir has killed bird-ACC.PL-DEF-ACC
'So Grettir went to mind the geese. There were fifty of them, and a number of goslings. Before long he began to find them troublesome, and the goslings would not come on quickly enough. This put him out, for he could never control his temper. Soon afterwards some wanderers found the goslings lying outside dead, and the geese with their wings broken. That was in the autumn. Asmund was very much annoyed and asked Grettir whether he had killed the birds.' (IS_Gret, Period I)

In (170) the hearer must apply their wider knowledge to successfully interpret the final definite NP in the anaphoric chain, i.e., they must know that geese and goslings are birds.

However, it is examples such as (171) below that seem to constitute the bridging context between direct and indirect anaphora. We quote the passage in full to give the reader an idea of the whole story, which we also summarize below.

(171) **Han** gik ena nat til hænne sæng ther hon soff mz
he went EN night to her bed where she slept with
barn-it Oc **myrdhe** sins brodher-s barn oc hænne
child-DEF and murdered his.REFL brother-GEN child and her
sofwande stak **han** knifw-in j hænna hand Æn hon
sleeping stuck he knife-DEF in her hand and she
waknadhe aff thy at blodh-it fløth vnder hænna sidho Hon
woke of this that blood-DEF flowed under her side she

byriadhe	*ropa*	*swa at*	*alt folk-it*		*waknadhe oc*	*komo thith*
started	scream	so that	all folk-DEF		woke	and came there
løpande oc	*funno*	*barn-it*	*dræpit oc*		*knifw-in*	*blodhoghan*
running and	found	child-DEF	killed and		knife-DEF	bloody
j	*hænna hand*	*Ther græt*	*badhe fadher*	*oc*	*modher oc*	*alle*
in	her hand	there cried	both father	and	mother and	all
the	*ther waro*	*Tha kom*	*ok*	**then ful-e**	**mordhar-in**	
they	there were	then came	also	DEF vile-WK	murderer-DEF	
løpande oc	*grep*	*the*	*ærlik-a*	*qwinn-o-n-a*		*j*
running and	seized	DEF	honest-WK	woman-ACC-DEF-ACC		in
har-it						
hair-DEF						

'One night he went to the bed, in which she slept with the child, and murdered his nephew and planted the knife in her hand. And she woke feeling blood flow under her side. She started to scream so that everybody woke and came running and found the child killed and the bloody knife in her hand. Mother, father and all that were there cried. Also the vile murderer came running and grabbed the honest woman by her hair.' (SV_ST, Period II)

In this story a young knight, brother to the emperor, fell in love with a woman who had found sanctuary at the emperor's court and was employed there to mind the emperor's child. As she spurned the knight's advances, he first tried to blacken her character, but as this did not work, he murdered the child in her care, leaving a bloodied knife beside her, so that she would be blamed for the deed. The knight is referred to as either *en unger riddare* 'a young knight', pronominally (*honom* 'him', *sin* 'his.REFL', *han* 'he') or, after he is described as the one who *myrdhe* 'murdered' his nephew, as *then fule mordharin* 'the vile murderer'. Although all NPs in this anaphoric chain are co-referential ('the young knight' is identical with 'the vile murderer', the latter being an instance of an unfaithful anaphor, see Lundquist 2007), without the intervening description of the murder we would not be able to place the last definite NP in the anaphoric chain. In other words, the final definite NP 'the vile murderer' is an indirect anaphor anchored by the verb 'murdered', while at the same time it is a direct anaphor, with a different lexical content, of the antecedent 'the young knight'. That the young knight was vile and a murderer is not just new information added by the speaker, it is actually anchored in the text and can be deduced from the text; an old referent is given a new role. We argue that this type of context is a bridging context, allowing the grammaticalizing definite to spread to indirect anaphoric contexts. In the following we will investigate the indirect anaphora, its typology, and the NPs used in this context in the corpus.

5.3.2.1   Indirect Anaphors—Typology

In 2.2.1 we presented a typology of indirect anaphors, noting that authors differ in their views on bridging reference, although, most of them distinguish between at least two major types of indirect anaphors: mereological indirect anaphors (the anchor is an established discourse referent; this includes part–whole relations and other thematic roles, e.g., *book—cover, book—author*) and frame-related indirect anaphors (the anchor is an eventuality or a frame present in the discourse model). The first major work on the subject, Clark and Haviland (1977), distinguishes between three types of indirect anaphors: meronymic relations, thematic relations and reasons/causes/consequences together with other relations between events. Schwarz's classification, based on her study of German texts (Schwarz M. 2000), largely follows this tripartite typology and includes four types: meronymy (part–whole relations), lexical/thematic type (thematic roles), scheme-based conceptual type, and inference-based conceptual type (complex inferencing). Irmer (2011) considers only meronymic and thematic types to be instances of bridging, while inference-based types are in his account excluded from the bridging types. Other notable studies of the context include Fraurud (1986), Gundel, Hedberg and Zacharski (1993), Cornish (1996, 1999), Poesio and Vieira (1998), Matsui (2000), Epstein (2002), Vieira and Poesio (2000), Poesio (2003), Löbner (2003), and an overview in Zhao (2014).

In the present study we largely follow M. Schwarz (2000) (a study based on actual language use and not constructed examples) and a simplified version of her typology in which we distinguish three major types of indirect anaphors: meronymic relations, thematic types (under which we subsume M. Schwarz's lexical/thematic type and scheme-based conceptual type) and inference-based conceptual type.

Meronymic relations are usually taken to be the canonical example of bridging in most studies. Gardent et al. (2003) demonstrate that part–whole relations indeed constitute a majority of all instances of bridging (in a study limited to cases with nominal and verbal antecedents). In 2.2.1.2 we presented a typology of meronymic types, consisting of necessary parts, probable parts and inducible parts (see examples 28–36, Chapter 2, section 2.2.1.2).

A typical feature of meronymic relations is that the antecedent is nominal. In many cases it is also natural to substitute a possessive NP for a definite NP, something which will be of consequence in our later analysis. The variation between defNP and possNP can be partly dependent on other factors, such as the animacy of the anchor. This applies especially to so-called inalienable possession, where the indirect anaphor constitutes a part of or is in close spatial relation with a whole that is a living body. We may observe that there are indeed differences between closely related article languages such as English and Swedish with respect to the marking of the indirect anaphor in this type of context (see also Lødrup 2009, 2010, 2014). While English utilizes possessive pronouns, Swedish (like other North Germanic languages) uses the definite article, as in (172).

Swedish
(172) *Jan stoppade* **hand-en** *i   ficka-n.*
       Jan put   hand-DEF in pocket-DEF
       'Jan put his hand in his pocket.'

English
(173) John put **his hand** in **his pocket**.

As regards thematic types, for Clark and Haviland (1977) and M. Schwarz (2000) this group consists of semantic roles, such as agent, object and instrument. In Clark and Haviland (1977) they are further subdivided into necessary and optional, such as the relation between *to murder—the murderer* (each murder has a murderer) and *to murder—the knife* (the instrument of a murder need not be a knife). As these examples indicate, the antecedent need no longer be nominal. Within this group we find different relations between anchor and anaphor, such as object—material (*bicycle—the steel*), object—component (*joke—the punchline*), collective—member (*deck—the card*), mass—portion (*pie—the slice*), etc. This group of indirect anaphors is less likely to be expressed by possessives.

Here we touch upon one of the puzzles which we presented in Chapter 1, i.e., the puzzle of success—why do demonstratives grammaticalize into definite articles but not any other potential candidates, such as possessive pronouns? The typology of indirect anaphora presented above, though very general, nevertheless reveals that the possessives are a viable alternative for a definite article only in a limited number of contexts, where nominal anchor is available, since it is not possible to use the possessives when the anchor is not a nominal. In order to be used in other types of indirect anaphora and, successively, in other definite contexts, the possessives would need to be bleached of the core of their meaning, i.e., the expression of possession, a link with another nominal. To our knowledge, such a process has not been observed in any language. The grammaticalization of the definite article out of a demonstrative, on the other hand, requires only the loss of proximal-distal distinctions, a process which is well-attested in a number of languages, and which seems to occur independent of the grammaticalization, as it is a natural development that such distinctions became blurred or lost with time.

Clark and Haviland distinguish a third group, which comprises types such as reasons, causes, consequences and other relations between events. M. Schwarz's third group is called inferential types, and comprises anaphors whose resolution builds on world knowledge and cannot be derived from the discourse alone. This group is not regarded as a type of bridging by Irmer (2011), who instead classifies it as a coherence device (see also Givón 1992 and 1995).

(174) Wussten Sie [...] dass *der Schrei in Hitchcocks „Psycho"* deshalb so echt wirkt, weil der Regisseur genau in dem Moment der Aufnahme eiskaltes Wasser durch **die Leitung** pumpen ließ?
'Did you know [...] that *the scream in Hitchcock's Psycho* seems so real because at the moment of filming the director allowed cold water to be pumped through **the pipe**?'
(Consten 2004:102)

To successfully interpret an anaphor of the inference-based conceptual type, some general knowledge is necessary. The interpretation of the definite NP *die Leitung* 'the pipe' relies on familiarity with the Hitchcock film and the fact that the famous scene with the scream takes place in a shower. In this context the indirect anaphor can only be expressed by a definite NP (in an article language), while demonstratives and possessives are disallowed in this context.

Traditionally, the point of departure for all classifications has been linked to definite NPs without an antecedent. Studies have aimed to explain their definiteness in the absence of an antecedent. However, in recent years, when the concept of bridging has become more established, more and more authors appreciate that bridging can occur also in the absence of definites (e.g., Asher and Lascarides 1998:107). In his discussion of totality (i.e., exhaustivity, completeness), Hawkins (1978) demonstrates that the definite can only occur in bridging when the referent is unique, e.g., *a car—the engine* but *a car—a tyre*, yet the underlying relationship between the engine and the car seems to be the same as that between a tyre and the car. It has also been demonstrated that possessives may introduce new, yet anchored referents (Willemse, Davidse and Heyvaert 2009). Those authors found that in a considerable number of cases the PM (= possessum) referents of possessive NPs are first mentions with inferential relations to the context (Willemse, Davidse and Heyvaert 2009:24), just as many definite NPs introduce new, grounded referents. It has in fact been noted that some contexts allow choice between defNP and possNP, as in example (175) (after Fraurud 2001:246).

(175) Beside the barn there is a little cottage. *The/Its roof* is leaking.
(but: *This roof is leaking)

There is, however, at least one obvious difference between bridging with definites and bridging with possessives: the definite article makes an implicit link with the other nominal, while the possessive makes an explicit link. Possessive NPs need a nominal antecedent, while definite NPs can be anchored by verbs, clauses or the text itself.

Bridging can be defined more or less broadly, depending on the types of relationships, the types of antecedents and the types of anaphors. For the present study we have chosen to adopt the following model of bridging relations:
- the anaphor can be any nominal NP: BN, defNP, indefNP, possNP or NP with a different determiner;
- the antecedent may be nominal or verbal, but the anaphor may also be resolved within the common ground (in the sense of Stalnaker 2002), thus lacking an explicit textual anchor.

We classify all indirect anaphors in the following groups:
1. meronymic relations
2. thematic types
3. inference-based conceptual types

We are also fully aware of the imperfections of the model and the crudeness of this typology. However, our goal is first and foremost to find the types of bridges that adopt the incipient definite article early, and those that adopt it later or perhaps express the bridging relation by other means. Only then will we be able to refine our classification.

Considering that there are so many subtypes of indirect anaphora, the next question to be asked is: do they all allow the incipient definite article at the same time, or do any of the types appear as definite NPs earlier? In other words, is there a greater affinity between one or more types of indirect anaphora and direct anaphora? In the remainder of this section, we will consider all three types of indirect anaphors separately, beginning with meronymic relations.

5.3.2.2   Semantic Types: Meronymic Relations

A number of examples of meronymic relations are found in the corpus. However, with limited material at our disposal, we were not able to find examples of each type of meronymic relation, which would enable a systematic study of all subtypes for all periods, and which would allow us to account for the possible differences of expression between necessary, probable and inducible parts. The examples which are best represented are those of inalienable possession, i.e., indirect anaphors referring to body-parts, items of clothing or weaponry, and anchors denoting human referents.

The types of NPs found in meronymic relations include bare nouns, possessive NPs and definite NPs, although in Period I inalienables seem to be found only as BNs (example 176) or possNPs (examples 177–178) and not as defNPs.

(176) *iak kom þa fuul sørhilika til miin kæra sun ok þahar iak*
I   came then fully sorrowful to my dear son and when I
sa hanum slaa-s   mæþ næua [...] *ok spytta-s   i **anlæt***
saw him   beat-REFL with fists   and spit-REFL in face
ok krona-s   mæþ þorna
and crown-REFL with thorns
'I came full of sorrow to my dear son and as I saw he was beaten with fists [...] and spat in the face and crowned with thorns' (DA_Mar, Period II)

(177) *Æn of swa worthær at   man mistær allæ sinæ   tændær af*
if of so becomes that man loses all his.REFL teeth of
sin   høs [...]
his.REFL head
'If so happens that a man loses all his teeth from his head [...]' (DA_VL, Period I)

(178) *at hon varþ   hauande mæþ gu-z   son ii **sino   liue***
that she became pregnant with God-GEN son in her.REFL womb
'That she became pregnant with God's son in her womb.' (SV_Bur, Period I)

In Period II inalienables no longer appear as BNs, but with either a (reflexive) possessive pronoun or the incipient definite article. It should be noted here that North Germanic languages have retained two possessive pronouns: the regular possessive *hans/hennes/dess*, corresponding to the English *his/her/its*, and the reflexive possessive, *sin/sitt*, which is used when the possessor is the subject of the clause. The default marking of inalienables in Period II seems to be the reflexive possessive, as in (179), and the incipient definite article is at first found with inalienables only in direct anaphora (i.e., such body-parts or items of clothing that are not only connected with an owner known from previous discourse, but have also been mentioned themselves).

(179) **Kwinna-n**   gik   bort   ok   faldadhe han j   **sinom**   **hwiff**
woman-DEF went away and folded   him in her.REFL scarf
som   **hon** hafdhe a   **sino**   **hofdhe**
which she had   on her.REFL head
'The woman went away and folded him in her scarf, which she had on her head'. (SV_Järt, Period II)

(180) Tha synti-s   quinn-onna   hwifwir allir blodhoghir ok
then see-REFL woman-DEF.GEN scarf   all   bloody   and
water aff blodh swa at   blodh-in   flöt   nidhir vm
wet of blood so that blood-DEF flowed down about
quinn-onna   kindir. Hulkit herra-n   saa, ropadhe ok.
woman-DEF.GEN cheeks which master-DEF saw screamed and
sagdhe hwar slo thik j   **thit**   änlite älla sarghadhe. Ok
said   who hit you in your face or hurt   and
quinnna-n   lypte vp **sina**   hand ok strök   sik   vm
woman-DEF lifted up her.REFL hand and stroked herself about
änlit-it   ok tha   hon tok   nidhir **hand-in-a**   tha war hon
face-DEF and when she took down hand-DEF-ACC then was she
al blodhogh.
all bloody
'Then the woman's scarf seemed all bloodied and wet with blood so that the blood flowed down the woman's cheeks. Which the master saw, screamed and said 'Who hit you in your face or hurt you?' And the woman lifted her hand and stroked her face and when she took the hand away it was all bloodied.' (SV_Järt, Period II)

Example (180) illustrates well the division of labour between the (reflexive) possessive and the incipient definite article. The possessive is used if the inalienable possessum is mentioned for the first time (indirect anaphora). The definite article is used only in further mentions, i.e., in direct anaphora (thus *your face—the face, her hand—the hand*). Naturally, we could simply treat such examples as direct anaphors. However, it is clear that they are both co-referential with an antecedent and accessible via their anchors. It seems that this double identity, as direct and indirect anaphors, constitutes a bridging context (in the sense of Heine 2002) for definite NPs to spread to indirect anaphora with meronyms. By the end of Period II and the beginning of Period III, the definite article begins also to be used in indirect anaphora (first mention of an inalienable possessum connected with a known discourse referent), as presented in (181) and (182).

(181) *Tha bar keysar-in   vp **hand**-en-a   oc slogh hona widh*
       then bore emperor-DEF up hand-DEF-ACC and hit her at
       ***kinben*-it**   *at hon størte til iordh-inna*
       cheekbone-DEF that she fell to earth-DEF
       'Then the emperor lifted his hand and hit her on the cheekbone so that she fell down.' (SV_ST, Period II)

(182) *Tha begynthe løffw-en som hwn war wan   gladeligh at løpe i*
       then began   lion-DEF as she was used.to gladly to run in
       closter-eth [...] *eller rørdhe **sticerth-en***
       monastery-DEF or wagged tail-DEF
       'Then the lion began, as she was accustomed to, to gladly run in the monastery [...] or wagged her tail.' (DA_Jer, Period III)

It should be noted that BNs are found in indirect anaphora even in Period III; however, as illustrated in examples (183) and (184), these occurrences may be lexicalizations rather than indirect anaphors.

(183) *Jamwnd-z   hoffuit bløde bodhe giømmen **mwn**   ok   **øren***
       Jamund-GEN head bled both through mouth and ears
       'Jamund's head bled both through mouth and ears.' (DA_KM, Period III)

(184) *badh   meth **mwndh** oc **hiœrthe***
       prayed with mouth and heart
       '[She] prayed with mouth and heart.' (DA_Kat, Period III)

5.3.2.3   Thematic Types

This type of indirect anaphora is based on our lexical knowledge of certain elements forming more or less stereotypical events or processes, and on our familiarity with stereotypical relations between objects or events and objects; for instance, a court case involves a judge, one or more hearings, a charge, a plaintiff, and so on. Thus, whenever such an event is presented in a text, the hearer will treat definite NPs such as *the judge*, *the hearings*, etc. as connected with that event.

In Period I we find mostly BNs in this type of indirect anaphora (examples 185 and 186), but, interestingly, a few instances of the incipient definite article occur as well (example 187).

(185)   Uærþær maþer *dræpin* [...] þa   skal **uighi**   a þingi lysæ
        be   man   killed   then shall murder on thing declare
        'If a man is killed [...] then the murder shall be made public on a thing'
        (SV_AVL, Period I)

(186)   Sitær konæ i bo   dör **bonde** [...]
        sits wife in house dies husband
        'If a wife is alive and the husband dies [...].' (SV_AVL, Period I)

(187)   Nu **dræpær** maþær   man   koma til arua
        now kills   man.NOM man.ACC come to heir
        man-zs-in-s   ok fa **drapar-an**   ok hugga þær niþær
        man-GEN-DEF-GEN and get killer-DEF.ACC and cut   there down
        a fötær þæs   döþ-a [...]
        on feet this.GEN dead-GEN
        'If a man kills another, the heirs of the deceased come and get the killer
        and cut him down at the feet of the deceased [...]' (SV_OgL, Period I)

This context allows definite NPs as early as Period I. In Period II the thematic types are regularly found as defNPs, in pairs such as *tjuven* 'the thief'—*stölden* 'the larceny', *wighia* 'to ordain'—*vixlenne* 'the ordination', *henger* 'hangs'—*galghan* 'the gallows', *rida* 'to ride'—*hästen* 'the horse', *fördes död* 'a dead (man) was carried'—*baren* 'the stretcher'. A characteristic of this type of indirect anaphora is that the anchor need not be nominal and the anaphor may be accessible through a VP.

Possessive NPs are seldom found in this type at all, independent of the period. We have located some examples of possNPs that may be considered indirect anaphors; it should be noted that, as in example (188), they sound natural with a reflexive possessive in Modern Swedish as well, and the choice between defNP and possNP may be a question of stylistics rather than grammatical correctness.

(188)   Diäfwl-en saa hans dirue oc reede   hanom snaru. [...] Oc
        devil-DEF saw his courage and prepared him   trap   and
        baþ   munk-in   sik   inläta i **sin**   cella.
        asked monk-DEF himself allow in his.REFL cell
        'The devil saw his courage and prepared a trap for him. [...] And he [the devil] asked the monk to let him in his [= the monk's] cell.' (SV_HML, Period II)

(189) *Ther sancta katherina thette fornam   tha luckthe hwn*
when saint   Catherine this   understood then locked she
*sik   hardeligh i **syn**   cellæ och badh jnderligh   till*
herself firmly   in her.REFL cell and prayed passionately to
gudh
God
'When saint Catherine understood this, she then locked herself firmly in her [own] cell and prayed passionately to God.' (DA_Kat, Period III)

5.3.2.4   Inference-Based Conceptual Types

This type of indirect anaphora is the least accessible. To correctly identify the referent, the hearer must not only consider textual information or stereotypical knowledge of the world, but also make inferences allowing them to resolve the anaphor. It should be noted that some authors do not consider this type anaphoric at all, e.g., Irmer (2011).

In the corpus, this type is expressed either by bare nouns or by definite NPs. No possessive NPs were found here. An interesting fact, though, is that defNPs may be found as early as Period I, as in (190).

(190) *Maþær far sær   aþalkono gætær uiþ barn dör sv fær*
man   gets himself wife   begets by child dies this gets
aþra   gætær viþ barn far hina þriðiu þör bonde þa   konæ
another gets   by child gets that third dies peasant then wife
er livændi þa   skal af takæ hemfylgh sinæ   alt þet ær
is alive   then shall of take dowry   her.REFL all that which
vnöt   ær hun ællær hænær börn   þa   skal hin ælsti
unused is she or   her   children then shall that oldest
*koldær boskipti kræfiæ   takær af þriþiung af **bo-no**.*
brood division demand take of third   of property-DEF.DAT
'A man gets himself a wife, she gets with child, then dies, he gets another, she gets with child, he gets a third wife and he dies. Then if a wife is alive, she shall take all her dowry which is not spent. If she or her children are alive, then the oldest brood shall demand division and take a third part of the estate.' (SV_AVL, Period I)

(191) *Nu j the stund-inne   for   ther framvm en prästir mz*
now in this hour-DEF.DAT travelled there forward en priest with
*gud-z   likama til en siuk-an   man ok **klokka-n** ringde for*
god-GEN body   to en sick-ACC man and bell-DEF rang   for

gud-z   likama.
God-GEN body
'At this hour a priest was travelling to a sick man, carrying the wafer and the bell rang to announce him.' (SV_Järt, Period II)

We have not found a single example of indirect anaphora that could be classified as a conceptual inference-based type being expressed by a possessive NP. In this type of anaphora defNPs occur early—they are found, though only sporadically, at the beginning of Period I, while, for instance, the meronymic type is not expressed by defNPs until the end of Period II. To begin with, however, BNs are prevalent. Gradually, they are replaced by definite NPs, without going through the possessive NP phase as the meronymic types seem to have done. This type of indirect anaphora may be considered to be reserved for the definite article, since no other element, possessive or demonstrative, can appear here.

5.3.2.5   Summary

Once the incipient definite article begins to occur in indirect anaphoric contexts, it is initially found with a group of contexts which is here referred to as thematic types. This observation ties in well with the type of direct anaphors which we identified as the bridging context between direct and indirect anaphora (example 171). These anaphors are direct in the sense that they have a formal antecedent in previous text, but also indirect in that they identify the discourse referent in a thematic role connected with some event mentioned earlier in the text.

The inferential types are infrequent, but from what we can observe, this context is also relatively early in allowing the incipient definite article. The type of indirect anaphora which lingers longest is the meronymic relation, i.e., the part–whole relation. Depending on the animacy of the possessor, they appear as possessive NPs (with animate possessors) or BNs (with inanimate entities). Eventually, the entire context adopts the incipient definite article.

5.3.3   *From Indirect Anaphora to Larger Situation Use*

The larger situation use of the definite article is based not on the familiarity, but the uniqueness of the discourse referent. There is nothing in the preceding discourse which may be identified as an anchor for the definite NP, thus making this definite article use different from indirect anaphora. To identify the referent, the hearer/reader needs to rely on their general knowledge.[1]

---

1 Section 5.3.3 is based on Piotrowska and Skrzypek (2020).

The unique referents that we have found in our corpus come from different domains. The major ones, with most frequently used referents, are nature (*sun, earth, air, nature, stars*, etc.), religion (*God, church, Bible, devil, heaven, hell, faith*, etc.), and law and rule (*law, king, mayor, emperor*, etc.). The majority of these belong to Hawkins' (1978, 1991) category of larger situation use, which relies on general (and not specific) knowledge. They may also be considered to be 'global' uniques, unvarying for all people and with their uniqueness being absolute (Lyons C. 1999:8).

The only unique reference NP that has survived as a bare noun until modern times in all North Germanic languages is *gud* 'God' (used solely with reference to the Christian God, other divine beings may be referred to as *gud-ar-na* 'god-PL-DEF'). Others have gradually adopted the definite article. We can, however, identify certain patterns.

First of all, in the domain 'religion' some referents are definite as early as in Period I; we find forms such as *kerki-an* 'church-NOM.DEF' or *kirki-unna* 'church-ACC.DEF' in Swedish, and *døth-æn-s* 'death-DEF-GEN' in Danish. In Period II we find a number of parallel forms, e.g., *himmell-en* 'heaven-DEF' vs. *himmel* 'heaven' in Danish. As late as in Period III, a number of unique referents from this domain can still occasionally be found as BNs, e.g., *and* 'spirit' and *skriffth* 'script' in both Danish and Swedish, but it should be noted that they most often appear in definite NPs with an adjectival modifier and a definite preposed article, as in example (192).

(192)   tror   tw   fadher tha   tror   tw   sønn-æn ok **then hælg-e
        believe you father then believe you son-DEF and DEF   holy-WK
        and**
        spirit
        'If you believe in father, then you also believe in the son and the holy spirit.' (Da_KM, Period III)

In the domain 'nature' some referents lag behind in adopting the definite article (for instance, bare nouns such as *sol* 'sun' in Swedish or *iord* 'earth' in Danish are frequent in Period II).

(193)   *Jach hauer i   thennæ vkæ   offræt   sannende offer til then gudh*
         I   have   in   this   week   offered   true   offer to this god
        *ther bodæ   skapeth **himmel** oc   **iordh** oc stiærnæ-r och haf oc*
        that   both   created heaven   and   earth   and star-PL   and sea and
        alt thet ther   fødh ær i   iørde-rige
        all   that which born is in earth-kingdom

'I have this week made true sacrifice to the god who created both heaven and earth and stars and the sea and all that is born on the earth.' (DA_Kerst, Period II)

Other referents, such as *wærld-æn* 'world-DEF', *wæruld-enna* 'world-DEF.GEN', i.e., 'the world', are definite already in the oldest Danish and Swedish texts from Period I. There are also a number of referents in this domain which adopt the definite article relatively early (Period II), and which may be considered either uniques or indirect anaphors, such as *skog* 'forest', *öken* 'wilderness, desert', *hav* 'sea'. Examples of such referents are found in (194) and (195).

(194) *Tha meth syne brødh-re-s raadh fick han løffw-en thet*
then with his.REFL brother-PL-GEN advice got he lion-DEF that
æmbeth at hwn skulle een asen som hænthe them weth
task that she should EN donkey which brought them wood
aff skoffw-en følghe till marck-en ther han thog syn
of forest-DEF follow to pasture-DEF where he took his.REFL
fødhe oc thaghe hannum till waræ
food and take him to care
'Then, by the advice of his brothers, he gave the lioness the task to guard the donkey which brought them wood from the forest and follow him to the pasture where he grazed.' (DA_Jer, Period III)

(195) *I rom var en keysare. han hafdhe ena dygdheliga oc*
in Rome was EN emperor he had EN virtuous and
gudhliga keysarinne. hon thiænte jomfru marie af allo hiærta.
godly empress she served virgin Mary of all heart
*keysar-en vilde fara ofvir **mær-it** til the hælgh-e graff.*
emperor-DEF wanted travel over sea-DEF to DEF holy-WK tomb
'There was an emperor in Rome who had a virtuous and pious wife who served Virgin Mary with all her heart. The emperor wanted to travel to the Holy Tomb over the sea.' (DA_ST, Period II)

The reason for treating them as potential indirect anaphors is that they usually appear in connection with some location (such as a city in which the narrative is taking place), and they could be understood as anchored by that location, with the definite article roughly corresponding to 'in the vicinity of the city'. On the other hand, it is not impossible to consider that at least some of them, such as the sea, may have been considered absolute uniques (like the sun). At the time when the texts were written, users of the language may not have been aware of there being more than one sea in the universe. What separated them from other uniques is also their affinity with the so-called 'definites of path' (see e.g., Roberts 2003), such as 'the elevator' in 'take the elevator', when there is more than one to choose from, and yet the NP is definite.

Finally, for the domain 'rule and law', we studied a context in which the difference between more local and more global unique referents and their formal representations may be studied diachronically. The context is co-ordinated NPs of the type 'to the king, the bishop and the district', which are regularly found in legal prose, stipulating to whom taxes or fines were to be paid. Since the payments were typically divided three ways, such co-ordinated NPs bring together a number of referents which are 'differently' unique. Furthermore, these NPs have a highly formulaic character and can therefore be expected to retain the original, article-less forms longer. The aim of this study was therefore to establish whether the definite article could be said to appear earlier with some types of referents than with other types. We assumed that the more 'local' uniques, such as *herad* 'district', *socken* 'parish' or *prest* 'priest', would be definite earlier than the more 'global' ones, such as *kung* 'king' or *biscop* 'bishop', considering that the former rely on familiarity as well as uniqueness.

This assumption was only partly borne out. True enough, in the oldest extant texts, the unique referents tend to be unmarked and appear as BNs, irrespective of the scope of their uniqueness, as in (196).

(196)   *Uerdher kyrkia brut-in   oc mæssu fat   stol-en* [...] *þat er*
       is   church break-PTCP and Mass   plate steal-PTCP this is
       *niv   march-a sak **kyrky**   swa **hærepe** sva **konogge**.*
       nine mark-PL fine church so   district so   king
       'If a church is broken into and the Mass plate stolen [...]. It is nine marks fine, to church, and so to district and so to king.' (SV_AVL, Period I)

The 'global' unique *kong* 'king' remains bare in the legal texts *Äldre Västgötalagen, Yngre Västgötalagen* and *Upplandslagen* (1225, 1280 and 1380 respectively), it is sporadically definite in *Östgötalagen* and *Dalalagen* (both ca. 1280), and the proportions do not differ for other legal texts. Overall, out of all instances of the lexeme 'king' in the legal texts studied here, 92.2% are bare NPs, while the remaining 8.8% are definite NPs. The first text in which a definite NP 'the king' is to be found in about 30% of the instances of that lexeme is *Kristoffers Landslag* (1440), and this is the highest score.

On the other hand, the more 'local' unique *höfding* 'chieftain' is also predominantly used as a bare noun throughout the legal prose, as in (197), even though instances of its use as a definite NP can be found as early as 1280 (*Yngre Västgötalagen*), as presented in example (198).

(197) vil han eig þa ræt göræ þa nempni **hæræz-höfþingi**
wants he not then right do then calls district-chieftain
ting
thing
'If he won't do what the law says, then the district chieftain calls a thing [assembly].' (SV_YVL, Period I)

(198) *kan man hittæ skiælikæn ældæræ kalli til sinæ grannæ*
can man find true vagabond calls to his.REFL neighbour.PL
*oc taki han oc före til **hæræz-höþingi-æn-s** æller*
and take he and lead to district-chieftain-DEF-GEN or
þes i hans staþ er satt-er.
this.GEN in his place is sit-PTCP
'If a man finds a true vagabond, he calls to his neighbours and they take the vagabond to the district chieftain or the one who acts in his stead.' (SV_YVL, Period I)

There is also a significant difference in the frequencies of both nouns. While *kung* 'king' appears in each legal text between ten and seventy times, *höfding* 'chieftain' appears sporadically in only four out of eighteen texts. This might partly explain why *kung* 'king' remains a bare noun for such a long time. However, all in all, it has to be concluded that the legal texts exhibit no clear pattern in the marking of these unique referents. It is only those referents that could well be considered cases of indirect anaphora that appear as definite NPs earlier, while other referents retain bare forms as late as the mid-15th century, as presented in example (199).

(199) *waren tha arfua-ne saklöse baade for **malsegende-n-om**,*
are then heir-DEF.PL innocent both for plaintiff-DEF-DAT
***konung-e** oc **hærade-n-o** [...]*
king-DAT and district-DEF-DAT
'If the heirs are then innocent both according to the plaintiff and king and the district [...]' (SV_Kris, Period II)

An interesting exception is the absolute unique *påven* 'the Pope', which appears as a definite NP already in one of the oldest extant legal texts (1225), as in (200).

(200) *All-um slik-um mal-um skal af land-i   skiptæ mæþ*
       all-DAT such-DAT case-DAT shall of country-DAT change with
       *brev-i   til **pavæ-n-s**   i rom þer skulu af*
       letter-DAT to pope-DEF-GEN in Rome there shall of
       ***pava-n-um**   bref till takæ*
       pope-DEF-DAT letter to take
       'All such cases of the country shall be changed with a letter to the Pope in Rome, there should a letter be taken from the Pope.' (SV_AVL, Period I)

For a statistical analysis of the larger situation use of the definite article in North Germanic the reader is directed to Piotrowska and Skrzypek (2020).

In conclusion, even though referents connected to the domain of nature are the least frequent among all unique referents in the corpus, they exhibit the largest proportion of definite forms. If we exclude the continuously bare referent *gud* 'God' from the results, it is the domain of law and rule that remains unmarked (bare) the longest, while the domain of nature is the first to demonstrate mostly definite referents. Based on these findings we may therefore state that within the larger situation uses, the more local unique referents (i.e., those based on specific knowledge), which could have been interpreted as indirect anaphors and thus textually anchored, seem to have served as a bridge from textual to non-textual definiteness in the grammaticalization of the definite article. The culmination of the grammaticalization is the use of the definite article with globally unique referents, a usage that is at odds with the original meaning of the demonstrative delimiting the referent from other potential referents.

5.3.4 Summary—A Review of the Grammaticalization Chain of the Definite Article

The data from the North Germanic corpus demonstrate how the successive stages of the grammaticalization chain of the definite article were reached. The original demonstrative was first used to mark direct anaphoric referents, especially those that were topical or reintroduced in the discourse. We find that the spread from direct to indirect anaphora was possible on the basis of contexts which could be read as either type, i.e., there was an antecedent for the anaphor, but the anaphor included new lexical information about the discourse referent. That information identified the referent as a thematic role for some event described earlier in the text.

The use of the incipient definite article in indirect anaphoric contexts marks the turning point in the development of the definite; from that point onwards, the demonstrative and the definite need to be studied separately. While the first stage of the grammaticalization process involved a shift from situational to textual deixis, this stage involves a shift from textual information to information that the speaker believes the hearer to possess and be able to activate in order to identify the referent of the definite NP, although the hearer is still guided by the text.

In Chapter 2, we mention Old French data and Carlier and Simonenko's hypothesis on the evolution of the definite article from expressing strong to weak definite semantics. In the French material the authors found that a critical context for the spread from direct to indirect anaphora may be the use of the incipient definite article followed by a restrictive relative clause. In our material, we have identified too few such instances to reinforce this insight; we would like to note, however, that there are no such uses in Period I. A handful of examples were found in Period II in Danish and in Swedish (and none in Icelandic). One Swedish and Danish example is actually identical, as it comes from two translations of the same text; see examples (201) and (202).

(201) *tak the **yrte-na** som stondir vndir thit hovith*
 take DEF herb-DEF that stands under your head
 'Take the herb that is under your head.' (DA_ST, Period II)

(202) *Tak the **yrte-na** som vnder thit hofwdh staar*
 take DEF herb-DEF which under your head stands
 'Take the herb that is under your head.' (SV_ST, Period II)

Two more Swedish examples were quoted above as (140) and (141).

Although we find examples discussed in Carlier and Simonenko, their frequency is low and their appearance later than the regular use of the definite article in indirect anaphoric contexts, which does not preclude that they did play a role in the evolution of definite article use from direct to indirect anaphora.

The final stage of the development discussed above involves a further shift away from the text and towards the general knowledge the hearer possesses and shares with the speaker. The data presented in the preceding section suggest that such a shift was again possible in contexts with potential double interpretation: on the one hand, as indirect anaphors (e.g., a town is discussed in the preceding discourse, the definite form of mayor may be taken to mean the mayor of that town), and on the other hand, as unique, text-independent reference ('locally' there is only one mayor, and no mention of the town is necessary for the identification of that referent).

We have not discussed the use of definite NPs in generic contexts. Such use marks the final stages of definite (and coincidentally, also indefinite) article grammaticalization. In other words, the articles must be well grammaticalized in other functions to be used generically. In the corpus, we find occasional examples of definite articles in generic contexts, as in (203). However, it is far more common to find BNs used generically as late as in Period III in all languages studied, as in (204) and (205).

(203) mærk pa en harpæ ther ær træth strenge ok hand-en ære
note on EN harp there is wood strings and hand-DEF are
iij tingh ok eth lydh so ær ok mandell nøt then først ær
three thing and one sound so is also almond nut then first is
skal-en ok swa fnas-et ok so kærn-in theære iij tingh
shell-DEF and so skin-DEF and so seed-DEF there three thing
ok eth
and one
'Note that as there are wood, strings and handle on a harp but one sound, and in an almond first there is the shell, then the skin, and then the seed, there are three things and one [entity].' (DA_KM, Period III)

(204) Wen jac haffwer atwakteliga hört tyn ordh, oc the gaffw-or
when I have carefully heard your words and DEF gift-PL
thyn konwng haffwer oss sänth epter **frome herr-a-s** sedh
your king has us sent after mighty lord-PL-GEN custom
'When I have carefully listened to your words and the gifts that your king has sent us in accordance with the customs of mighty lords.' (SV_Troj, Period III)

(205) Roland sade **madkæ fyskæ fwglæ by** worde ok leffue aff
Roland said worms fish birds bees be and live off
søl-æn ok ander tingh wdhen mand-z samlende
sun-DEF and other thing without man-GEN union
'Roland said worms, fish, birds, bees live off the sun and other things without people coming together' (DA_KM, Period III)

We will touch upon generic reference in the final section of this chapter, but for a more in-depth account of genericity in North Germanic the reader is directed to Skrzypek and Kurek (2018) and Skrzypek, Kurek-Przybilski and Piotrowska (2020).

5.4 Grammaticalization of the Indefinite Article

We noted in Chapter 1 (section 1.1; see also section 2.3) that the model of indefinite article grammaticalization has been tested against data from a number of languages and has been shown to predict correctly the development of the article from the numeral 'one' (see also Brandtler and Delsing 2010, Skrzypek 2012 and 2013 for an account of the development in Swedish). With respect to the indefinite article, there is one major difference amongst the North Germanic languages, namely that the indefinite article has not evolved in Icelandic, although it is present in all other North Germanic languages, including Faroese, an insular language which has retained a number of archaic traits and is typologically similar to Icelandic.

In this section we will therefore briefly present the data from Danish and Swedish, which illustrate the development of the indefinite article in these languages. We will also consider the Icelandic data to determine whether grammaticalization of the indefinite article was initiated in that language, or whether there were no such tendencies in the studied time-frame.

5.4.1 The Presentative Marker

The first article-like function of the numeral 'one' is that of a presentative marker, i.e., a signal to the hearer that the introduced discourse referent will be salient, and will be referred to at least once more in the remaining text. It should be noted that it is not always easy to classify a given use of the numeral 'one' unequivocally as numeral or presentative. We chose to treat all instances of 'one' which were not contrasted with a different numeral or quantifier as presentative. In (206) and (208), 'one' is contrasted with 'all' or 'both' and is thus treated as a numeral.

(206) *En þau váru öll í svefni í* **skemmu einni**, *Þorbjörn ok*
and they were all in sleep in bedroom EN Thorbjörn and
syn-ir hans ok Þórdís
son-PL his and Thordis
'And they were all asleep in one bedroom, Thorbjörn and his sons and Thordis.' (IS_Gis, Period III)

(207) *Og er þau komu á Eyri settust þau niður á* **einn stól**
and as they came to Eyri seat.REFL they down on EN chair
fyrir Þorgeiri og Urðarköttur milli þeirra
for Thorgeir and Urðarköttur between them
'And as they came to Eyri, they were seated on one chair with Thorgeir and Urðarköttur [Stone-cat] between them.' (IS_Finn, Period II)

(208)   ællær at   the   brænnæ **bathæ** i   **et hus.**
        or   that they burn   both   in EN house
        'or that they burn both in one house.' (DA_VL, Period I)

The presentative use is therefore not so much about the numeral value, but rather about the topicality of the new discourse referent. The incipient indefinite article is typically found at the beginning of a tale, introducing its main hero or heroine, as in (209).

(209)   Thet   war **en** timæ en hellugh møø aff tyræ ther hob hafdæ
        There was EN time EN holy   maid of Tyr who hope had
        til Vorherræ [...]
        to Our.Lord
        'There was one time a holy maid of Tyr who hoped to Our Lord [...].'
        (DA_Kerst, Period II)

However, we notice a change in the placement of the presentative NP. In the oldest extant texts (1200–1350), they were placed clause-initially, as in examples (210–212).

(210)   **En riddar** rik ok væl burin gaf-s   i   clostar
        EN knight rich and well born gave-REFL in monastery
        'A rich and well-born knight was given in a monastery.' (SV_Bur, Period I)

(211)   **En diäkne** war j   enom stadh som   heet   montepessolanus
        EN deacon was in EN   city   which was.called Montepessolanus
        'There was a deacon in a city called Montepessolanus.' (SV_Järt, Period II)

(212)   **Kona   ein** fór of morgun snemma að kanna fjöru því að
        woman EN went of morning early   to search shore for that
        búandi   hennar var eigi heima.
        husband her   was not home
        'There was a woman who went out early one morning in search of her husband who was not at home.' (IS_Jart, Period I)

In Modern Swedish and Danish clause-initial indefinite NPs are avoided, unless they are adverbials of time or place, such as *en dag*, which translates naturally as 'one day' rather than 'a day'. If the subject is indefinite, usually some other element is placed clause-initially, e.g., an adverbial, or a presentative construction is used, as in (213).

(213) a. *?En katt satt i trappa-n.*
 INDF cat sat on stairs-DEF
 'A cat sat on the stairs.'

 b. *I trappa-n satt en katt.*
 on stairs-DEF sat INDF cat
 'On the stairs sat a cat.'

 c. *Det satt en katt i trappa-n.*
 there sat INDF cat on stairs-DEF
 'There sat a cat on the stairs.'

Interestingly enough, clause-initial indefinite NPs are found in Swedish in both Period I and II, but gradually disappear in favour of other presentative constructions, as in examples (214–216).

(214) *War **en** iuþe ioachim at namne i nazareth*
 was EN Jew Joachim to name in Nazareth
 'There was a Jew whose name was Joachim in Nazareth.' (SV_Bur, Period I)

(215) *Thät war **en** riddare som het troillus*
 there was EN knight who was.called Troillus
 'There was a knight who was called Troillus.' (SV_Järt, Period II)

(216) *I them daghomen war **en hälogher biskopp**-er i en stadh*
 in those days was EN holy bishop-NOM in EN city
 som heth traiectum
 that was.called Traiectum
 'In those days there was a holy bishop in a city that was called Traiectum.' (SV_Linc, Period III)

We found no clause-initial presentative indefinite NPs in Danish, not even in Period I, as examples (217) and (218) illustrate.

(217) *Thet var en timæ **en værliz** man oc han haffde **en dotter***
there was EN time EN worldly man and he had EN daughter
'There was one time a worldly man and he had a daughter.' (DA_Mar, Period II)

(218) *Saa wor ther **een presth** han heet abrathar*
so was there EN priest he was.called Abrathar
'So was there a priest he was called Abrathar.' (DA_Jesu, Period III)

In Icelandic the presentative use of EN is limited to Periods I and II, as shown in examples (219) and (220).

(219) *Við þann stein-boga er **kastali einn**, er heitir Briktan*
by this stone-arch is castle EN which is.called Briktan
'By this stonearch, there is a castle which is called Briktan.' (IS_Did, Period I)

(220) *Grímur hét **einn bóndi**, mikils hátt-ar og vel járeigandi.*
Grim was.called EN yeoman great kind-GEN and well sheep.owner
'Grim was called a yeoman, he was of great kind and a good sheep owner.' (IS_Jart, Period I)

(221) *Var í þessu liði **ein blóð-sjúk kona**, sú er hann segir eftir orðum Ambrósíus-ar Mörtu verið hafa*
was in this group EN blood-sick woman this which he says after words Ambrosius-GEN Marta be have
'There was in this group a blood-sick woman, which, according to Ambrosius' words, was Marta.' (IS_Marta, Period II)

We find the numeral 'one' used presentatively in all languages studied, but in Icelandic the examples are limited to Periods I and II, as in examples (219–221). Otherwise, it is common to present new referents by BNs, as in (222) below.

(222) *Maðr hét Ölvir inn hvíti.*
Man was.called Ölvir DEF white
'A man was called Ölvir the white.' (IS_To, Period I)

While it is not impossible that 'one' continued to be used as a presentative marker in Icelandic (the lack of examples in our corpus does not rule it out), it does not seem to have become a marker that is used with new, salient discourse referents; rather, it remained optional and never proceeded to the next stage of grammaticalization.

The Swedish data reveal that 'one' was first used as a presentative marker under specific circumstances, i.e., clause-initially and with subjects (see also Skrzypek 2013). As early as in Period II the clause-initial position was no longer the only option, and presentative NPs appear later in sentences as well as in first position. The Danish data do not exhibit a similar phase in the development, since there are no presentative indefinite NPs placed clause-initially in the corpus. In the material, we have only found examples of presentative constructions similar to the modern ones.

5.4.2 *The Specificity Marker*

After grammaticalizing as the presentative marker, the incipient indefinite article may be used to introduce any new referent into the discourse, irrespective of its salience or topicality. We find occasional instances of such use of the original numeral 'one' as early as in Period I (examples 223–224), but it is in Period II that new discourse referents are first generally presented as indefinite NPs in Danish and Swedish (examples 225–230).

(223)   *Innæn en stath i thæt land tha hørthæ en ærlik conæ*
        within EN town in this land there belonged EN honest woman
        en strætæ til oc wæl hus-æt.
        EN street to and well house-DEF
        'In a town in this land, there a street belonged to an honest woman and also the house.' (DA_ML, Period I, the only example of specificity in Period I in Danish)

(224)   *oc kombir j mesopotamia landh j **ena borgh** som   aatte*
        and comes in Mesopotamia land in EN   castle which owned
        nakor abraham-s   brodhir
        some Abraham-GEN brother
        'And comes to Mesopotamia land to a castle which one of Abraham's brothers owned.' (SV_Pent, Period I, the only example of specificity in Period I in Swedish)

(225)   *Tha lod vrbanus hennis fadær muræ vp **eth torn***
        then let Urbanus her   father build up EN tower
        'Then let Urbanus her father build up a tower.' (DA_Kerst, Period II)

(226) *Hoss thæt closter   var haffuer oc   **eth market** var thære hoos*
by   this monastery was sea   and EN market was there by
thre milæ fran closter
three miles from monastery
'By this monastery, there was a sea and a market was there three miles from the monastery.' (DA_Mar, Period II)

(227) *Nu j   the samu stund-inne tha   gingo twe brödhir   aff thy*
now in DEF same hour-DEF then went two brothers of DEF
*sama klostr-ino   j   **en-om   skoogh** som   la-def näär thy*
same monastery-DEF in EN-DAT forest which lay   near DEF
klostr-eno.
monastery-DEF
'Now at the same time, went two brothers from the same monastery in a forest which lay near this monastery.' (SV_Järt, Period II)

(228) *Ok gik   ginstan bort til **en biscop** ok   skriptadhe sik*
and went instantly away to EN bishop and confessed himself
mz   storom angir
with great remorse
'And went instantly away to a bishop and confessed with great remorse.' (SV_Järt, Period II)

(229) *Tha satto the   hona vth aff skip-it   oppa **eet litit   skær***
then sat they her   out of ship-DEF upon EN small islet
som   laa mit   j hafw-it
which lay middle in sea-DEF
'Then they forced her out of the ship upon a small islet which lay in the middle of the sea.' (SV_ST, Period II)

(230) *Ok aff henna root wäxte op **en litin   gran**   aff hwilke*
and of her   root grew up EN small spruce of which
borghare-n gladdis
citizen-DEF gladdened
'And out of the root grew up a small spruce of which the citizen was very glad.' (SV_SVM, Period II)

In Period III, in both Danish and Swedish, all new discourse referents (which are not anchored in the preceding discourse or unique) are introduced by means of indefinite NPs, as in (231) and (232).

(231) oc   thedhe henne **eth bliith anleth** meth ale the thegn som
       and showed her   EN mild face   with all DEF signs which
       hwn kunne gøre
       she could do
       'And showed her a mild face with all the signs which she could make.'
       (DA_Kat, Period III)

(232) han hauer **en godan skiold** then will jak haffua
       he has   EN good shield this want I   have
       'He has a good shield that I want to have.' (SV_Did, Period III)

While it is not always easy to tell the presentative and specific uses of the incipient indefinite article apart, we may note that the presentative NPs are overwhelmingly animate, singular, and masculine subjects. Those NPs have the same semantic make-up as the first NPs to appear with the definite article. Here we find a parallel between the two developments. The specific use, on the other hand, is not limited in the same way, and here we also find NPs that are inanimate, plural, neuter and so forth. The discourse referents that are introduced in this way form background for the main agents in the text.

So far, we have discussed the Danish and Swedish data alone. The Icelandic data differ significantly. As we have indicated in Chapter 4 (section 4.2, Table 23), the frequency of the numeral 'one' remains stable throughout the three periods studied, in contrast to Danish and Swedish, where we observed a noticeable rise in frequency, which often accompanies grammaticalization of an item. In the usage of the numeral 'one' in Icelandic, we find occasional examples which could be classified as specific, i.e., introducing a new discourse referent which is neither salient nor topical. Some such examples are presented in (233–234) below.

(233) *Er önnur löng leið ok dálig, en önnur miklu skemmri ok*
       is other long road and bad and other much shorter and
       *betri. En á   þessi inni skemmri er **annmarki nokkurr** svá. Þat*
       better and on this DEF shorter is obstacle some   so that
       *er á   **ein**, er eigi má yfir koma-st   nema at **einum***
       is river EN which not may over come-DEP but   by EN
       *stein-boga. Við þann stein-boga er **kastali einn**, er   heitir*
       stone-arch by that stone-arch is castle   EN   which is.called
       Briktan. Þann kastala halda tólf   skotmenn
       Briktan that castle   holds twelve shooters

'There is one long and bad road, and another much shorter and better. And on the shorter one there are some obstacles. There is one river, which may not be traversed, but for a place by one stone arch. By this stone arch, there is one castle which is called Briktan. This castle holds twelve shooters.' (IS_Did, Period I)

Note that both the stone arch and the castle are presented as indefinite and are picked up later in the text; therefore, the use of *en* 'one' could be taken to be presentative (the subsequent mentions are topicalized). The numeral could be pre- or postposed, seemingly with no difference in meaning (compare example 148 section 5.3.1 on direct anaphora in Polish). The NP *á ein* 'river one' introduces a new discourse referent which is not mentioned again, and the numeral could be construed as an example of a specificity marker. Similarly, in example (234) from Period II, the new discourse referent does not appear in subsequent mentions.

(234)   *Kolur sagði þá:*   *Sá*   *eg*   *þá*   *bræður, Helga og Gunnar, í*
        Kolur said   then   saw   I   them brothers Helgi and Gunnar in
        hell-i   **ein-um** *norður með á-nni.*
        cave-DAT EN-DAT north   with   river-DEF.DAT
        'Kolur said then: I saw these brothers, Helgi and Gunnar, in a cave north downstream.' (IS_Gun, Period II)

However, these two examples are the only ones found in the entire Icelandic corpus where the numeral 'one' is seemingly used as a specificity marker. No other examples of such uses were found in the material chosen for this study.

5.4.3   The Non-specificity Marker

The use of EN with non-specific discourse referents is occasionally found in Period II, but it is first in Period III that we find more examples. The typical contexts include similes (comparisons, e.g., *as bright as a sun*), conditionals, negations, etc. Examples of the incipient indefinite article used in these contexts are quoted in (235–239).

(235)   *Hwar meghet meræ bær menneske at arbeydhe for hwer*
        how   much   more   must man   to work   for each
        andhre-s siele-s salighet at swadanth **eth wæænth**
        other-GEN soul-GEN holiness that such   EN beautiful
        creaturæ *skall ey forkaste-s*
        creature shall not reject-REFL

'How much more must people work for each other's soul's holiness so that such a beautiful creature should not be rejected.' (DA_Kat, Period III)

(236) *færekude swaret hwore motthæ* **en** *jomffrv barn føde*
Farekunde answered how could EN virgin child bear
'Farekunde answered: How could a virgin bear a child?' (DA_KM, Period III)

(237) *ok diäfwl-en vppinbaradhi-s j* **enna quinn-o** *liknilse ok*
and devil-DEF revealed-REFL in EN woman-GEN likeness and
synti-s hanum idhkelika j tholiko liknilse
showed-REFL him incessant in such likeness
'And the devil revealed himself in one woman's form and showed himself to him incessantly in such form.' (SV_Järt, Period II)

(238) *Tha gör iak som* **en folsker man** *än frankis land skal tappa*
then do I as EN false man if French land shall lose
sit loff fore mina skuld
its.REFL praise for my sake
'Then I act like a false man if France shall lose its praise for my sake.' (SV_KM, Period II)

(239) *hans nampn war willebrordus, han aktadhe at visitera* **eth**
his name was Willebrordus he intended to visit EN
iomffrw closter, *huilket han siälffwer fordhom haffdhe bygth*
maiden monastery which he himself before had built
oc stiktat
and established
'His name was Willebrordus, he intended to visit a female monastery, which he himself had built and established.' (SV_Linc, Period III)

In the Icelandic data we found no examples of the use of EN in which it could be classified as a non-specific marker.

5.4.4 Summary

The model of the indefinite article grammaticalization is well-confirmed by the Danish and Swedish data. The interesting fact, however, is that the topicality of the new referent is also marked by other means, not only the incipient indefinite article, but also by the subject role and position in the sentence. Further, it is interesting to note that, despite their close relationship, Icelandic exhibits a different development than Danish and Swedish. There are isolated uses of the numeral EN in Icelandic which could be treated as presentative, but no further developments can be discerned. Indeed, it seems that some development towards an indefinite article first occurs later in the history of Icelandic history (Kliś 2019), but it never quite takes off.

As with the definite article, we have found occasional instances of indefinite NPs used with generic reference; see examples (240) and (241). They all come from Period III and mark the final stage of indefinite article grammaticalization.

(240) *Jtem kære fadher haffde i seeth eller kunne see **een**
therefore dear father had you seen or could see EN
mænneske-s sieell the thwiffler mik enckthet ther paa*
man-GEN soul that doubt me nothing there on
'Therefore, dear father, had you seen or could see a man's soul, you would not doubt me on that.' (DA_Kat, Period III)

(241) *Enghen thingh er j wærdh-en ther kan ighne-s with **een**
no thing is in world-DEF which can liken-REFL with EN
sieel-s delighet*
soul-GEN beauty
'Nothing in this world can be compared with the beauty of a soul.' (DA_Kat, Period III)

They all come from Period III and mark the final stage of indefinite article grammaticalization. This indicates that the grammaticalization of the indefinite article has by that time progressed to the final stage, however, generics may also appear as BNs at that time.

5.5 Grammaticalization of Definiteness—A Larger Chain

At the beginning of our study, we pointed out a number of puzzles that remain unsolved in research on the diachrony of (in)definiteness. Apart from the puzzles concerning the stages of development of each article, we also find that the interplay between the two developments is far from clear.

Typological data suggest that if a language has grammaticalized the indefinite article, it is likely to have grammaticalized the definite as well. The reverse does not seem to hold, i.e., we find article languages with only the definite article, where the morphological zero is used in indefinite contexts. Diachronically, there is ample evidence that the grammaticalization of the definite article precedes the grammaticalization of the indefinite. It would thus seem that the two developments are interconnected in such a way that, when the definite article grammaticalizes, the indefinite may, but need not, grammaticalize as well.

As we have demonstrated above, the origins of both grammaticalizations lie in textual use: the demonstrative as a direct anaphoric marker, and the numeral 'one' as a presentative marker. While direct anaphora typically points backwards, instructing the hearer to seek an antecedent in the preceding discourse, the presentative marker's function is to arrest the attention of the hearer and direct it towards a new but salient or topical discourse referent. In this sense the presentative marker may be said to be cataphoric, as it directs the hearer forward in the text.

It should be noted that, as the incipient definite article progresses on the grammaticalization scale to mark all known discourse referents and not just topical ones, so does the incipient indefinite article come to mark all new discourse referents. In this sense the two grammaticalizations go hand in hand, and their joint result is a system of marking of specific, textually-anchored discourse referents which are accessible to the hearer through the discourse alone. Nevertheless, as the Icelandic case indicates, at this stage the grammaticalization of the indefinite article is an option, but not a necessity. We therefore have a number of languages which have grammaticalized the definite article only.

Once we leave the textual ground and come to other uses of the definite article, in larger situation use, there is no obvious parallel between the development of the definite article and that of the indefinite. However, both grammaticalizations conclude with the same article usage, i.e., in generic reference. Genericity, as the final stage of grammaticalization of each article, seems to neutralize the definite–indefinite distinction.

At this point we must note that, despite the similarities in their developments with respect to article grammaticalization, modern North Germanic languages exhibit surprising discrepancies in article use with generic referents. Even though all NP types can be used generically (BNs, defNPs in singular and plural, plural NPs and, in the Continental languages, indefNPs), each language has its own preferences. In Norwegian (*bokmål*) the default form of generic NP is BN, while Danish exhibits a strong preference for singular defNPs, with Swedish results giving a multifaceted picture, though with a preference for defNPs as well (Skrzypek, Kurek-Przybilski and Piotrowska 2020).

This suggests that even though the grammaticalization models present some universal tendencies, they do not exclude language-specific developments, which may result in idiosyncratic distribution of the articles. For instance, the definite articles in some Romance languages acquire at an early stage, from the 12th century onwards, a generic interpretation in contexts where this is still impossible for English, German, and Dutch (e.g., English (*The) *Whales are mammals* vs. French *Les baleines sont des mammifères*; De Mulder and Carlier 2011:534).

If both articles evolve in a language, the definite seems to always predate the indefinite (which may not grammaticalize at all, as in Icelandic), although the two developments may overlap to some extent. In Danish and Swedish the grammaticalization of the definite article is not complete before the grammaticalization of the indefinite is initiated (see also Skrzypek 2012). As a result, the development of the definite article is at least partly conditioned by the development of the indefinite. In the absence of the indefinite article, the definite is also more likely to evolve into a specific article (Greenberg 1991, De Mulder and Carlier 2011:525), though as the Icelandic example indicates, again this is not a necessity.

Finally, both grammaticalizations involve a gradual reduction in the scope of the use of BNs. In a language with no articles—most Slavic languages, for example—BNs are the default NP forms, irrespective of intended definite or indefinite meaning. In a language with just the definite but no indefinite article, e.g., Icelandic, BNs are used where Danish, Swedish and Norwegian would use the indefinite article. However, as noted in Borthen (2003) and Asudeh and Mikkelsen (2000), the use of BNs in Mainland Scandinavian languages exceeds the use of BNs in other Germanic languages, such as English or German. BNs seem to have undergone a secondary grammaticalization (see also Berezowski 2009, Rosén and Borthen 2017, Kinn 2019), in contrast to the definite and indefinite articles, whereby the articles can be omitted to create a non-morphic, non-specific effect.

5.6   *Excursus*: The Incipient Indefinite Article in Icelandic beyond 1500

The data retrieved from our corpus includes examples of the presentative use of the numeral 'one' in Icelandic and some instances of its use as a specific marker, but the development as documented here does not seem to go beyond the first stage of grammaticalization. As we have noted, the two grammaticalizations, of the definite and of the indefinite article, are interdependent—or more correctly, the grammaticalization of the indefinite article follows that of the definite, initially mirroring it in terms of the factors affecting the selection of the grammaticalizing item. We have also concluded that while the Continental languages Danish and Swedish have developed the indefinite article, the

Insular language Icelandic has not. The question remains open as to whether the rise of the indefinite article is in any way aligned with that of the definite; in other words, whether there is in fact a 'window of opportunity', a timeframe in which the grammaticalization of the indefinite is possible while the definite is still at the early stages of grammaticalization, or whether the indefinite article can develop at any moment in the history of a language. We have the benefit of hindsight knowing that Modern Icelandic does not possess an indefinite article; however, it would be interesting to extend our search for possible grammaticalization further than the present study allows, to establish whether there were in fact any developments toward indefinite article grammaticalization.

A claim to this effect has been made in the literature before, in particular by Leijström (1934). Previous research has also revealed an increased frequency of *einn* 'one' in Old Icelandic (1200–1400). The increase reported is from 0.77 instances per 1000 words in the 13th century to 1.27 in the 15th century (Rögnvaldsson et al. 2012, Table 2). However, from the 16th to the 19th century the frequency is decidedly lower (Rögnvaldsson et al. 2012, Table 3). Although a rise in the frequency of an item is not in itself a diagnostic of the grammaticalization of that item, it often accompanies changes in its use, which may be part of the grammaticalization process. Therefore, this rise does not seem irrelevant. Our corpus, which spans the years 1200–1500, reveals similar results: very similar values in Period I (1200–1350) and Period III (1450–1550), but double those values in Period II (1350–1450) (see Chapter 4.2). As we have found in our analysis, the most likely reason for this increase is the use of *einn* as a presentative marker. Rögnvaldsson et al. (2012) do not analyse the uses of *einn*, so we have no way of comparing our data with theirs. It has been noted in the literature that the function of *einn* was not merely cardinal (*ein, ikkje to* 'one, not two'), but also deictic: *ein eller annan, ein viss* 'one or another, a certain' (Haugen 2006:268). This demonstrates the form's potential to develop into an indefinite article. However, it was not obligatory in the latter types of contexts.

Interestingly enough, there is hardly any account of *einn* in Icelandic from a diachronic perspective. It seems that, based on its use in Old Icelandic and the lack of an indefinite article in Modern Icelandic, the history of *einn* has not come under the spotlight of historical linguistics. The only major work that touches upon the subject is the now somewhat dated 1934 monograph by Gunnar Leijström *Om obestämda artikeln: ett bidrag till nordisk språkhistoria* 'On the indefinite article: a contribution to Nordic language history', to which we will return shortly. It is noted in the literature that *einn* may have the indefinite meaning if it is postposed, for example *einn maður* means 'one man' (cardinal meaning), while *maður einn* means 'some man', corresponding to the indefinite pronouns *einhverr* 'some, someone' and *nokkur* 'some', for which it may be exchanged; compare with Swedish *någon* 'some' (Bandle 1956:330; see also Nivre 2002).

However, Leijström notes that during the Reformation, from ca. 1520, there is evidence of the use of *einn* in the written standard in article-like functions. He attributes this to Danish and German influence (Leijström 1934:71). The article-like use is found mainly in religious prose, and Leijström quotes relevant passages from the New Testament:

(242) þu   ert einn Iude enn eg em ein samuersk kona
       you are EN   Jew   and I   am EN   Samaritan woman
       'You are a Jew and I am a Samaritan woman.' (John 4.9, Helgason 1929:116)

This use of (preposed) *einn* persisted until the early 1800s (Bandle et al. 2002: 1268), but beyond that period the preposed *einn* becomes less frequent in the written standard. The reason for this seems to lie in the strong purist tendencies of the mid-1800s, whose explicit goal was to make the language free of any foreign influence, as proclaimed in among others *Fjölnir*, an annually published journal (1835–1844) with ambitions to revive Icelandic national consciousness and gain support for Icelandic independence (Leijström 1934:71). Part of the process was a preference for the word order noun + *einn*, present in Icelandic in the first extant texts with the meaning 'some x', which would create an antipole for the Danish order *en* + noun (Kristjánsson 2009:199).

It is important to observe that the only evidence of the article-like use of the numeral *einn* in Icelandic comes from written texts representing high literary style. It does seem as though this use was indeed a copy of the Danish and German pattern rather than a spontaneous innovation. Leijström not only rejects the idea that such use could be an archaism from Old Icelandic times, but also draws a line between the Old Icelandic uses of *einn* as indefinite pronoun and the modern Continental languages' use of the indefinite article, at the same time attributing the rise of indefinite article in Danish and Swedish to language contact with Low German, a contact which the Icelandic community, due to its isolated geographical position, escaped (Leijström 1934:171). Leijström notes also that the endemic use of *einn* as indefinite pronoun is most clearly visible in the Sagas of Icelanders (*Íslendinga sögur*), as this genre is quite free of foreign linguistic influence, as opposed to contemporary (*samtíðarsögur*) or chivalric sagas (*riddarasögur*), which may have been written with Continental literature as their model (Leijström 1934:85).

There are no other major works in which Icelandic *einn* is considered as a potential indefinite article. Some scattered information is to be found in studies of Old Norse and Icelandic syntax. Similarly to Leijström, also Westergård-Nielsen (1946) dismisses the possibility of the indefinite use of *einn*, and finds that such use in the 17th century was a result of Danish and German influence (Westergård-Nielsen 1946:58), while Hanssen et al. state [*u*]*bestemt artikkel i moderne mening har det eldre norrøne mål ikke* 'the indefinite article in the modern meaning is not found in Old Norse' (Hanssen et al. 1975:136). As an argument against the indefinite article interpretation, it is noted that the form is not obligatory, and that there is apparently free variation between BN and *einn* with nouns; for example, *maðr er nefndr Emundr* 'a man is called Emundr' is compared with a number of examples with *einn* (Iversen 1972:125). This view is also found in Falk and Torp (1900). On the other hand, Nygaard admits that some occurrences of *einn* are better described as an indefinite article (in its early stages). It is also Nygaard who describes the preposition of *einn* with a new, article-like meaning (Nygaard 1905).

Interestingly, it is in more recent literature that the indefinite article interpretation is found more acceptable. Bandle considers *einn* to be the indefinite article in Old Icelandic (Bandle 1956:330), Einar Haugen emphasizes the form's potential to grammaticalize into the indefinite article (Haugen 2006:268), and Haugen states that the indefinite article was on the verge of grammaticalization in the 14th century, but did not come into wide use and was gradually abandoned, the only texts with significant occurrence of *einn* being those translated from Middle Low German (Haugen 1976:299).

In summary, it may be said that opinions on the status of *einn* have evolved hand in hand with theoretical developments that allow a more dynamic interpretation of language. The fact that it is known today that the potential development towards an indefinite article did not go any further, and that there is now no indefinite article in Icelandic, does not rule out the possibility that its grammaticalization was underway at some point.

One attempt to verify this hypothesis is found in a 2015 BA thesis by Phil Beier. The author chose four Sagas of Icelanders, as these are expected to be free of foreign influence and thus include the original, endemic use of *einn* (Beier 2015:21; see also Kristjánsson 2009:218 and Leijström 1934:85). The texts have a largely narrative character and document historical events. The sagas chosen for the study were *Egils saga Skalla-Grímssonar* (13th century), *Finnboga saga ramma* and *Flóamanna saga* (14th century) and *Fljótsdæla saga* (15th century). The second of these is also part of our corpus, and the timeframe of the study is identical to ours.

Beier's quantitative results reveal that preposed *einn* is on the rise in the 14th century compared with the 13th century material, but its frequency is lower again in the 15th century.

TABLE 63   *Einn* in four Sagas of Icelanders, after Beier (2015)

Text	*einn* in preposition	*einn* in postposition	Total
Egils saga, 13th century	47	34	81
Finnboga saga, 14th century	37	10	47
Flóamanna saga, 14th century	28	14	42
Fljótsdæla saga, 15th century	32	27	59
Total	144	85	229

Although not directly reported in relation to the overall length of each text, the results nevertheless indicate that the frequency of *einn* rises in the 14th century in the selected corpus. Beier (2015) states that none of the uses of *einn* in either text can be shown to be indefinite article use; he notes, however, that some examples from *Fljótsdæla saga* could possibly be considered quasi-article uses.

(243) *Eg sá **járn-súlu** eina standa upp í hell-i-n-um undir*
I saw iron-column EN stand up in cave-DAT-DEF-DAT under
*ræfur en við þessa súlu var bundin **ein kona**.*
roof which by this column was bound EN woman
'I saw an iron column in the middle of the cave which bore the cave's roof and to which a woman was tied.' (Fljótsdæla saga, Beier 2015:32)

(244) *Þeir sáu út frá Mýnesi hvar **einn stakkgarður** stóð fram*
They saw out from Mýnes where EN fence stood fore
í vatn-ið Lagarfljót.
in water-DEF Lagarfljót
'Outwards Mýnes they saw a fence protruding into the waters of Lagarfljót.' (Fljótsdæla saga, Beier 2015:32)

Both the position of *einn* and its individualizing meaning in *ein kona* 'a woman' and *einn stakkgarður* 'a fence' suggest that this is a potential case of an incipient indefinite article (see also Falk and Torp 1900:61).

As we mentioned before, apart from Leijström's monograph, which deals with the indefinite article in all Scandinavian languages and not only Icelandic, there is hardly any research into the history of *einn* in Icelandic. The present study concludes with texts from the 16th century, and although it confirms the form's potential to undergo grammaticalization, it does not indicate that such grammaticalization in fact took place. In our study, which is based on material from three languages, we would like to pay more attention to the differences between the languages which may result in different article systems. We shall therefore make a closer inspection of the Icelandic *einn*.[2]

To investigate the hypothesis that the numeral 'one' may have progressed further in its grammaticalization into an indefinite article, we have prepared a complementary corpus of Icelandic texts, which is an excerpt from The Icelandic Parsed Historical Corpus (IcePaHC; Wallenberg et al. 2011). IcePaHC includes a number of Icelandic texts, representing a variety of genres, written between 1100 and 2000. The corpus is still being updated; for the purpose of the present study, we used the version 0.9 from 2011.

The texts chosen for this supplementary study represent different periods and genres. A short description of each is given below.

1. *Fyrsta málfræðiritgerðin* (FM), 'The First Grammatical Treatise', is a study of Icelandic phonology; it was most likely composed in the 12th century and is among the first written texts in Icelandic. It is found in *Codex Wormianus*, which includes three other texts, with FM being the first; this is the reason for its being named First Grammatical Treatise. It represents academic prose.
2. *Miðaldaævintýri* (M), 'Medieval Adventure', written ca. 1475, is a translation from English. It is a collection of morality tales and represents religious prose (Viðarsson 2007:12–13).
3. *Okur: Hvörinn það er fyrirboðið og bannað í guðsorði* (Okur). 'Usury. Whether it is forbidden and banned in gospel'. This text was written 1611 by Guðmundur Einarsson. It considers religious matters, but does not have a narrative character like the morality tales in M.
4. *Reisubók Jóns Ólafssonar Indíafara* (RJOI), 'Travel book by Jón Ólafsson India-traveller'. Jón Ólafsson was a famous Icelandic traveller, mainly known for his voyage to the Danish settlement of Tranquebar (Tharangambadi) in India. The text is an autobiography written in 1660, documenting Ólafsson's life and travels, with the final part written by his son. The text is available from a number of sources, and has also been published in Danish and English (Neijmann 2006:219–220).
5. *Nikulás Klím* (NK) is a satirical novel by the Norwegian–Danish author Ludvig Holberg, originally published in Latin in 1741, which gave it a world-

---

[2] This section is partly based on an unpublished MA thesis by Karolina Kliś, written in 2017–2019 in connection with the current project.

TABLE 64   *Einn* in the supplementary Icelandic corpus (Kliś 2019:57)

Texts	Frequency per 1000 words	Cardinal	Potential cardinal	Temporal adverbial	Presentative marker	Specificity marker	Non-specificity marker	Total
FM (1150)	11.8	18	3	–	5	–	–	26
M (1475)	8.9	2	8	17	91	–	29	147
Okur (1611)	5.9	2	6	4	8	–	34	54
RJOI (1661)	9.0	4	10	38	51	–	65	168
N (1745)	7.5	4	13	19	27	–	95	158
Total	–	30	40	78	182	–	223	553

wide audience. The Icelandic version was published in 1745 in a translation from German (Viðarsson 2007:10–11).

The supplementary corpus consists of both original Icelandic texts and translations from other languages, where some influence in the choice of *einn* as an equivalent of the indefinite article could be expected, both M and NK being translated from article languages with developed indefinite articles. We have included FM, even though it is dated to the period already studied in our main corpus, so as to have a viable collection of similar texts representing all periods in this supplementary study of Icelandic. Translations were included as the most likely place for foreign-influenced indefinite article-like uses of *einn* to appear.

Each text was excerpted in its entirety using the KWIC concordance creator, and the results were then sorted manually. Taking Heine's (1997) model of the grammaticalization of the indefinite article (see Chapter 2) and the earlier observations on the distribution of *einn* (among others its propensity to appear with temporal adverbials), the excerpted instances of *einn* were sorted into the following categories: cardinal, potential cardinal, temporal adverbial, presentative marker, specific marker, non-specific marker. The numeral–potential numeral dichotomy served to sort the obvious cardinal uses of *einn*, typically when a contrasting cardinal could be found in the context, from those that included no such contrast but were nonetheless possibly cardinal and not presentative. An overview of the results is given in Table 64.

Firstly, we note that even though the frequencies per 1000 words are not markedly different for each text, there are substantial differences with respect to each type of use. The highest frequency is found in FM, the oldest text in the sample. The instances of *einn* in this text comprise mainly conspicuous cardinal uses and a few instances of the presentative marker. These results largely confirm the findings of the present study and the main corpus.

Secondly, the younger texts exhibit lower frequencies of *einn* than FM, but the occurrences of *einn* there belong to entirely different categories: there are a number of examples of presentative use and, surprisingly, relatively many examples of use as a non-specific marker. In fact, this latter use turns out to be the most frequent in the supplementary corpus, quite contrary to the intuitions expressed in earlier treatments of *einn*. The original cardinal use of *einn* is equally represented in each of the younger texts, ranging between 10 and 17 instances (cardinals and potential cardinals taken together). The temporal adverbials are also relatively frequently used with *einn*, as the results in Table 64 indicate; there are also many instances of the presentative use of *einn*, with the highest number in M (from 1475). Gradually, the non-specific use takes over as the dominant use of *einn* in Okur, RJOI and NK. As regards the the two translations, M and NK, the latter stands out in terms of the non-specific use of *einn*. However, there is also a considerable time gap between the two, making M an example of quite advanced development for its time.

5.6.1   Cardinal Uses

As we have discussed the cardinal usage of *einn* in detail based on the main corpus, we will only quote a handful of relevant examples here from the supplementary corpus.

(245)   og   gjöri   ég   **einn staf**   af   báðum
       and   make   I   EN   letter   of   two
       'And I spell two letters as one.' (IS_FM, 1150)

(246)   og   lætur   þau   liggja   saman   í   **einni sæng**,   svo   lengi   að
       and   let   them   lie   together   in   EN   bed   so   long   that
       hans   systir   varð   með   barn
       his   sister   was   with   child
       'And they let them lie together in one bed until his sister was with child.' (IS_M, 1475)

(247)   að   hjálpa   þeim   þurfuga   um   **eina mjöltunnu**   fyrir   3   vættir
       to   help   the   needy   by   EN   flour.barrel   for   three   parts
       fiska   í   einkaupi
       fish   in   retail
       'To help the poor by selling one barrel of flour for the equivalent of several pounds fish in retail.' (IS_Okur, 1611)

(248) *að vega sjálfur í metum púðr-ið   í **einni skál-inni** en*
       to weigh self   in measure powder-DEF in EN   bowl-DEF but
       lóð-ið   í annarri
       solder-DEF in other
       'To weigh by yourself the measure of the powder in one bowl but the solder in another.' (IS_RJOI, 1661)

(249) *að **allir** innbúar   þessa pláneta tala **ein-u   tungumál-i***
       that all   inhabitants this planet speak EN-DAT tongue-DAT
       'That all who inhabit this planet shall speak one language.' (IS_NK, 1745)

Note that in example (248) the numeral *einn* is joined with the definite form of the noun *skál* 'bowl'. Similar co-occurrences of the numeral 'one' with the definite forms have also been noted in Old Swedish.

(250) *Falder klocka rummi nither i houoth manni böte sokn   fore*
       falls bell   room down in head man   pay parish for
       *III   marker **arfua-nom enom** æn han dör aff*
       three marks heir-DAT   EN if he dies of
       'If a church bell falls down on a man's head, the parish shall pay three marks to the heir if the man dies of it.' (YVL, Period I; quoted after Skrzypek 2012:190)

This type of construction in Icelandic, including other indefinites (*suman mjoð-inn* 'some honey-DEF', *hvern fugl-inn* 'each bird-DEF'), is discussed in Perridon (1989:197), as well as in Sigurðsson (2006) and Pfaff (2017). This construction is part of a larger pattern of partitive constructions, in which a definite noun is combined with a quantifier. Sigurðsson calls these Full Concord Constructions (Sigurðsson 2006) and Pfaff calls them Little Partitives (Pfaff 2017).

5.6.2 *Potential Cardinal Use*

The contexts in which *einn* is used as a potential cardinal differ from straightforward cardinal uses, as in these contexts it is not always obvious whether 'one' is indeed the intended reading. Such contexts usually have the property that *einn* is not contrasted with any quantifiers. As an example of such use, we quote a passage from NK, the most recent text in the supplementary corpus.

(251) *að þeir væru hinir vitugustu og sanngjörnustu dómarar, þeir*
       that they were the wisest   and fairest   judges   their

eð   hverki   gengist fyrir gjöfum   né   hótunum að víkja   **eina**
oath neither goes   for presents nor threats   to depart   EN
fingurs-breidd frá   *sannleik-n-um*
finger-breadth from truth-DEF-DAT
'That they were the wisest and fairest judges, their oath would not be broken for presents nor threats and they would not depart from the truth by one millimetre.' (IS_NK, 1745)

The context is ambiguous, it is possible that EN here is a cardinal but an indefinite article is equally possible.

5.6.3   *Temporal Adverbials and Presentative Marker*

The third category includes the use of *einn* in temporal adverbials. Such use has already been noted in previous work; Leijström states that it was quite frequent in Old Norse (Leijström 1934:39). It is not surprising that this use is absent from FM, it being an academic rather than a narrative text. Below follows a selection of examples from the remaining four texts in the supplementary corpus.

(252)   *Á* ***einum tíma*** *var einn ríkur maður.*
        on EN   time was EN rich man
        'Once upon a time there was a rich man.' (IS_M, 1475)

(253)   *Gleði þeirra ómildu og óguðlegu varir um* ***eitt augna-blik***
        joy their unkind and ungodly lasts on   EN eye-blink
        'Their unkind and ungodly joy lasts only for a blink of an eye.' (IS_Okur, 1611)

(254)   ***Einn tíma*** *bar svo við 1617 um   sumar-ið,   á   ein-um*
        EN   time was so by 1617 about summer-DEF on EN-DAT
        torg-deg-i   sem   var laugardag, að einn maður [...]
        market-day-DAT which was Saturday that EN man.NOM
        'One time, in the summer of 1617, it so happened on a market day that was Saturday, that one man [...]' (IS_RJOI, 1661)

(255)   *sem   þeir* ***einu sinni*** *heyra*
        which they EN   time   hear
        'which they one time hear' (IS_NK, 1745)

The use of *einn* with temporal adverbials is widespread throughout all of the texts in the supplementary corpus.

(256) *Svo segist af íkorn-a-n-um   að   hann rennur eftir **ein-um***
so   says of squirrel-DAT-DEF-DAT that he   runs   after EN-DAT
***mann-i.** Maður-inn flýði fast   undan fyrir hræðsl-u sakir*
man-DAT   man-DEF   fled quickly away for fear-OBL sake
'It is told of the squirrel that he hunted one man. The man fled quickly for the sake of fear.' (IS_M, 1475)

(257) *Það skrifa-st   um   **einn náttúru-stein** sem   Chalazias er*
it   write-REFL about EN   nature-stone   which chalazias is
nefndur að   hann sé   harð-ur   sem demant
called that he   be.SUBJ hard-NOM as diamond
'It is said about a natural (magical) stone called chalazias (named by Pliny, most likely a type of quartz) that it is as hard as diamond.' (IS_Okur, 1611)

(258) *Þar   kom   **einn maður**,   Andrés Sandvík að nafn-i* [...]
there came EN   man.NOM, Andrés Sandvík to name-DAT
'There came a man called Andrés Sandvík [...]' (IS_RJOI, 1661)

(259) *Í   þess-um stað var   **eitt akademíum eður gymnasium**. Þar*
in this-DAT town was   EN   academy   or   gymnasium there
voru kenndar frí-kúnstir með bestu siðsemi.
were known free-arts   with best propriety
'In this town, there was an academy or a gymnasium. Free arts with highest propriety were famous there.' (IS_NK, 1745)

There is, however, no reason to suppose that the use of EN here is a diagnostic of progressing indefinite article grammaticalization. Nor does the abundant presentative use seem to be such a diagnostic, as it is also found throughout the texts studied. Some examples of the presentative marker follow below. Note that no such examples were found in FM.

5.6.4 Marker of Specificity

The marker of specific reference cannot be easily distinguished from the presentative marker, as both introduce new discourse referents. The only difference seems to lie in the discourse referent's topicality or lack thereof. Discourse referents introduced by the presentative marker are salient and likely to be anaphorically referred to later in the text, while those introduced by the specificity marker may be backgrounded and need not receive any subsequent mentions. By this definition, if the discourse referent is mentioned in subsequent text, the marker used to introduce it (if any) may be classified as presentative; if not, it is classed as specific. This distinction is extremely crude; taking the presence of subsequent mentions as the only feature distinguishing the two uses, we located only two examples of the specific use of *einn* in the supplementary corpus.

(260) *Í ein-um stað er   Lundún heitir   í Englandi bar   svo*
      in EN-DAT town which London is.named in England carried so
      til að einn rík-ur   maður   og annar órík-ur
      to that EN rich-NOM man.NOM and other unrich-NOM
      kærðust   við   um   eitt lítið land
      quarrelled with about EN small land
      'In a town called London which lies in England it so happened that a rich and a poor man quarrelled over a small piece of land.' (IS_M, 1475)

Neither discourse referent is referred to in the remaining text, based on this we could argue the use of EN to be as marker of specificity rather than a presentative one.

5.6.5   Marker of Non-specificity
As we have discussed in Chapter 2, the spread of the numeral 'one' to non-specific contexts is a turning point in the grammaticalization of the indefinite article, since the numeral cannot usually be used in such a context. What we refer to as a 'non-specific context' includes in fact a number of different contexts. Similarly to indirect anaphora, with such heterogeneity we expect some of the contexts to admit the incipient indefinite article sooner than others.

One such context is similes. It has been noted previously that *einn* can be found in similes relatively often (Leijström 1934; see also Skafte Jensen 2016 for similar results in Danish), and this observation is borne out by the data from the supplementary corpus. While no such examples could be found in FM, the other texts include a number of relevant instances.

(261) *Hann kallaði til sín einn fjanda, hver   eð   vera skyldi svo sem*
      he   called to self EN devil   which oath be   guilty so   as
      hans meistari, hafandi á   sínu höfði eina kórónu, og eitt tré í
      his master   having on his head EN   crown and EN   tree in
      hendi-n-ni, og sitja á stól-i   sem einn kóngur.
      hand-DEF-DAT and sit on chair-DAT as EN   king
      'He summoned a devil who owed him an oath as to his master, who had a crown on his head, a tree in his hand and sat on a chair as a king.' (IS_M, 1475)

(262) *Því   þar   evangelium predika-st,   þar   er mesta uggleysi*
therefore where Evangelia   preach-REFL there is most fearless
hjá þeim sem hlýða eiga, ein-s   og í Nóa tíð   og
by them who obey must EN-GEN and in Noah time and
Loth-s, og allmörgum af þeim er svo þvers   um
Lot-GEN and some   of them are so oppose about
*geð   kristilega að lýsa,   sem **ein-um soltn-um***
temperament Christian to proclaim as   EN-DAT hungry-DAT
hund-i   að fasta.
dog-DAT to fast
'Thus, where the gospel is preached, there is the least fear in those who obey and in the time of Noah and Lot, and some of them are as much against claiming the Christian temperament as a hungry dog is opposed to fasting.' (IS_Okur, 1611)

(263) *hversu þær gæti   gjört   mig sem líkastan **einni eik***
how   they could made me as like   EN   oak
'How they could make me like an oak.' (IS_NK, 1745)

(264) *þá   sýndist þú öll-um oss sem **ein ónýt***
then seemed you all-DAT us as   EN unnecessary
jarðar-byrð-i
earth-burden-DAT
'Then you seemed to all of us as an unnecessary earthly burden.' (IS_NK, 1745)

Admittedly, the use of *einn* in this particular context is perhaps in itself no diagnostic of indefinite article grammaticalization either, as we occasionally find indefinite pronouns here. In this sense, one could argue that the use of *einn* in the examples above is no more than that of the indefinite pronoun. A counterargument is found in the position of *einn*, namely its preposition, which, according to Nygaard, is a hallmark of the beginning of grammaticalization in this article-like use of the numeral. However, we must note that similes constitute the majority of examples classified as non-specific here.

Unequivocally, the use of *einn* in negative polarity contexts, for example in the scope of negation, must be considered non-specific. A handful of such examples were retrieved from the supplementary corpus.

(265) *þó   þeir geti   ei lagt af við sig nema   **eina***
though they could not laid off by self but.NEG EN

túbaks-pípu   sér   til heilsubótar.
tobacco-pipe self.DAT to healing
'Though they could not quit but one pipe for the sake of health.'
(IS_Okur, 1611)

As with the specific uses, there are too few instances of EN used in non-specific contexts to make any claims about the grammaticalization process. They could be isolated instances, dismissed as errors or the result of foreign language influence.

5.6.6   Other Types of Non-specific Contexts

There are a number of other non-specific contexts, such as constructions with conditionals and verbs of volition, or reported speech where the distance from the reported dialogue is marked by the subjunctive mood.

(266)   *og þess   vegna   út-send-u   eina kvinnu er   þeirra*
        and this.GEN reason out-send-PL EN woman which their
        lín-klæði   hafði að vakta, og báð-u   hana trúlega   einn
        linen-clothes had to watch   and asked-PL her presumably EN
        örugga-n   og fróma-n   man-n   að útvega
        trustworthy-ACC and pious-ACC man-ACC to choose
        'And for this reason, they sent a woman who had watched their linens, and asked her to choose a trustworthy and pious man.' (IS_RJOI, 1661)

Example (266) is an opaque context, i.e., it could be interpreted as either specific (there was a certain pious and trustworthy man to be chosen) or non-specific (any such man would be eligible). The context suggests a non-specific reading.

(267)   *því þeir meina, að   ein respublica eður landsstjórn kunni*
        for they mean   that EN republic   or   government   could
        ómögulega að standast, þar sem   hver og einn má
        impossibly to stand   there which each and one may
        umbreyta lög-u-n-um   og aftaka þau, eftir eigin
        change   law-DAT.PL-DEF-DAT and refuse them after own
        velþóknan
        gratification
        'For they mean that a republic or a government could not possibly exist where everybody could change the laws or refuse to adhere to them for their own gratification.' (IS_NK, 1745)

In example (267) a cardinal reading is possible, if we assume that the intended meaning was that a single lone republic would not survive if men were allowed to change the laws according to their whims; but it seems a far-fetched one, since it would imply a contrast between such a system and a hypothetical one with more than one republic or government, which could better weather such adverse circumstances. The most neutral and natural reading is non-specific, especially considering the presence of the negated adverb *ómögulega* 'impossibly'. A further curiosity is the presence of *einn* before *respublica* 'republic' (a loan word) and its absence before *landstjórn* 'government'. This may reflect the influence of the original German text from which the Icelandic version was translated, with a single use of the indefinite article to render the whole NP indefinite.

Specific
(268) Ég   minnist   hér   um   leið **graf-skrift-ar**   **einn-ar** yfir
       I   remembered   here about way   grave-script-GEN   EN-GEN   over
       bond-a   **nokkur-n**, sem   þeir í Keba gjörðu yfir hann,
       yeoman-OBL   some-DAT   which   they in Keba made   over him
       og   svo   hljóðar [...]
       and   which   proclaimed
       'Here I was reminded of an inscription on a grave of some yeoman, which they made for him in Kebi and which said [...]' (IS_NK, 1745)

Observe the contrast between *einn* 'one' and *nokkur* 'some' in (268) above. The specific reference is rendered by means of *einn*—the speaker recalls a certain grave inscription once seen. On the other hand, the person that was commemorated by this inscription is presented as 'some yeoman' by means of *nokkur*. This use of the indefinite pronoun is reminiscent of the spesumptive use of *någon* (a cognate of *nokkur*) in Modern Swedish, in positive polarity contexts, e.g., *Jag talade med någon medicinsk expert*. 'I spoke with some medical expert' (Nivre 2002:12, the paper also includes a discussion of these uses of *någon* and its cognates in Continental Scandinavian languages). The use of *någon* rather than the indefinite article indicates that the speaker is unable or unwilling to give further information about the referent; it also prevents the referent from being established in the discourse and referred to in the following text. The Icelandic data does not allow us to pursue the subject, but we note that two forms are chosen in the text, treating two discourse referents differently—the one introduced with *einn* is referred to in the rest of the text, the one introduced with *nokkur* is not.

(269) *Soddan kauphöndlan við   hinn fátæka, nauðstadda, kalla-st*
      such   negotation   with the   poor   necessitous   call-REFL
      *okur og   er **eitt fordæðuverk** meðal kristinna mann-a   og*
      okur and is EN witchcraft   among Christian man-GEN.PL and
      viðurstyggð fyrir guð-i
      vileness   for god-DAT
      'Such negotiations with the poor, the necessitous, are called okur 'usury' and it is a witchcraft when driven among Christian men and a vileness before God.' (IS_Okur, 1611)

Conditional

(270) *hefðu þeir meint, að   ég hefði viljað   nauðga **einni frú**   af*
      had they meant that I   had wanted compel EN   woman of
      því ypparlegasta standi
      this highest   station
      'They thought that I had wanted to force a woman of the highest class.' (IS_NK, 1745)

(271) *því   mér sýndust þeir heldur spila **eina comædiu**, en   þeir*
      therefore me seemed they rather play EN   comedy   than they
      héldi réttargang
      hold trial
      'It therefore seemed to me that they would rather play a comedy than hold a trial.' (IS_NK, 1745)

Non-referential
Finally, there are a number of examples where *einn* is used in a predicative NP, as (under some restrictions) the indefinite article is used in the modern Continental languages.

(272) *Severin-s   talsmann-s   dóttir   sem er **ein vel-talandi***
      Severin-GEN speaker-GEN daughter who is EN well-spoken
      jungfrú
      woman
      'The daughter of speaker Severin, who is a well-spoken young woman.' (IS_NK, 1745)

We may observe that it is not inconceivable that the form is still a cardinal here, as one can say in English, emphatically, 'she was one fine woman'. Similar examples from the same text are presented in (273) and (274).

(273) *Því   hann var   einn tilvalinn   höfuð-disputant*
it.DAT he   was   EN   appointed head-disputant
'For he was an appointed main disputant.' (IS_NK, 1745)

(274) *þá   getur hann allvel   dugað til að vera   einn*
 then can he   nevertheless suffice to to be   EN
hof-hlaupari
court-messenger
'Nevertheless, he can then suffice to be a court messenger.' (IS_NK, 1745)

One can note, however, that such an abundant use of *einn* in this position points towards a more neutral rather than emphatic use. It most certainly seems also to be a case of influence of the original.

5.6.7 Generic Reference

The models of grammaticalization of both the definite and the indefinite article identify the use of the articles with generic reference as the ultimate stage of the development: in Heine's (1997) terms, the conventionalized article. We have observed before that this final stage seems to neutralize the definite–indefinite distinction. We have also found a number of generic uses of the numeral 'one' in the Continental languages. However, the supplementary Icelandic corpus did not supply any such examples.

Undoubtedly, we have only touched upon the story of *einn* in Icelandic, given the limitations of our main and supplementary corpora. Nevertheless, we have demonstrated that the development of *einn* into the indefinite article, though obviously unsuccessful, was underway, at least to some extent, in the course of Icelandic history. It might have originated, as it did in the other North Germanic languages, due to internal processes, as a reaction to the early stages of the grammaticalization of the definite article, or it could have been instigated by intensive contact with languages with well-formed indefinite articles, such as Danish and German. If the former is true, then there are a number of possible explanations for why it never really took hold. Firstly, it seems that while *einn* undoubtedly can serve as a presentative marker, it is not obligatory in this function in texts from 1200–1550, while the definite article continues to grammaticalize and spread to new contexts. It is not inconceivable that there is a 'window of opportunity' for the grammaticalization of the indefinite article, defined by the stage of definite article grammaticalization. We may further consider the position of *einn* with respect to the main noun. Characteristically, Icelandic is not only the sole representative of the North Germanic (and all Germanic) languages which did not grammaticalize the indefinite article, it is also the only one with a very limited use of the preposed definite article. Even though it is possible to prepose the definite article *hinn*, it is by no means stylistically neutral. The preposed definite article can be used only if the noun is modified by an adjective (as in the other North Germanic languages); it is traditionally viewed as characteristic of formal or written Icelandic, although stylistic considerations are not the only ones; and the two forms of the article (pre- and postposed) are not completely equivalent from a semantic point of view (Thráinsson 2007:4–6). When a non-restrictive reading of a definite noun phrase is intended, the preposed definite article is required and the postposed one excluded (Sigurðsson 2006, Thráinsson 2007, Pfaff 2015, Ingason 2016b, Harðarson 2017).

If, on the other hand, the origins of indefinite article grammaticalization in Icelandic lie in language contact with Danish and German, we may easily understand how the strong purist tendencies of the 18th century might have put a stop to this development. A question that remains open in this scenario is to what extent language policies may affect language change, but with a highly literate population such as that of Iceland, it is not inconceivable that such policies may be successful.

The two scenarios are not mutually exclusive. It is possible that the potential of *einn* to grammaticalize was to some extent realized in the early history of Icelandic, and that at a later stage, in contact with closely related and typologically close languages (German in particular), this potential was re-activated. Whether language policy alone could be responsible for checking this development, or whether it was still at odds with the general make-up of the language, is a topic for a further, more in-depth study, taking into account spoken as well as written varieties of Icelandic.

5.7 Summary

In this chapter, we have considered the corpus material qualitatively, with particular reference to the models of article grammaticalization proposed in the literature, for definite articles arising out of demonstratives and for indefinite articles arising out of the numeral 'one'. While the indefinite article grammaticalization model has been successfully tested against data from a number of languages, the definite article grammaticalization model still presents some puzzles, in particular that concerning the major switch from familiarity-based, strong definite semantics uses at the early stages of grammaticalization to the uniqueness-based, weak definite semantics uses at the subsequent stages of the process.

Our data suggest that the incipient definite article is first used in direct anaphoric contexts, as marker of high accessibility of the discourse referent. However, it is not impossible to use BNs anaphorically throughout Period I in all languages. It is first in Period II that their use becomes limited to referents that are unique and do not need an antecedent to be identified. We have further found that the distance between the anaphor and the antecedent, measured by a number of intervening syntagms, may affect the choice of the anaphoric marking.

We have also demonstrated that the bridging context, i.e., one that is ambiguous between direct and indirect anaphoric reading, can be found in anaphoric chains, in which the same discourse referent may find a different representation (pronominal, nominal) and the hearer may be informed of its new properties. In this sense, the reference builds both on the direct anaphora (repetition of the antecedent) and on the indirect anaphora (anchoring the anaphor in other information).

The indirect anaphora proved to be a complex and heterogenous context and the definite marking was not acquired simultaneously in all its sub-types. In particular, the data provide us with strong arguments that the inalienable possession (body parts, items of clothing), which is an example of a part–whole relation, was marked with reflexive possessive pronouns rather than the incipient definite article as late as in Period II. Only in Period III did the use of the definite article stabilize in this type of context.

The grammaticalization of the indefinite article, as documented in the North Germanic sources, conforms to the proposed model and proceeds through the presentative use of the nominal 'one' (to introduce new and salient discourse referents), the marking of specificity and, finally, the marking of non-specificity. This process does not take place in Icelandic. However, our study of a supplementary corpus of Icelandic texts from 1200–1745 has revealed that the numeral 'one' can, in fact, be found in article-like uses. It can also be speculated that the grammaticalization process started but never reached the stage of the obligatory use of 'one' in these contexts.

In the final chapter we will bring together the quantitative and the qualitative results and propose a refined model of the grammaticalization of the definite article, while discussing the interdependencies between the two grammaticalization processes.

CHAPTER 6

Discussion and Conclusions

6.1   Introduction

The aim of this book has been to study the grammaticalization of the definite and indefinite articles in the North Germanic languages between 1200 and 1550, and to use this close inspection of their development to offer new insights into the rise of articles. We have considered the current state of research and the theoretical models of both types of grammaticalizations. We have found that while the model of the development of the indefinite article seems to be confirmed by a number of empirical studies (of, among others, Danish and Swedish), the model of the development of the definite article leaves a number of questions unanswered, a fact also noted in the literature on the diachrony of definiteness in other languages (e.g., Carlier and Simonenko 2016). To refine the model, we have employed a relatively new theory that posits two kinds of definiteness, strong and weak, and have found evidence that it is strong definite semantics that finds grammaticalized representation first, a fact known and postulated in previous research, but not formulated in terms of this dichotomy. We then examined the most elusive type of use of the definite article, namely indirect anaphora, and its many subtypes. In terms of the strong–weak distinction, this context can be classified as neither strong nor weak (semantically), but some types of indirect anaphora fall closer to one or the other. In the material studied we found, somewhat surprisingly, that the strong definite semantics type grammaticalizes later than the weak type with respect to indirect anaphora.

6.2   Grammaticalization of the Definite Article

The proposed first stage of definite article grammaticalization is the use of the demonstrative with direct anaphoric reference. In Chapter 4 we demonstrated that direct anaphora is the strongest predictor of definite article use in all of the languages studied here, throughout all periods. Even though the use itself is not evidence of grammaticalization, the high frequency of such use is. At the same time, we note that in Period I not all direct anaphors are definite. The statistical data reveal that the incipient definite article is preferred with discourse referents that are animate, singular, and syntactic subjects. A closer inspection of the texts reveals further that more salient referents receive definite marking earlier than less salient ones.

The development from direct to indirect anaphora constitutes the crucial switch and the true hallmark of grammaticalization. The data suggest that the first indirect anaphors to appear as definite NPs are those that were here defined as thematic types, i.e., semantic relations other than the meronymic ones. Meronymic relations appear as possessive NPs or BNs before appearing as defNPs, by which time the definite article is well established with thematic roles.

The North Germanic data suggest that this crucial switch took place within anaphoric chains (series of anaphoric links) in which the same discourse referent is presented, on the one hand, by means of two (or more) co-referring NPs, and on the other hand, as filling a thematic role for some event or process also presented in the text. Thus, the defNP received a double reading—as a direct anaphor with an antecedent, and at the same time as an indirect anaphor with an anchor. For the sake of the argument, we repeat example (171) here as (275), which illustrates this point.

(275)   **Han** gik   ena nat   til hænne sæng ther   hon soff   mz
        he   went EN   night to her   bed   where she slept with
        barn-it   Oc **myrdhe**   sins   brodher-s   barn oc   hænne
        child-DEF and murdered his.REFL brother-GEN child and her
        sofwande stak **han** knifw-in j   hænna hand Æn   hon
        sleeping stuck he   knife-DEF in her   hand and she
        waknadhe aff thy at   blodh-it   fløth   vnder hænna sidho Hon
        woke   of this that blood-DEF flowed under her   side she
        byriadhe ropa   swa at   alt folk-it   waknadhe oc   komo thith
        started scream so that all folk-DEF woke   and came there
        løpande oc   funno barn-it   dræpit oc   knifw-in   blodhoghan
        running and found child-DEF killed and knife-DEF bloody
        j   hænna hand Ther   græt badhe fadher oc   modher oc   alle
        in   her   hand there cried both   father and mother and all
        the   ther   waro Tha   kom   ok   **then ful-e**   mordhar-in
        they there were then came also DEF   vile-WK murderer-DEF
        løpande oc   grep   the   ærlik-a   qwinn-o-n-a   j
        running and seized DEF honest-WK woman-ACC-DEF-ACC in
        har-it
        hair-DEF

'One night he went to the bed, in which she slept with the child, and murdered his nephew and planted the knife in her hand. And she woke feeling blood flow under her side. She started to scream so that everybody woke and came running and found the child killed and the bloody knife in her hand. Mother, father and all that were there cried. Also the vile murderer came running and grabbed the honest woman by her hair.' (SV_ST, Period II)

This explains further why we do not seem to find the most commonly discussed examples of indirect anaphora, i.e., part–whole relations, as definite NPs as early as other types, i.e., the thematic roles and inference-based conceptual types. The formal representation of meronymic relations is dependent on the animacy of the possessor: for animate possessors the preferred form is a possNP (with reflexive possessive pronoun), while for inanimate possessors the preferred form is a BN. It is not until definite marking is adopted for thematic roles that part–whole relations also allow defNPs.

This observation may be of some consequence for the strong–weak dichotomy within definiteness. F. Schwarz (2009, 2013) suggests that indirect anaphora may include both strong definite semantics (part–whole relations) and weak definite semantics (thematic roles). We do not challenge this assumption, in particular since it is founded on strong empirical data. We must note, however, that if this typology is correct, the grammaticalization of the definite article (if there is only one such article) progresses in a zigzag manner, as in (276).[1]

(276) strong definite semantics—weak definite semantics—strong definite semantics—weak definite semantics
direct anaphora—indirect anaphora / thematic—indirect anaphora / meronymic—larger situation use

This model is also intuitively compelling: while we can understand the potential link between direct anaphora and thematic roles, we are less likely to see parts receive the same marking as wholes may do when repeated. It is not a coincidence that meronymic relations are almost the last to receive regular definite marking, since for animates there is the alternative of reflexive

---

[1] If two definite articles grammaticalize we would still see the zigzag pattern, but with two different forms. Dahl's study on the two grammaticalizations in Swedish shows that the preposed and the postposed definite article may have developed from different semantics: the weak vs. the strong. In standard language, however, the two articles are united in one defNP (with modifiers).

possessives, as in example (179) repeated here as (277), and for inanimates BNs persist, as in (279).

(277) **Kwinna-n** gik bort ok faldadhe han j **sinom** **hwiff**
woman-DEF went away and folded him in her.REFL scarf
som **hon** hafdhe a **sino** **hofdhe**
which she had on her.REFL head
'The woman went away and folded him in her scarf, which she had on her head'. (SV_Järt, Period II)

(278) Tha bar keysar-in vp **hand-en-a** oc slogh hona widh
then bore emperor-DEF up hand-DEF-ACC and hit her at
kinben-it at hon størte til iordh-inna
cheekbone-DEF that she fell to earth-DEF
'Then the emperor lifted his hand and hit her on the cheekbone so that she fell down.' (SV_ST, Period II)

(279) Jak skal lydha idhart radh oc bidha til morghin-s oc
I shall follow your advice and bide until morning-GEN and
lät han swa läggia i **mörka-stoffwo**
let him so lie in dark-cellar
'I shall follow your advice and wait until the morning and keep him imprisoned until then.' (SV_SVM, Period II)

Similar examples are noted for Norwegian as well, as in (280).

(280) oc vt ad **dør** gek oc Hiarandher Stæffansson bondh-en
and out of door went and Hiarander Stæffansson master-DEF
i gord-en med honum
in farm-DEF with him
'And the master of the household, Hiarandher Stæffansson, also went out through the door with him.' (DN II 1016, 1501, after Kinn 2016; see also Kinn 2019)

However, in Danish and Swedish in Period II, when placed in anaphoric chains, the subsequent mentions of the indirect anaphor are treated as direct anaphors and receive definite marking. This is the crucial difference between the Period II system in these languages and that of Modern English, for instance, where every subsequent reference to an inalienable possessum is made by means of a possessive NP.

DISCUSSION AND CONCLUSIONS 227

(281) *Tha synti-s   quinn-onna   hwifwir allir blodhoghir ok*
       then see-REFL woman-DEF.GEN scarf   all   bloody   and
       *water aff **blodh** swa at   **blodh-in** flöt   nidhir vm*
       wet   of   blood so   that   blood-DEF flowed down about
       quinn-onna   kindir. Hulkit herra-n   saa, ropadhe ok.
       woman-DEF.GEN cheeks which master-DEF saw screamed and
       *sagdhe hwar slo thik j   **thit** änlite älla sarghadhe. Ok*
       said   who hit you in your face   or   hurt   and
       *quinnna-n   lypte vp **sina**   hand ok strök   sik   vm*
       woman-DEF lifted up her.REFL hand and stroked herself about
       ***änlit-it**   ok   tha   hon tok nidhir **hand-in-a**   tha war hon*
       face-DEF and when she took down hand-DEF-ACC then was she
       al blodhogh.
       all bloody
       'Then the woman's scarf seemed all bloodied and wet with blood so
       that the blood flowed down the woman's cheeks. Which the master
       saw, screamed and said 'Who hit you in your face or hurt you?' And
       the woman lifted her hand and stroked her face and when she took the
       hand away it was all bloodied.' (SV_Järt, Period II)

Once the definite article has been established as an indirect anaphoric marker, it spreads even further to encompass also larger situation use. Judging from the data presented in Chapter 5, this development originated most likely with more local larger situation uses, pertaining to the local village or parish, for instance. The definite discourse referents present ambiguous readings: as larger situation use, but also as indirect anaphora, which may be anchored in previous discourse by some mention of a given location. Examples (194) and (195), illustrating this, are repeated here as (282) and (283).

(282) *Tha meth syne   brødh-re-s   raadh fick han løffw-en thet*
       then with his.REFL brother-PL-GEN advice got he lion-DEF that
       æmbeth at   hwn skulle een asen   som   hænthe them weth
       task   that she should EN donkey which brought them wood
       *aff **skoffw-en** følghe till marck-en   ther   han thog syn*
       of forest-DEF follow to pasture-DEF where he took his.REFL
       fødhe oc   thaghe hannum till waræ
       food and take   him   to care
       'Then, by the advice of his brothers, he gave the lioness the task to guard
       the donkey which brought them wood from the forest and follow him
       to the pasture where he grazed.' (DA_Jer, Period III)

(283) *I rom   var en keysare. han hafdhe ena dygdheliga oc*
in Rome was EN emperor he had   EN virtuous and
gudhliga keysarinne. hon thiænte jomfru marie af allo hiærta.
godly   empress   she served virgin Mary of all heart
*keysar-en   vilde   fara   ofvir **mær-it** til the hælgh-e graff.*
emperor-DEF wanted travel over sea-DEF to DEF holy-WK tomb
'There was an emperor in Rome who had a virtuous and pious wife who served Virgin Mary with all her heart. The emperor wanted to travel to the Holy Tomb over the sea.' (DA_ST, Period II)

Examples of such ambiguous contexts illustrate how language change comes about in language acquisition. While the parent generation may use the definite form as a signal that the discourse referent is identical with the one mentioned earlier (direct anaphora), the child generation may understand the definite form as a means to signal that the discourse referent is connected with an event or process mentioned earlier and fills a thematic role in that event. As both uses are felicitous—the discourse referent is correctly identified by the hearer—the child does not realize parents may mean something different and adopts this use in his or her language, passing it on to the next generation.[2] Equally, the next switch, from indirect anaphora to larger situation use, is made possible in language acquisition. This stage also constitutes a major step in definite article grammaticalization, as it makes possible the use of the definite article without any connection to the text. Nevertheless, especially in its more local uses, the definite article retains the link with the original demonstrative, as it can be interpreted in connection with the utterance situation.

Finally, we should stress the fact that by the time the first North Germanic texts were written (in the Latin alphabet), the original demonstrative could already be cliticized to the noun, judging by the fact that it is spelled together with the noun. In fact, Danish and Swedish texts display only the cliticized form, while in Icelandic writing some variation can still be found: the form appears sometimes spelled together with the noun and sometimes separately. The development seems to be well underway, resulting in a formal split between the demonstrative and the article.

At the same time, the statistical results for Icelandic are more uniform in all three periods studied than those for Danish and Swedish, which exhibit more fluctuations with respect to factors influencing the choice of the definite

---

2 On language acquisition as the locus of language change see in particular Lightfoot (2010).

form and its distribution between different types of reference. This discrepancy might be explained by the difference in text genres and origins between Icelandic, on the one hand, and Danish and Swedish, on the other. The oldest extant Danish and Swedish texts are either legal texts or translations, mostly from Latin. It is conceivable that neither the legal genre nor the Latin original favoured the use of the (incipient) definite article. Icelandic texts, on the other hand, are both some years older and indigenous, without foreign sources. The majority represent profane prose, a genre which includes some dialogue and is more likely to have been closer to everyday speech than a legal text. It is not unlikely that they imply the process of article grammaticalization to have been more advanced than in Danish or Swedish as early as Period I, without this necessarily having been the case.

6.3   Grammaticalization of the Indefinite Article

As we have observed before, the model of indefinite article grammaticalization does not present the same puzzles as the definite case, as it has been shown to correctly predict developments in a number of languages, including Swedish. Similarly to the definite article grammaticalization model, it involves a major shift in the use of the original numeral 'one', namely its extension to use with non-specific discourse referents.

To some extent the grammaticalization of the indefinite article mirrors that of the definite, as it originates with salient discourse referents. Factors that were found important for selection of the definite article at the onset of grammaticalization, such as case, gender and syntactic function, are also important for selection of the incipient indefinite article, but only at the earliest stages of grammaticalization. The fact that they are of importance seems to be a result of their importance for the selection of the definite article (as a means to keep track of salient discourse referents) and not of the indefinite article per se, as this article is used presentatively, to mark discourse referents that will be salient in the following discourse.

The presentative use of the numeral 'one' is not a diagnostic of ongoing grammaticalization. In fact, there are a number of such uses of EN in the Icelandic corpus, without the form progressing to the next stage of grammaticalization. We find examples where there is a contrast in how salient referents are introduced against how other new referents are presented, as in (284).

(284)   **Kona   ein** fór   of morgun snemma að kanna fjöru því að
        woman   EN   went of morning early   to search shore for that

búandi   hennar var   eigi heima. Sér   hún síðan   **örkn** mikið liggja
husband her   was not home   sees she then   seal large lie
á   **steini** skammt frá   sér og   svaf   en   hún hafði ekki   í
on stone close   from her and slept but she   had   nothing in
hendi sér.   Fékk hún síðan   lurk   nekkvern er   lá í
hand she.DAT got   she then cudgel some   which lay in
fjöru-nni   og   stillti að sel-num   og   laust í   höfuð honum.
shore-DEF and crept to   seal-DEF and hit   in head   him
'There was a woman who went out early one morning in search of her husband who was not at home. She saw a large seal lying on a stone not far from her, sleeping. But she had nothing with her. She then found some cudgel which was lying on the shore, crept towards the seal and hit him on the head.' (IS_Jart, Period I)

The text fragment (which continues for several more sentences) has one main character, the woman who slays a seal, and a secondary character in the seal itself. Although both protagonists are subsequently referred to by pronouns or definite NPs, the introductions differ: only the main character, the woman, is presented by means of EN. It is not impossible to find EN with minor characters as well, but the presentative use is mainly found with the most salient referents.

Once the presentative marker stage is passed and the incipient indefinite article is used to introduce all new discourse referents, irrespective of their salience, it may continue to grammaticalize into a non-specific marker. A diagnostic of this stage of grammaticalization is the possibility to use the article in negative polarity contexts, such as conditionals, negation, and after verbs of volition. This development is documented in both the Danish and Swedish corpora, as in examples (285–287).

(285)   oc   taghe theris staff-ue [...]   oc   hwilken staff som fluer **een** dwæ
and take   their staff-PL   and which   staff that flies EN dove
aff end-en   oc   op til hemmel-in   then scaltu   sætte til ath
of end-DEF and up to heaven-DEF this shall.you set   to to
gøme   mariam.
protect Mary
'And they shall take their staffs [...] and the staff from which end a dove will fly out towards heaven is the staff you shall use to protect Mary.' (DA_Jesu, Period III)

(286) *færekude   swaret   hwore motthæ* **en** *jomffrv barn føde*
Farekunde answered how   could   EN virgin child bear
'Farekunde answered: How could a virgin bear a child?' (DA_KM, Period III)

(287) *ok diäfwl-en vppinbaradhi-s j* **enna** *quinn-o   liknilse*
and devil-DEF revealed-REFL in   EN   woman-GEN likeness
'And the devil revealed himself in one woman's form.' (SV_Järt, Period II)

Chronologically, the use of 'one' as a presentative marker can be found as early as in Period I, but the use of 'one' as a non-specific marker is first found in Period II, occasionally, and regularly in Period III.

6.4   The Puzzles Revisited

In Chapter 1 we opened with a list of puzzles concerning the developments of articles, which remain unsolved despite a vast body of research into their diachrony. We quote them below in summary form.

Puzzle 1:   'the puzzle of uniformity of sources', i.e., the near-universal tendency for definite articles to grammaticalize out of deictic elements and for indefinite articles to stem from the numeral 'one'.

Puzzle 2:   'the puzzle of success', closely connected with Puzzle 1, i.e., what makes these original forms better candidates for articles than the forms they compete against, such as possessive pronouns or indefinite pronouns.

Puzzle 3:   'the puzzle of definite first', i.e., why the grammaticalization of the indefinite article always seems to follow that of the definite, and not the other way around.

Puzzle 4:   'the puzzle of indirect anaphora', i.e., how exactly the grammaticalization proceeds from direct to indirect anaphora, given that this is the defining point in definite article grammaticalization, and has not yet been satisfactorily explained.

Of these four as yet unanswered questions, we have largely focused on the last, giving greater scope to the classification and description of the indirect anaphoric use of the definite article (see sections 5.3.2 and 6.2). We will now consider the remaining puzzles and discuss them with reference to the data obtained in our study.

Puzzles 1 and 2 are in fact two sides of the same coin. There are a number of potential candidates for the role of definite article, the most likely ones including the demonstrative and the possessive pronouns. Similarly to the indefinite article, the indefinite pronouns 'some' and 'such' make good candidates, and they have been used as presentative markers in some languages. However, only the demonstrative (or some other deictic element) and the numeral 'one' seem to grammaticalize fully, i.e., beyond the first stages of purely textual use as direct anaphoric marker and presentative marker respectively.

With the grammaticalization of the definite article, the answer to the 'puzzle of success' seems to lie in the dichotomy of its use with strong or weak definites. It has been pointed out before that in some uses of the definite article the speaker may exchange it freely for a demonstrative (strong definite semantics) or for a possessive pronoun (weak definite semantics). We repeat examples (51) and (52) from section 2.2.1.2 here as (288) and (289) respectively.

(288)   Beside the barn there is *a little cottage*. The/**This** cottage was built in 1875.
(but *Its cottage)

(289)   Beside the barn there is *a little cottage*. The/**Its** roof is leaking.
(but *This roof)
(Skrzypek 2012:45, after Fraurud 2001:246)

The two categories, definiteness and possession, share their exponents to some extent. In North Germanic, the definite article is used with inalienable possession (in contrast to English, for instance, where only the possessive is possible). Possessives may be stylistically preferred in some indirect anaphoric contexts, including inalienables.

However, the two categories are semantically different. While definiteness is primarily about the identifiability of a discourse referent, possession is about a relation between two entities. They may overlap, and indeed do in terms of morphology, when the identifiability of the discourse referent relies on its relations with a previously mentioned other entity. Seemingly, it is such uses of the possessives, reminiscent of definite article use in article languages, that have led some scholars to postulate that possessives may be a source of definite articles. However, as Bechert (1993) so pertinently observes, the analysis of possessives as definites may just be the result of applying the morphological representation of a category in one language onto another.

We may further note that in languages with two definite articles, even if they are etymologically different, both seem to stem from demonstratives, as

DISCUSSION AND CONCLUSIONS

with Fering *a* and *di* (Standard German, in F. Schwarz's description, exhibits a different distribution of article with preposition and not two etymologically different articles). They are not cases of two definites of which one originates in a demonstrative and the other in a possessive.

As regards the grammaticalization of the indefinite article, it is important to bear in mind that it does not occur in a void (as, of course, no grammaticalization process does), but that it follows the grammaticalization of the definite article. It seems that the obligatorification of definite marking in direct anaphoric contexts with salient discourse referents exerts pressure to use a symmetric marker to introduce such salient referents into the discourse. The symmetry of the two developments was clearly demonstrated in Chapter 4, where the same factors were at play and the presentative indefinite NPs were overwhelmingly subjects, with animate, singular and masculine head nouns. What are the other shared characteristics of the use of the two articles?

To answer this question, we may first consider the use of BNs in Modern Danish and Swedish (the use of BNs in Icelandic coincides partly with that of indefNPs in Danish and Swedish, as Icelandic has no indefinite article). Apart from lexicalized phrases such as *spela piano* 'play the piano' or *sitta i fängelse* lit. 'sit in jail', i.e., 'be imprisoned', BNs can be used productively to give a count noun a mass reading. Consider the examples in (290–293).

(290) *Tydliga spår både av **älg** och **hund** fanns i den*
clear traces both of elk and dog were in DEF
ny-grusade vägbana-n.
newly-gravelled road-DEF
'There were clear traces of both elk and dog in the newly gravelled road.'

(291) *Den luktade både **får** och **get**.*
it smelled both sheep and goat
'It smelled of both sheep and goat.' (Teleman et al. 2010:19)

(292) *Vi såg spår av tre älg-ar.*
we saw traces of three elk-PL
'We saw traces of three elks.'

(293) *Vi såg **en** stor älg. Den stor-a älg-en tittade på oss.*
we saw INDF big elk DEF big-WK elk-DEF looked on us
'We saw a large elk. The large elk stared at us.' (Skrzypek 2012:33)

The lack of articles or other determiners renders a noun uncountable: in (290) the phrase *spår av älg* 'traces of elk' (or even *älgspår* 'elk traces') makes no reference to the number of elks who left them. In that sentence, it is rather the case that the imprints remind one of those usually left by elks, but they could actually have been left by a different creature or a device of some sort. This makes the example different from (292) and (293), in which the presence of numerals or articles makes the elk in question countable.

BNs are neutral with respect to the definite–indefinite opposition—they are not definite and they are not indefinite. Further, they are neutral with respect to number—they are neither singular nor plural. By using a BN, the speaker may even suppress gender classification; consider (295).

(294) *Han ska köpa bil.*
       he   will buy car.UTR
       'He will buy a car.'

(295) ***Bil***   *är   dyr-t.*
       car.UTR is   expensive-N
       'It is expensive to buy a car.' (Delsing 1993:58–59)

Not all nouns can be used in this way; it seems that the noun must signify a referent whose purchase is not trivial, thus e.g., *köpa bok* 'buy book' is not possible (Delsing 1993:59).

We may therefore conclude that the common feature of the articles is their effect on the noun, namely that they give it a countable interpretation. By using an article, the speaker declares that the discourse referent in question has boundaries—that it can be considered in its entirety. This is particularly clear with plural or mass referents used with the definite article, which creates an effect of totality (Hawkins 1978; see examples quoted at the end of section 2.2.5).

Puzzle 3—why the definite article grammaticalizes first, before the indefinite—seems to find its answer in the fact that the grammaticalization of the indefinite, which begins with the presentative use of the numeral 'one', is a secondary process, which may only be initiated when the grammaticalization of the definite has gone beyond the first stage, the marking of all salient discourse referents. It seems that if there are indefinite articles that have developed in the absence of the definite, at least their origin must be different from the presentative use.

6.5 Concluding Remarks

The aim of the present study was to explore the rise of articles in three closely related languages, employing both quantitative and qualitative methods. The results largely confirm earlier studies which identify pragmatic factors as those of greatest importance at the onset of both grammaticalizations. There is strong statistical evidence that the article-like use of both the demonstrative and the numeral, which gradually evolved into articles, originated with prominent discourse referents, to which the speaker wished to draw the hearer's attention. The qualitative study of the chosen corpus has enabled the identification of bridging contexts which made the grammaticalization possible, in particular that of the definite article.

A number of issues still remain open and worthy of separate studies; in particular, the developments beyond the timeframe of this study, that is, after 1550. It is then that the modern use of BNs is grammaticalized, a use which sets North Germanic apart from other Germanic languages. It is also after 1550 that the differences in generic expressions arose which we observe in modern North Germanic languages. These questions surely merit a study of their own.

Finally, a few words against teleology. Despite formulations such as: initiation of the process, etc., the developments should not be considered teleological in nature. Rather, a cyclical character of grammaticalizations should be accentuated. On the one hand, the system seems to have been stable for some centuries now. However, the case of the indefinite article in Icelandic indicates that despite similarities between the linguistic systems at two discrete points in time, linguistic change may take place in between. Between 1550 and 2000 other changes take place: the BNs undergo a secondary grammaticalization, genericity marking is formed (differently in each language!), etc. On the other, a long-term stability may nevertheless come to an end. Standardization and wide-spread literacy may have had a conserving effect on the article systems in North Germanic. However, this does not preclude that these systems will undergo some changes in the future.

Sources

Swedish

AVL   Äldre Västgötalagen. 1827. *Samling af Sweriges gamla lagar* (Vol. 1), ed. by Hans S. Collin, & Carl J. Schlyter. Stockholm: Haeggström. Manuscript Holm B 59.

Bur   Codex Bureanus. 1847. *Ett fornsvenskt legendarium*, ed. by George Stephens. Stockholm: Norstedt. Manuscript Holm A 34.

Did   *Sagan om Didrik af Bern*. 1850–1854. Ed. by Gunnar O. Hyltén-Cavallius. Stockholm: Norstedt. Manuscript Skokloster 115, 116 HAND A.

DL   Dalalagen. 1827. *Samling af Sweriges gamla lagar* (Vol. 5), ed. by Hans S. Collin, & Carl J. Schlyter. Stockholm: Haeggström. Manuscript Holm B 54.

HML   Helga manna lefverne. 1877–1878. *Klosterläsning*, ed. by Gustaf E. Klemming. Stockholm: Norstedt. Manuscript Holm A 110 (Codex Oxenstierna).

Järt   Järteckensboken. 1877–1878. *Klosterläsning*, ed. by Gustaf E. Klemming. Stockholm: Norstedt. Manuscript Holm A 110 (Codex Oxenstierna).

KM   Karl Magnus. 1887–1889. *Prosadikter från Sveriges medeltid*, ed. by Gustaf E. Klemming. Stockholm: Norstedt. Manuscript Holm D 4.

Kris   Kristoffers Landslag. 1869. *Samling Af Sweriges Gamla Lagar* (Vol. 12), ed. by Carl J. Schlyter. Lund. Manuscript Holm B 23a.

Linc   Linköpingslegendariet, Legenden om Sankt Amalberga. 1847. *Ett fornsvenskt legendarium*, ed. by George Stephens. Stockholm: Norstedt. Manuscript Linc B 70a.

OgL   Östgötalagen. 1827. *Samling af Sweriges gamla lagar* (Vol. 2), ed. by Hans S. Collin, & Carl J. Schlyter. Stockholm: Haeggström. Manuscript Holm B 50.

Pent   Pentateukparafrasen. 1955. *Fem Möseböcker på fornsvenska*, ed. by Olof Thorell. Uppsala: Almqvist & Wiksell. Manuscript Codex Thott (Köpenhamn).

ST   *Själens tröst: Tio Guds bud förklarade genom legender, berättelser och exempel*. 1873. Ed. by Gustaf E. Klemming. Stockholm: Norstedt. Manuscript Holm A 108.

SVM   Sju vise mästare. 1887–1889. *Prosadikter från Sveriges medeltid*, ed. by Gustaf E. Klemming. Stockholm: Norstedt. Manuscript Holm D 4.

Troja   *Historia Trojana*. 1892. Ed. by Robert Geete. Stockholm: Norstedt. Manuscript Holm D 3a.

YVL   Yngre Västgötalagen. 1827. *Samling af Sweriges gamla lagar* (Vol. 1), ed. by Hans S. Collin, & Carl J. Schlyter. Stockholm: Haeggström. Manuscript Holm B 58.

All texts are available on *Fornsvenska textbanken*, at https://project2.sol.lu.se/fornsvenska/.

Danish

ErL   Eriks Lov. 1933–1961. *Danmarks gamle Landskabslove med Kirkelovene I–VIII*, ed. by Johannes Brøndum-Nielsen, Svend Aakjær, Erik Kroman & Peter Skautrup, et al. Manuscript AM 455 12mo. https://tekstnet.dk/eriks-lov/1/4.

GD   *Gesta danorum på dansk*. 2015. Ed. by Marita Akhøj Nielsen. Copenhagen: Det Danske Sprog- og Litteraturselskab. Manuscript C67. https://tekstnet.dk/gesta-danorum-c67/1.

Jer   Af Jeronimi levned. 1917–1930. *Samfund til Udgivelse af gammel nordisk Litteratur*, ed. by G. Knudsen. Copenhagen: S.L. Møllers Bogtrykkeri. Manuscript Gl. kgl. Saml. 1586 4to.

Jesu   *Jesu Barndoms Bog*. 2015. Ed. by Simon Skovgaard Boeck. Copenhagen: Det Danske Sprog- og Litteraturselskab. Based on Gotfred af Ghemen's print of *Jesu Barndomsbog* (Copenhagen 1508). https://tekstnet.dk/jesu-barndomsbog/metadata.

Kat   Af Katherine legende. 1917–1930. *Samfund til Udgivelse af gammel nordisk Litteratur*, ed. by G. Knudsen. Copenhagen: S.L. Møllers Bogtrykkeri. Manuscript Gl. kgl. Saml. 1586 4to.

Kerst   Aff Sancte Kerstine hennis pyne. 1859. *De hellige Kvinder, en Legende-Samling*, ed. by Carl J. Brandt, 38–51. Copenhagen. Manuscript Cod. Holm. K4.

KM   Karl Magnus Krønike. 1960. *Udg. for Universitets-Jubilæets Danske Samfund*, ed. by Poul Lindegård Hjorth, 138–170. Copenhagen: J.H. Schultz Forlag. https://cst.dk/dighumlab/duds/DSST/XML/KM1480.xml.

Mar   Aff Sancta Marina. 1859. *De hellige Kvinder, en Legende-Samling*, ed. by Carl J. Brandt, 88–91. Copenhagen. Manuscript Cod. Holm. K4.

MK   *Mariaklagen efter et runeskrevet Haandskrift-Fragment i Stockholms Kgl. Bibliotek*. 1929. Ed. by Johannes Brøndum-Nielsen, & Aage Rohmann. Copenhagen. Manuscript Cod. Holm. A120.

ML   Marialegende. 1931–1937. *Fragmenter af gammeldanske Haandskrifter*, ed. by Paul Diderichsen. Copenhagen. Manuscript K 48. https://tekstnet.dk/legendefragmenter-k48/metadata.

SKL   *Skånske Kirkelov*. 2015. Ed. by Simon Skovgaard Boeck. Copenhagen: Det Danske Sprog- og Litteraturselskab. Manuscript AM 28, 8vo. https://tekstnet.dk/skaanske-kirkelov-am28/metadata.

SL   Skånske lov. 1859. *Samling af Sweriges gamla lagar* (Vol. 9), ed. by Carl J. Schlyter. Stockholm: Haeggström. Manuscript Holm B 76. Available on *Fornsvenska textbanken*.

SMB   *Skriftemålsbøn*. 2015. Ed. by Marita Akhøj Nielsen. Copenhagen: Det Danske Sprog- og Litteraturselskab. Manuscript K 48. https://tekstnet.dk/skriftemaalsboen/metadata.

ST Sjalens trost. 1937. Udg. for Universitets-Jubilæets Danske Samfund v. Niels Nielsen. Copenhagen: J.H. Schultz Forlag, https://cst.dk/dighumlab/duds/DSS T/XML/HOLMA109.xml

Pouel Huoel Sancte Pouel vort pint. 1859. De hellige Kvinder, en Legende-Samling, ed. by Carl J. Brandt, 24–28. Copenhagen. Manuscript Cod. Holm. K4.

VL Valdemars Lov. 2015. Ed. by Simon Skovgaard Boeck. Copenhagen: Det Danske Sprog- og Litteraturselskab. Manuscript AM 455, 12mo. https://tekstnet.dk/valdemars-lov/metadata

Icelandic

Arna Árna saga biskups. 1988. Sturlunga saga: Árna saga biskups. Hrafns saga Sveinbjarnarsonar hin sérsaka, ed. by Örnólfur Thorsson, et al. Reykjavík: Svart á hvítu.

Band Bandamanna saga (Konungsbók text). 1985. Íslendinga sögur (Vol. I), ed. by Jón Torfason, et al., 27–45. Reykjavík: Svart á hvítu.

Did Þiðreks saga af Bern. 1954. Ed. by Guðni Jónsson. Reykjavík: Íslendingasagnaútgáfan. Chapters 82–86. https://heimskringla.no/wiki/%C3%9Ei%C3%B oreks_saga_af_Bern_-_Vi%C3%B0ga_%C3%BE%C3%A1ttr_Velentssonar.

Egil Þetubrot Egils Sögu (Theta manuscript of Egils Saga) by Snorri Sturluson. 2008. Egils saga Skallagrímssonar, ed. by B. Jónsson. Copenhagen: C.A. Reitzels Forlag.

Finn Finnboga saga ramma. 1985. Íslendinga sögur (Vol. I), ed. by Jón Torfason, et al., 625–673. Reykjavík: Svart á hvítu.

Ge Geirmundar þáttr heljarskinns. 1954. Sturlunga saga, ed. by Guðni Jónsson. Reykjavík: Íslendingasagnaútgáfan. Chapters 1–7. https://heimskringla.no/wiki/Geirmundar_%C3%BE%C3%A1ttr_heljarskinns

Gis Gísla saga Súrssonar. 1953. Vestfirðinga sǫgur, ed. by Björn K. Þórólfsson & Guðni Jónsson. Íslenzk fornrit VI. Reykjavík: Hið íslenzka fornritafélag. https://heimskringla.no/wiki/G%C3%ADsla_saga_S%C3%BArssonar.

Gragas Grágás. Lagasafn íslenska þjóðveldisins. 1992. Ed. by Gunnar Karlsson, Kristján Sveinsson & Mórður Árnason, 209–262. Reykjavík: Mál og menning,

Gret Grettis saga Ásmundarsonar. 1985. Íslendinga sögur (Vol. I), ed. by Jón Torfason, et al., 968–1015. Reykjavík: Svart á hvítu.

Gun Gunnars saga Keldugnúpsfífls. 1985. Íslendinga sögur (Vol. I), ed. by Jón Torfason, et al. Reykjavík: Svart á hvítu.

Jarl Jarlmanns saga og Hermanns. 1963. Late Medieval Icelandic Romances III, ed. by Agnete Loth, 3–66. Copenhagen: Munksgaard.

Jart Jarteinabók. 1989. Þorláks saga helga. Elsta gerð Þorláks sögu helga ásamt

    jarteinabók og efni úr yngri gerðum sögunnar, ed. by Ásdís Egilsdóttir, 59–108. Reykjavík: Þorlákssjóður.
Marta Mörtu saga og Maríu Magdalenu. 2003. *Heilagra meyja sögur*, ed. by Kirsten Wolf, et al., 50–92. Reykjavík: Bókmenntafræðistofnun Háskóla Íslands.
Torlak Þorláks saga helga. 1989. *Þorláks saga helga. Elsta gerð Þorláks sögu helga ásamt jarteinabók og efni úr yngri gerðum sögunnar*, ed. by Ásdís Egilsdóttir, 111–165. Reykjavík: Þorlákssjóður.
To Þorsteins saga hvíta. 1947. *Íslendinga sögur. Bd 10, Austfirðinga sögur*, ed. by Guðni Jónsson. Reykjavík: Íslendingasagnaútgáfan.
Vig Víglundar saga. 1986. *Íslendinga sögur* (Vol. II), ed. by Jón Torfason, et al. Reykjavík: Svart á hvítu.
Vil Vilhjálms saga Sjóðs. 1964. *Late Medieval Icelandic Romances IV*, ed. by Agnete Loth. Copenhagen: Munksgaard.

All texts apart from Did, Ge, Gis and To are available thanks to the IcePaHC project (Wallenberg et al. 2011, version 0.9).

References

Abbott, Barbara. 2002. Donkey demonstratives. *Natural language semantics* 10(4): 285–298.

Abraham, Werner. 2007. Discourse binding: DP and pronouns in German, Dutch, and English. *Nominal Determination: Typology, Context Constraints and Historical Emergence*, ed. by Elisabeth Stark, Elisabeth Leiss & Werner Abraham, 21–48. Amsterdam: John Benjamins.

Akhøj Nielsen, Marita (ed.). 2015. *Gesta danorum på dansk*. Copenhagen: Det Danske Sprog- og Litteraturselskab.

Anderson, Stephen R. & Edward Keenan. 1985. Deixis. *Language Typology and Syntactic Description: Grammatical categories and the lexicon*, ed. by Timothy Shopen, 259–308. Cambridge: Cambridge University Press.

Andersson, Erik. 1979. Balansen mellan grammatiskt och semantiskt genus i svenskan. *Folkmålsstudier* 22: 27–48.

Apothéloz, Denis & Marie-José Reichler-Béguelin. 1999. Interpretations and functions of demonstrative NPs in indirect anaphora. *Journal of Pragmatics* 31(3): 363–397. doi:10.1016/S0378-2166(98)00073-3.

Ariel, Mira. 1988. Referring and Accessibility. *Journal of Linguistics* 24(1): 65–87.

Ariel, Mira. 1994. Interpreting Anaphoric Expressions: A Cognitive versus a Pragmatic Approach. *Journal of Linguistics* 30(1): 3–42.

Ariel, Mira. 2014. *Accessing Noun-Phrase Antecedents*. London: Routledge. doi:10.4324/9781315857473.

Asher, Nicholas & Alex Lascarides. 1998. Bridging. *Journal of Semantics* 15(1): 83–113. doi:10.1093/jos/15.1.83.

Askedal, John Ole. 2012. Germansk artikkeltypologi: Bestemte og ubestemte artikler i germanske språk. *Germansk filologi og norske ord: festskrift til Harald Bjorvand på 70-årsdagen den 30. juli 2012*, ed. by John Ole Askedal, Harald Bjorvand, Tom Schmidt & Rolf Theil, 70–93. Oslo: Instituttet for sammenlignende kulturforskning.

Asudeh, Ash & Line Hove Mikkelsen. 2000. Incorporation in Danish: Implications for interfaces. *Grammatical interfaces in HPSG*, ed. by Ronnie Cann, Claire Grover & Philip Miller, 1–15. Stanford: CSLI Publications.

Bandle, Oskar. 1956. *Die Sprache der Guðbrandsbiblía: Orthographie und Laute, Formen*. Copenhagen: Ejnar Munksgaard.

Bandle, Oskar, Kurt Braunmüller, Ernst Hakon Jahr, Allan Karker, Hans-Peter Naumann, Ulf Teleman, Lennart Elmevik & Gun Widmark. 2002. *The Nordic Languages: An International Handbook of the History of the North Germanic Languages*. Berlin/Boston: De Gruyter Mouton Barnes.

Barðdal, Jóhanna. 2001. *Case in Icelandic: A Synchronic, Diachronic and Comparative Approach*. Lund: Department of Scandinavian Languages, Lund University.

Barðdal, Jóhanna. 2009. The Development of Case in Germanic. *The Role of Semantic, Pragmatic and Discourse Factors in the Development of Case*, ed. by Jóhanna Barðdal & Shobhana L. Chelliah, 123–125. Amsterdam: John Benjamins.

Barnes, Michael P. 2008. *A new introduction to Old Norse, part 1: Grammar*. 3rd ed. London: Viking Society for Northern Research.

Bechert, Johannes. 1993. *Definiteness and article systems*. EUROTYP Working Papers, vol. 1. Strassbourg: European Science Foundation.

Beier, Phil. 2015. *Einn, uppkomst och utveckling: Den obestämda artikeln i Íslendinga sögur*. Uppsala: Uppsala University, unpublished BA thesis.

Berezowski, Leszek. 2009. *The Myth of the Zero Article*. London/New York: Continuum International Publication Company.

Boor, Helmut de. 1928. Nordische Sprachprobleme. *Deutsch-Nordische Zeitschrift* 1: 186–201.

Börjars, Kersti. 1994. Swedish Double Determination in a European Typological Perspective. *Nordic Journal of Linguistics* 17(2): 219–252. doi:10.1017/S0332586500003024.

Börjars, Kersti & Pauline Harries. 2008. The Clitic-Affix Distinction, Historical Change, and Scandinavian Bound Definiteness Marking. *Journal of Germanic Linguistics* 20(4): 289–350. doi:10.1017/S1470542708000068.

Borthen, Kaja. 2003. *Norwegian Bare Singulars*. PhD dissertation, Norges vetenskaplige universitet.

Brandtler, Johan & Lars-Olof Delsing. 2010. Framväxten av obestämd artikel i svenska: Definithet, specificitet och polaritet. *Svensson och svenskan: med sinnen känsliga för språk: Festskrift till Jan Svensson den 24 januari 2010*, ed. by Gunilla Byrman, Anna Gustafsson & Henrik Rahm, 24–36. Lund: Lund University.

Braunmüller, Kurt. 1982. *Syntaxtypologische Studien zum Skandinavischen*. Tübingen: Narr.

Brøndum-Nielsen, Johannes & Aage Rohmann (eds.). 1929. *Mariaklagen efter et runeskrevet Haandskrift-Fragment i Stockholms Kgl. Bibliotek*. Copenhagen: J.H. Schultz Forlag.

Bullitta, Dario. 2017. Sources, Context, and English Provenance of the Old Danish Visio Pauli. *The Journal of English and Germanic Philology* 116(1): 1–23. doi:10.5406/jenglger mphil.116.1.0001.

Carlier, Anne & Walter De Mulder. 2010. The emergence of the definite article in Late Latin: ille in competition with ipse. *Subjectification, intersubjectification and grammaticalization*, ed. by Hubert Cuykens, Kristin Davidse & Lieven Vandelanotte, 241–275. The Hague: Mouton de Gruyter.

Carlier, Anne & Alexandra Simonenko. 2016. The evolution of the French definite article: from strong to weak. *Paper presentation at Formal Diachronic Semantics 2016, University of Konstanz, September 12–14, 2016.*

Carlsson, Yvonne. 2012. *Genericitet i text*. PhD dissertation, Stockholm University, Faculty of Humanities, Department of Scandinavian Languages.

Charolles, Michel. 1990. L'anaphore associative: problèmes de délimitation. *Verbum* 13(3): 119–148.

Christophersen, Paul. 1939. *The articles: A study of their theory and use in English*. Copenhagen: Munksgaard.

Clark, Herbert H. 1983. Bridging. *Thinking: Readings in Cognitive Science*, ed. by Philip N. Johnson-Laird & Peter C. Wason, 311–326. Cambridge: Cambridge University Press.

Clark, Herbert H. & Susan E. Haviland. 1977. Comprehension and the given-new contrast. *Discourse Production and Comprehension*, ed. by Roy O. Freedle, 1–40. Norwood, NJ: Ablex.

Comrie, Bernard. 1981. *Language universals and linguistic typology: Syntax and morphology*. 2nd edition. Chicago: University of Chicago Press.

Consten, Manfred. 2004. *Anaphorisch oder deiktisch? Zu einem integrativen Modell domanengebundener Referenz*. Tübingen: Niemeyer.

Corbett, Greville G. 2000. *Number*. Cambridge Textbooks in Linguistics. Cambridge: Cambridge University Press. doi:10.1017/CBO9781139164344.

Cornish, Francis. 1996. "Antecedentless" Anaphors: Deixis, Anaphora, or What? Some Evidence from English and French. *Journal of Linguistics* 32(1): 19–41.

Cornish, Francis. 1999. *Anaphora, Discourse, and Understanding: Evidence from English and French*. Oxford: Clarendon Press.

Dahl, Östen. 2003. Competing definite articles in Scandinavian. *Dialectology meets Typology*, ed. by Bernd Kortmann, 147–180. Berlin: Mouton de Gruyter.

Dahl, Östen. 2004. Definite articles in Scandinavian: Competing grammaticalization processes in standard and non-standard varieties. *Dialectology meets Typology*, ed. by Bernd Kortmann, 147–180. Berlin/New York: Mouton de Gruyter. doi:10.1515/9783110197327.147.

Dahl, Östen. 2015. *Grammaticalization in the North: Noun phrase morphosyntax in Scandinavian vernaculars*. Berlin: Language Science Press. doi:10.26530/OAPEN_559871.

Dahl, Östen & Kari Fraurud. 1996. Animacy in Grammar and Discourse. *Reference and Referent Accessibility*, ed. by Thorstein Fretheim & Jeanette K. Gundel, 47–64. Amsterdam: John Benjamins. doi:10.1075/pbns.38.04dah.

Davidson, Herbert. 1990. *Han hon den: genusutvecklingen i svenskan under nysvensk tid*. Lund: Lund University.

De Mulder, Walter & Anne Carlier. 2011. The grammaticalization of definite articles. *The Oxford Handbook of Grammaticalization*, ed. by Bernd Heine & Heiko Narrog, 522–535. Oxford: Oxford University Press. doi:10.1093/oxfordhb/9780199586783.013.0042.

Delbrück, Bertold. 1916. *Der altisländische Artikel: Germanische Syntax III*. Leipzig: Teubner.

Delsing, Lars-Olof. 1993. *The Internal Structure of Noun Phrases in the Scandinavian Languages: A comparative Study*. Lund: Lund University.

Delsing, Lars-Olof. 1994. Hans siukt ben: Om starka och svaga adjektiv i fornsvenskan. *Språkbruk, grammatik och språkförändring: En festskrift til Ulf Teleman*, ed. by Nils Jörgensen, Christer Platzack & Jan Svensson, 99–108. Lund: Lund University, Department of Scandinavian Languages.

Delsing, Lars-Olof. 1999. Från OV-ordföljd till VO-ordföljd: En språkförändring med förhinder. *Arkiv för nordisk filologi* 114: 151–232.

Delsing, Lars-Olof. 2002. The morphology of Old Nordic II: Old Swedish and Old Danish. *The Nordic Languages: An International Handbook of the History of the North Germanic Languages*, ed. by Oskar Bandle, Kurt Braunmüller, Ernst Hakon Jahr, Allan Karker, Hans-Peter Naumann, Ulf Teleman, Lennart Elmevik & Gun Widmark, 925–939. Berlin/Boston: De Gruyter Mouton.

Delsing, Lars-Olof. 2014. Den stora katastrofen med för- och efterskalv: om kasussammanfallet i fornsvenska. *Studier i svensk språkhistoria 12*, ed. by Cecilia Falk & Maria Bylin, 9–29. Stockholm: Stockholm University.

Delsing, Lars-Olof, Øystein Alexander Vangsnes & Anders Holmerg. 2003. *Dialektsyntaktiska studier av den nordiska nominalfrasen*. Oslo: Novus.

Diessel, Holger. 1999. *Demonstratives: Form, function and grammaticalization*. Philadelphia: John Benjamins.

Diewald, Gabriele. 2002. A model for relevant types of contexts in grammaticalization. *New Reflections on Grammaticalization*, ed. by Ilse Wischer & Gabriele Diewald, 103–120. Typological studies in language 49. Amsterdam/Philadelphia: John Benjamins.

Diewald, Gabriele. 2006. Context types in grammaticalizations as constructions. *Constructions all over—case studies and theoretical implications*, ed. by Doris Schönefeld. Düsseldorf: Heinrich-Heine-Universität Düsseldorf.

Dryer, Matthew S. 1989. Article-Noun Order. *Papers from the 25th Regional Meeting of the Chicago Linguistic Society*, 83–97.

Dryer, Matthew S. 2013a. Definite Articles. *The World Atlas of Language Structures Online*, ed. by Matthew S. Dryer & Martin Haspelmath. Leipzig: Max Planck Institute for Evolutionary Anthropology.

Dryer, Matthew S. 2013b. Indefinite Articles. *The World Atlas of Language Structures Online*, ed. by Matthew S. Dryer & Martin Haspelmath. Leipzig: Max Planck Institute for Evolutionary Anthropology.

Dvorak, Jan. 2019. The emerging definite article ten in spoken Czech: a further analysis in terms of 'semantic' and 'pragmatic' definiteness. *Paper presentation at The 41st Annual Conference of the German Linguistic Society (DGfS), 6–8 March 2019*. Bremen, Germany.

Ebert, Karen. 1971a. *Referenz, Sprechsituation und die bestimmten Artikel in einem Nordfriesischen Dialekt (Fering)*. PhD dissertation, Christian-Albrechts-Universität zu Kiel.

Ebert, Karen. 1971b. Zwei Formen des bestimmten Artikels. *Probleme und Fortschritte der Transformationsgrammatik*, ed. by Dieter Wunderlich, 159–174. Munich: Hueber.

Epstein, Richard. 1993. The definite article: early stages of development. *Historical Linguistics*, ed. by Jaap van Marle, 111–134. Amsterdam: John Benjamins.

Epstein, Richard. 2002. The definite article, accessibility, and the construction of discourse referents. *Cognitive Linguistics* 12: 333–378.

Faarlund, Jan Terje. 2007. From clitic to affix: The Norwegian definite article. *Working Papers in Scandinavian Syntax* 79: 21–46.

Faarlund, Jan Terje. 2009. On the history of definiteness marking in Scandinavian. *Journal of Linguistics* 45(3): 617–639. doi:10.1017/S0022226709990041.

Faingold, Eduardo D. 2003. *The Development of Grammar in Spanish and The Romance Languages*. London: Palgrave Macmillan UK. doi:10.1057/9780230006218.

Falk, Hjalmar & Alf Torp. 1900. *Dansk-norskens syntax i historisk fremstilling*. Kristiania: H. Aschehoug & Co. (W. Nygaard).

Fischer, Olga & Anette Rosenbach. 2000. Introduction. *Pathways of Change: Grammaticalization in English*, ed. by Olga Fischer, Anette Rosenbach & Dieter Stien, 1–37. Amsterdam/Philadelphia: John Benjamins.

Fraurud, Kari. 1986. The introduction and maintenance of discourse referents. *Papers from the Ninth Scandinavian Conference on Linguistics, Stockholm, January 9–11, 1986*, ed. by Östen Dahl, 111–122. Stockholm: Stockholm University.

Fraurud, Kari. 1990. Definiteness and the processing of noun phrases in natural discourse. *Journal of Semantics* 7: 395–433.

Fraurud, Kari. 2001. Possessives with extensive use: a source of definite articles? *Dimensions of Possession*, ed. by Irene Baron, Michael Herslund & Finn Sørensen, 243–268. Typological Studies in Language 47. Amsterdam/Philadelphia: John Benjamins.

Frege, Gottlob. 1892. On Sense and Reference. *Translations from the Philosophical Writings of Gottlob Frege*, ed. by Peter Geach & Max Black, 56–78. Oxford: Blackwell.

Friðriksson, Finnur. 2008. *Language change vs. Stability in conservative language communities: A case study of Icelandic*. Gothenburg: University of Gothenburg Press.

Gardent, Claire, Hélène Manuélian & Eric Kow. 2003. Which Bridges for Bridging Definite Descriptions? *Paper presentation at 4th International Workshop on Linguistically Interpreted Corpora—LINC'03*. Budapest, Hungary.

Givón, Talmy. 1981. On the development of the numeral 'one' as an indefinite marker. *Folia Linguistica Historica* 2: 35–53.

Givón, Talmy. 1992. The grammar of referential coherence as mental processing instructions. *Linguistics* 30: 5–55.

Givón, Talmy. 1995. Coherence in text vs. coherence in mind. *Coherence in Spontaneous*

Text, ed. by Morton Ann Gernsbacher & Talmy Givón, 59–115. Amsterdam: John Benjamins.

Gjerdman, Olof. 1924. Till frågan om bestämda artikelns uppkomst och placering. *Festskrift till H. Pipping*, 122–147. Helsingfors: Svenska Litteratursällskapet i Finland.

Goodwin Davies, Amy. 2016. Definiteness Morphology in Swedish Determiner Phrases. *University of Pennsylvania Working Papers in Linguistics* 22(1): 119–128.

Greenberg, Joseph H. 1978. How does a language acquire gender markers? *Universals of Human Language 3*, ed. by Joseph H. Greenberg, 47–82. Stanford: Stanford University Press.

Greenberg, Joseph H. 1991. The last stages of grammatical elements: contractive and expansive desemanticization. *Approaches to grammaticalization*, ed. by Elizabeth Closs Traugott & Bernd Heine, 301–314. Amsterdam: John Benjamins.

Grice, Paul. 1967. Logic and conversation. *Studies in the Way of Words*, ed. by Paul Grice, 41–58. Harvard: Harvard University Press.

Grimm, Jakob. 1898. *Deutsche Grammatik IV*. Berlin: Gütersloh.

Gundel, Jeanette K., Nancy Hedberg & Ron Zacharski. 1993. Cognitive Status and the form of referring expressions in discourse. *Language* 69: 274–307.

Gunnarsson, Britt-Louise. 1982. *Lagtexters begriplighet: en språkfunktionell studie av medbestämmandelagen*. Stockholm: LiberFörlag.

Haig, Geoffrey & Stefan Schnell. 2015. *Multi-CAST: Multilingual Corpus of Annotated Spoken Texts*. https://multicast.aspra.uni-bamberg.de/.

Håkansson, David. 2008. *Syntaktisk variation och förändring: En studie av subjektslösa satser i fornsvenska*. Lundastudier i nordisk språkvetenskap. Lund: Lund University.

Hansen, Aage. 1927. *Bestemt og ubestemt substantiv*. Copenhagen: Busk.

Hanssen, Eskil, Else Mundal & Kåre Skadberg. 1975. *Norrøn grammatikk: lydlære, formlære og syntaks i historisk framstilling*. Oslo: Universitetsforlaget.

Harbert, Wayne. 2006. *The Germanic Languages*. Cambridge: Cambridge University Press. doi:10.1017/CBO9780511755071.

Harðarson, Gísli R. 2017. *Cycling through grammar: On compounds, noun phrases and domains*. PhD dissertation, University of Conneticut.

Hartmann, Dietrich. 1967. *Studien zum bestimmten Artikel in "Morant und Galie" und anderen rheinischen Denkmälern des Mittelalters*. Giessen: Wilhelm Schmitz Verlag.

Hartmann, Dietrich. 1978. Verschmelzungen als Varianten des bestimmten Artikels? *Sprache in Gegenwart und Geschichte: Festschrift Für Heinrich Matthias Heinrichs*, ed. by Dietrich Hartmann, Hansjürgen Linke & Otto Ludwig, 68–81. Köln: Böhlau.

Hartmann, Dietrich. 1980. Über Verschmelzungen von Präposition und bestimmtem Artikel: Untersuchungen zu ihrer Form und Funktion in gesprochenen und geschriebenen Varietäten des heutigen Deutsch. *Zeitschrift für Dialektologie und Linguistik* 47: 160–183.

Hartmann, Dietrich. 1982. Deixis and anaphora in German dialects: The semantics and pragmatics of two denite articles in dialectal varieties. *Here and There: Crosslinguistic studies on deixis and demonstration*, ed. by Jürgen Weissenborn & Wolfgang Klein, 187–207. Amsterdam: John Benjamins.

Haskå, Inger. 1972. *Studier över bestämdhet i attributförsedda nominalfraser: uttryckstyperna det vida hav, vida havet osv. i svensk poesi 1500–1940*. Lund: Studentlitteratur.

Haugen, Einar. 1976. *The Scandinavian Languages: An Introduction to their History*. London: Faber and Faber Limited.

Haugen, Einar. 2006. *Grunnbok i norrønt språk*. Gyldendal: Akademisk Forlag.

Hawkins, John A. 1978. *Definiteness and indefiniteness: a study in reference and grammaticality prediction*. London: Croom Helm.

Hawkins, John A. 1991. On (in)definite articles: Implicatures and (un)grammaticality prediction. *Journal of Linguistics* 27(2): 405–442. doi:10.1017/S0022226700012731.

Heim, Irene. 1988. *The Semantics of Definite and Indefinite Noun Phrases*. New York/London: Garland Publishing, Inc.

Heine, Bernd. 1997. *Cognitive Foundations of Grammar*. Oxford: Oxford University Press.

Heine, Bernd. 2002. On the role of context in grammaticalization. *New Reflections on Grammaticalizations*, ed. by Ilse Wischer & Gabriele Diewald, 83–101. Typological Studies in Language 49. Amsterdam/Philadelphia: John Benjamins.

Heine, Bernd & Tania Kuteva. 2002. *World Lexicon of Grammaticalization*. Cambridge: Cambridge University Press.

Heine, Bernd & Tania Kuteva. 2005. *Language Contact and Grammatical Change*. Cambridge: Cambridge University Press. doi:10.1017/CBO9780511614132.

Heine, Bernd & Heiko Narrog. 2011. *The Oxford Handbook of Grammaticalization*. Oxford: Oxford University Press. doi:10.1093/oxfordhb/9780199586783.013.0001.

Heinrichs, Heinrich Matthias. 1954. *Studien zum bestimmten Artikel in den germanischen Sprachen*. Giessen: Schmitz.

Helgason, Jón. 1929. *Málið á Nýja testamenti Odds Gottskálkssonar*. Safn Fræðafjelagsins um Ísland og Íslendinga 7. Copenhagen: S.L. Möller.

Henning, Bengt. 1970. *Didrikskrönikan: Handskriftsrelationer, översättningsteknik och stildrag*. Stockholm Studies in Scandinavian Philology: New Series, 8. Stockholm: Almqvist & Wiksell.

Herslund, Michael. 2012. Grammaticalisation and the internal logic of the indefinite article. *Folia Linguistica* 46(2): 341–358. doi:10.1515/flin.2012.012.

Heusler, Andreas. 1950. *Altisländisches Elementarbuch*. Heidelberg: C. Winter

Himmelmann, Nikolaus P. 1997. *Deiktikon, Artikel, Nominalphrase: Zur Emergenz syntaktischer Struktur*. Tübingen: Max Niemeyer Verlag.

Himmelmann, Nikolaus P. 2001. Articles. *Language Typology and Language Universals*, ed. by Martin Haspelmath, Ekkehard König, Wulf Oesterriecher & Wolfgang Raible, 831–841. Berlin: Mouton de Gruyter.

Hirvonen, Ilkka. 1987. *Konstruktionstyperna denne man och denne mannen i svenskan:*

En språkhistorisk undersökning. Studier i nordisk filologi 69. Helsinki: Svenska Litteratursällskapet i Finland.

Hirvonen, Ilkka. 1997. *Konstruktionstyperna gamle man, den gamle man och den gamle mannen: Studier i nordisk filologi.* Studier i nordisk filologi 75. Helsinki: Svenska Litteratursällskapet i Finland.

Hodler, Werner. 1954. *Grundzüge einer germanischen Artikellehre.* Heidelberg: Winter Universitätsverlag.

Holmbäck, Åke & Elias Wessén. 1979. *Svenska landskapslagar tolkade och förklarade för nutidens svenskar.* Stockholm: AWE/GEBERS.

Holmberg, Per. 2015. Svaren på Rökstenens gåtor: En socialsemiotisk analys av meningsskapande och rumslighet. *Futhark: International Journal of Runic Studies* 6: 65–106.

Hopper, Paul J. & Janice Martin. 1987. Structuralism and diachrony: The development of the indefinite article in English. *Papers from the Seventh International Conference on Historical Linguistics*, ed. by Anna G. Ramat, Onofrio Carruba & Giuliano Bernini, 295–304. Amsterdam: John Benjamins.

Hopper, Paul J. & Elizabeth Closs Traugott. 2003. *Grammaticalization.* Cambridge: Cambridge University Press.

Huang, Yan. 2000. *Anaphora: a cross-linguistic approach.* Oxford: Oxford University Press.

Ingason, Anton Karl. 2016a. *Realizing morphemes in the Icelandic noun phrase.* PhD dissertation, University of Pennsylvania.

Ingason, Anton Karl. 2016b. Suffixation under structural adjacency: the case of Icelandic the-support. *Proceedings of NELS 46*, ed. by Christopher Hammerly & Brandon Prickett, 147–160. Amherst, MA: GLSA.

Irmer, Matthias. 2011. *Bridging Inferences: Constraining and Resolving Underspecification in Discourse Interpretation.* Berlin/Boston: De Gruyter Mouton.

Iversen, Ragnvald. 1972. *Norrøn grammatikk.* Oslo: Aschehoug.

Jansson, Valter. 1934. *Fornsvenska legendariet: Handskrifter och språk.* Stockholm/Copenhagen: Almqvist & Wiksell.

Jenset, Gard B. & Barbara McGillivray. 2017. *Quantitative Historical Linguistics: A Corpus Framework.* Oxford Studies in Diachronic and Historical Linguistics. Oxford/New York: Oxford University Press.

Johnsen, Gail Perkins. 1975. *The development of the definite article in Old Norse.* PhD dissertation, The University of Rochester.

Julien, Marit. 2005. *Nominal phrases from a Scandinavian perspective.* Linguistik aktuell, Linguistics today 87. Amsterdam/Philadelphia: John Benjamins.

Kibrik, Andrej A. 2011. *Reference in discourse.* Oxford: Oxford University Press.

King, Jeffrey C. 2001. *Complex demonstratives: A quantificational account.* Vol. 2. Cambridge, MA: MIT Press.

Kinn, Kari. 2016. Bare nouns in Middle Norwegian. *Paper presentation at The 18th Diachronic Generative Syntax conference, 28 June 2016*. Ghent.

Kinn, Kari. 2019. Bare singular nouns in Middle Norwegian. *Cycles in Language Change*, ed. by Miriam Bouzouita, Anne Breitbarth, Lieven Danckaert & Elisabeth Witzenhausen, 109–130. Oxford Studies in Diachronic and Historical Linguistics. Oxford/New York: Oxford University Press.

Kleiber, Georges. 1990. Sur l'anaphore associative: article défini et adjektif démonstratif. *Rivista di Linguistica* 2: 155–175.

Klemming, Gustaf E. 1848. *Svenska medeltidens Bibel-arbeten*. Vol. 9. Samlingar utgivna av Svenska Fornskrift-sällskapet (SSFS). Stockholm: P.A. Norstedt & söner.

Kliś, Karolina. 2019. *Grammatikalisering av obestämd artikel i fornisländska*. Adam Mickiewicz University, Poznań, unpublished MA thesis.

Kock, Axel. 1919. Fornnordiska böjningsformer. *Arkiv för nordisk filologi* 35: 55–99.

Kołaczek, Natalia. 2019. *Bestämdhet och indirekta anaforer i svenskan ur främmandespråksperspektiv: en studie av polska studenters svenska*. PhD dissertation, Adam Mickiewicz University, Poznań.

Kovari, Geoffrey. 1984. *Studien zum germanischen Artikel: Entstehung und Verwendung des Artikels im Gotischen*. Vienna: Karl M. Halosar.

Krahe, Hans. 1948. *Germanische Sprachwissenschaft II. Formenlehre*. Berlin: Walter de Gruyter.

Kristjánsson, Jónas. 2009. *Málrækt og Málrýrð*. Reykjavík: Hið Íslenska Bókmenntafélag.

Kurek-Przybilski, Anna. 2020. *Generics in Norwegian—a Cognitive Analysis*. PhD dissertation, Adam Mickiewicz University, Poznań.

Kuryłowicz, Jerzy. 1965. The Evolution of Grammatical Categories. *Diogenes* 13(51): 55–71. doi:10.1177/039219216501305105.

LaCara, Nicholas. 2011. A Definite Problem: The Morphosyntax of Double Definiteness in Swedish. *Morphology at Santa Cruz: Papers in Honor of Jorge Hankamer*, 55–83.

Larm, Karl. 1936. *Den bestämda artikeln i äldre fornsvenska*. Stockholm: Bonniers.

Lehmann, Christian. 1995. *Thoughts on Grammaticalization*. LINCOM Studies in Theoretical Linguistics 1. Münich: LINCOM Europa.

Lehmann, Christian. 2004. Theory and Method in Grammaticalization. *Zeitschrift für Germanische Linguistik* 32(2): 152–187.

Leijström, Gunnar. 1934. *Om obestämda artikeln: ett bidrag till nordisk språkhistoria*. Stockholm: Hugo Gebers Förlag.

Leiss, Elisabeth. 2000. *Artikel und Aspekt: die grammatischen Muster von Definitheit*. Berlin: Mouton de Gruyter.

Leiss, Elisabeth. 2007. Covert patterns of definiteness/indefiniteness and aspectuality in Old Icelandic, Gothic and Old High German. *Nominal Determination: Typology,*

Context Constraints and Historical Emergence, ed. by Elisabeth Stark, Elisabeth Leiss & Werner Abraham, 73–102. Amsterdam: John Benjamins.

Lightfoot, David. 2010. Language acquisition and language change. *WIREs Cognitive Science* 1(5): 677–684.

Löbner, Sebastian. 1985. Definites. *Journal of Semantics* 4(4): 279–326.

Löbner, Sebastian. 2003. *Definite Associative Anaphora*. Düsseldorf: Heinrich-Heine-Universität, Ms.

Lødrup, Helge. 2009. External and Internal Possessors with Body Part Nouns: The Case of Norwegian. *SKY Journal of Linguistics* 22: 221–250.

Lødrup, Helge. 2010. Implicit possessives and reflexive binding in Norwegian. *Transactions of the Philological Society* 108(2): 89–109. doi:10.1111/j.1467-968X.2010.01235.x.

Lødrup, Helge. 2014. Split possession and the syntax of kinship nouns in Norwegian. *The Journal of Comparative Germanic Linguistics* 17(1): 35–57. doi:10.1007/s10828-014-9065-7.

Lohrmann, Susanne. 2010. *The structure of the DP and its reflex in Scandinavian*. PhD dissertation, University of Stuttgart.

Lundeby, Einar. 1965. *Overbestemt substantiv i norsk og de andre nordiske språk*. Oslo: Universitetsforlaget.

Lundquist, Lita. 2007. Lexical anaphors in Danish and French. *Anaphors in Text: Cognitive, formal and applied approaches to anaphoric reference*, ed. by Monika Schwarz-Friesel, Manfred Consten & Mareile Knees, 37–48. Amsterdam/Philadelphia: John Benjamins.

Lyons, Christopher. 1999. *Definiteness*. Cambridge: Cambridge University Press.

Lyons, John. 1975. Deixis as the source of reference. *Formal semantics of natural language*, ed. by Edward Keenan, 61–83. Cambridge: Cambridge University Press.

Magerøy, Hallvard (ed.) 1981. *Bandamanna Saga*. Oslo: Dreyers Forlag, Viking society for northern research, University College London.

Maling, Joan. 2002. Icelandic Verbs with Dative Objects. *Working Papers in Scandinavian Syntax* 70: 1–60.

Matsui, Tomoko. 2000. *Bridging and Relevance*. Amsterdam: John Benjamins.

Mattsson, Ola. 1957. *Helga manna leverne: Studier i den fornsvenska översättningen av Vitae Patrum*. Helsingfors: Svenska Litteratursällskapet i Finland.

McColl Millar, Robert. 2000. Some suggestions for explaining the origin and development of the definite article in English. *Pathways of change: Grammaticalization in English*, ed. by Olga Fischer & Anette Rosenbach. Amsterdam: John Benjamins.

Møller, Kristen. 1945. *Nordiske artikelproblemer*. Copenhagen: J.H. Schultz forlag.

Møller, Kristen. 1974. *Vestjyske artikelproblemer*. Dialektstudier udgivne af Institut for Dansk Dialektforskning 3. Copenhagen: Akademisk Forlag.

Moravcsik, Edith A. 1969. Determination. *Working Papers on Language Universals* 1: 64–98.

Musinowicz, Alexander. 1911. *Die Stellung des attributiven Adjektivs im Altisländischen und Altnorwegischen.* Riga: N. Kymmel.

Naert, Pierre. 1969. Góður maðurinn: En studie över den syntaktiska kombinationen obestämt—bestämt i isländskan, särskilt den nyare isländskan. *Arkiv för nordisk filologi* 84: 115–130.

Neckel, Gustav. 1924. Die Entwicklung von schwachtonigem altnordischem *u* (o) vor *m* aus helleren Vokalen und der altnordische Substantivartikel. *Festschrift für Eugen Mogk zum 70. Geburtstag*, 387–412. Halle: Niemeyer.

Neijmann, Daisy L. (ed.). 2006. *A history of Icelandic literature*. Histories of Scandinavian literature 5. Lincoln/London: University of Nebraska Press.

Nivre, Joakim. 2002. Three Perspectives on Swedish Indefinite Determiners. *Nordic Journal of Linguistics* 25(1): 3–47. doi:10.1080/03325860213069.

Norde, Muriel. 1997. *The history of the genitive in Swedish: A case study in degrammaticalization*. PhD dissertation, University of Amsterdam.

Nygaard, Marius. 1905. *Norrøn syntax*. Kristiania: Aschehoug.

Osthoff, Hermann. 1876. *Zur Geschichte des schwachen deutschen Adjectivums: eine sprachwissenschaftliche Untersuchung*. Vol. 2. Jena: Costenoble.

Perridon, Harry. 1989. *Reference, definiteness and the noun phrase in Swedish*. PhD dissertation, University of Amsterdam.

Perridon, Harry. 1996. Noun phrases in Runic Swedish. *The Nordic Languages and Modern Linguistics: Proceedings of the Ninth International Conference of Nordic and General Linguistics*, ed. by Kjartan G. Ottósson, Ruth V. Fjeld & Arne Torp, 248–261. Oslo: Novus.

Perridon, Harry. 2009. Is the definite article in Jutlandic a borrowing from Low German? *Multilingua—Journal of Cross-Cultural and Interlanguage Communication* 16(4): 351–364.

Pettersson, Thore. 1976. Bestämda och obestämda former. *Kontrastiv fonetik och syntax med svenska i centrum*, ed. by Eva Gårding, 119–142. Lund: LiberLäromedel.

Pfaff, Alexander. 2015. *Adjectival and Genitival Modification in Definite Noun Phrases in Icelandic: A Tale of Outsiders and Inside Jobs*. PhD dissertation, University of Tromso.

Pfaff, Alexander. 2017. Adjectival inflection as diagnostic for structural position: inside and outside the Icelandic definiteness domain. *The Journal of Comparative Germanic Linguistics* 20(3): 283–322.

Pfaff, Alexander. 2019. Reunited after 1000 years: The development of definite articles in Icelandic. *Nordic Journal of Linguistics* 42(2): 165–207. doi:10.1017/S0332586519000155.

Piotrowska, Alicja. 2020. Animacy and other determinants of genitive variation in Swedish: s-genitive vs. prepositional construction. Manuscript in review.

Piotrowska, Alicja. In press. Possessive Expressions in Old Swedish and Present-day

Swedish—A Comparative Analysis. *Exploring Variation in Linguistic Patterns*, ed. by Karolina Drabikowska & Anna Prażmowska, 116–134. Lublin: Wydawnictwo KUL.

Piotrowska, Alicja & Dominika Skrzypek. 2020. Familar vs. unique in a diachronic perspective. Manuscript in review.

Poesio, Massimo. 2003. Associative Descriptions and Salience. *Proceedings of the EACL Workshop on Computational Treatments of Anaphora, Budapest, April 2003*, 31–38.

Poesio, Massimo & Renata Vieira. 1998. A Corpus-based Investigation of Definite Description Use. *Computational Linguistics* 24(2): 183–216.

Pollack, Hans W. 1912. Zur Stellung des Attributes im Urgermanischen: (Ein Beitrag zur Geschichte des suffigierten Artikel im Altnordischen und der germanischen Kasuskomposita). *Indogermanische Forschungen* 30: 283–302.

Pozas-Loyo, Julia. 2010. *The Development of the Indefinite Article in Medieval and Golden-Age Spanish*. London: University of London.

Prince, Ellen. 1981a. On the inferencing of indefinite-this NPs. *Elements of discourse understanding*, ed. by Joshi K. Aravind, Bonnie L. Webber & Ivan A. Sag, 231–250. Cambridge: Cambridge University Press.

Prince, Ellen. 1981b. Toward a taxonomy of given-new information. *Radical Pragmatics*, ed. by Peter Cole, 223–255. New York: Academic Press.

Prokosch, Eduard. 1939. *A Comparative Germanic Grammar*. Philadelphia: Linguistic society of America, University of Pennsylvania.

Quine, Willard van O. 1940. *Mathematical logic*. Cambridge/Massachusetts: Harvard University Press.

Quine, Willard van O. 1953. *Reference and Modality*. Cambridge/Massachusetts: Harvard University Press.

Ralph, Bo. 2007. Gåtan som lösning. *Maal og minne* 20: 133–157.

Ringe, Don. 2006. *From Proto-Indo-European to Proto-Germanic*. Oxford: Oxford University Press.

Ringgaard, Kristian. 1986. Flektionssystemets forenkling og middelnedertysk. *Arkiv för nordisk filologi* 101: 173–183.

Roberts, Craige. 2003. Uniqueness in Definite Noun Phrases. *Linguistics and Philosophy* 26(3): 287–350. doi:10.1023/A:1024157132393.

Rögnvaldsson, Eiríkur, Anton Karl Ingason, Einar Freyr Sigurðsson & Joel C. Wallenberg. 2012. Sögulegi íslenski trjábankinn. *Gripla* 23: 331–350.

Rosén, Victoria & Kaja Borthen. 2017. Norwegian bare singulars revisited. *Bergen Language and Linguistics Studies* 8(1): 220–240. doi:10.15845/bells.v8i1.1330.

Scheutz, Hannes. 1988. Determinantien und Definitheitsarten im Bairischen und Standarddeutschen. *Festschrift für Ingo Reiffenstein zum 60. Geburtstag*, 231–258. Göppingen: Kümmerle.

Schuh, Russel G. 1983. The evolution of determiners in Chadic. *Studies in Chadic and Afroasiatic linguistics*, ed. by Ekkehard Wolff & Hilke Meyer-Bahlburg, 157–210. Hamburg: Buske.

Schütte, Gudmund. 1922. *Jysk og Østdansk artikelbrug*. Copenhagen: Shlonsky.

Schwager, Magdalena. 2007. (Non-)functional concepts: Denite articles in Bavarian. *Paper presentation at The 8th Szklarska Poreba Workshop*.

Schwarz, Florian. 2009. *Two types of definites in natural language*. PhD dissertation, The Graduate School of the University of Massachusetts Amherst.

Schwarz, Florian. 2013. Two Kinds of Definites Cross-linguistically. *Language and Linguistics Compass* 7(10): 534–559. doi:10.1111/lnc3.12048.

Schwarz, Monika. 2000. *Indirekte Anaphern in Texten: Studien zur domänengebundenen Referenz und Kohärenz im Deutschen*. Tübingen: Niemeyer.

Schwarz-Friesel, Monika. 2007. Indirect anaphora in text: A cognitive account. *Anaphors in Text: Cognitive, formal and applied approaches to anaphoric reference*, ed. by Monika Schwarz-Friesel, Manfred Consten & Mareile Knees, 3–20. Amsterdam/Philadelphia: John Benjamins.

Seip, Didrik A. 1958. Den etterhengte artikkel i nordisk. *NTS XVII*: 231–261.

Selig, Maria. 1992. *Die Entwicklung der Nominaldeterminanten im Spätlatein: Romanische Sprachwandel und lateinische Schriftlichkeit*. Tübingen: G. Narr.

Sigurðsson, Halldór Ármann. 2006. The Icelandic noun phrase: central traits. *Arkiv för nordisk filologi* 121: 193–236.

Silverstein, Michael. 1976. Hierarchy of features and ergativity. *Grammatical categories in Australian languages*, ed. by Robert M.W. Dixon, 112–171. Atlantic Highlands, NJ: Humanities Press.

Skafte Jensen, Eva. 2006. Far thæn man kunu ær børn hafwær—On the Use of Demonstratives, Nouns and Articles in the Scanic Law of Old Danish. *Oppa swänzsko oc oppa dansko: Studien zum Altostnordischen*, ed. by Harry Perridon & Arend Quak, 123–151. Amsterdam: Amsterdamer Beiträge zur Älteren Germanistik.

Skafte Jensen, Eva. 2007a. Der var engang en mand: om markeret og umarkeret artikelbrug i moderne dansk og gammeldansk. *Det bedre argument: Festskrift til Ole Togeby*, ed. by Henrik Jørgensen & Peter Widell, 299–320. Aarhus: Forlaget Wessel and Huitfeldt, Nordisk Institut.

Skafte Jensen, Eva. 2007b. Om udviklingen af den ubestemte artikel. *Ny forskning i grammatik 14*, ed. by Merete Birkelund, Susana S. Fernández, Alexandra Kratschmer & Henning Nølke, 145–162. Odense: Syddansk Universitetsforlag.

Skafte Jensen, Eva. 2016. Changes in the properties of the noun in Danish—evidence from the indefinite article. *Let us have articles betwixt us—Papers in Historical and Comparative Linguistics in Honour of Johanna L. Wood*, ed. by Sten Vikner, Henrik Jørgensen & Elly van Gelderen, 261–280. Aarhus: Dept. of English, School of Communication & Culture, Aarhus University.

Skovgaard Boeck, Simon (ed.). 2015. *Jesu Barndoms Bog (Ghemen, ca. 1508)*. Copenhagen: Det Danske Sprog- og Litteraturselskab.

Skrzypek, Dominika. 2005. *The Decline of Nominal Inflection in Old Swedish: The Loss of Dative Case*. Lund: Lund University.

Skrzypek, Dominika. 2009. Äldre and Yngre Västgötalagen—some linguistic evidence. *Folia Scandinavica Posnaniensia* 10: 205–218.

Skrzypek, Dominika. 2012. *Grammaticalization of (in)definiteness in Swedish*. Poznań: Wydawnictwo Naukowe UAM.

Skrzypek, Dominika. 2013. Textual Origins of the Indefinite Article in Swedish. *Folia Scandinavica Posnaniensia* 15(1): 31–45. doi:10.2478/fsp-2013-0003.

Skrzypek, Dominika. 2020. Indirect anaphora in a diachronic perspective: The case of Danish and Swedish. *Nominal Anchoring*, ed. by Robert Van Valin & Kata Balogh, 171–193. Berlin: Language Science Press.

Skrzypek, Dominika & Anna Kurek. 2018. Generics in Mainland Scandinavian languages. *European Journal of Scandinavian Studies* 48(2): 253–266. doi:10.1515/ejss-2018-0019.

Skrzypek, Dominika, Anna Kurek-Przybilski & Alicja Piotrowska. 2020. Expressions of genericity in Mainland Scandinavian languages: A case study. Manuscript in review. Poznań: Adam Mickiewicz University.

Smith-Stark, Thomas C. 1974. The plurality split. *Papers from the Tenth Regional Meeting, Chicago Linguistic Society, April 19–21, 1974*, ed. by Michael W. La Galy, Robert A. Fox & Anthony Bruck, 657–671. Chicago: Chicago Linguistic Society.

Sprenger, Ulrike. 1977. *Untersuchungen zum Gebrauch von sá und nachgestelltem inn in der altisländischen Prosa*. Basel: Helbing & Lichtenhahn.

Ståhle, Carl Ivar. 1967. Medeltidens profana litteratur. *Ny illustrerad svensk litteraturhistoria*, ed. by Eugène N. Tigerstedt, 37–124. Stockholm: Natur och kultur.

Stalnaker, Robert. 2002. Common ground. *Linguistics and Philosophy* 25(5–6): 701–721. doi:10.1023/A:1020867916902.

Stark, Elisabeth. 2002. Indefiniteness and Specificity in Old Italian Texts. *Journal of Semantics* 19(3): 315–332. doi:10.1093/jos/19.3.315.

Stark, Elisabeth, Elisabeth Leiss & Werner Abraham (eds.). 2007. *Nominal Determination: Typology, Context Constraints, and Historical Emergence*. Amsterdam: John Benjamins.

Stendahl, Anders. 2013. *Användningen av "en" som indefinit artikel i fornsvenskan*. Åbo: Åbo Akademis förlag.

Stirling, Lesley & Rodney Huddleston. 2002. Deixis and Anaphora. *The Cambridge Grammar of the English Language*, ed. by Rodney Huddleston & Geoffrey K. Pullum, 1449–1564. Cambridge: Cambridge University Press.

Stroh-Wollin, Ulla. 2009. On the development of definite markers in Scandinavian. *Working Papers in Scandinavian Syntax* 83: 1–25.

Stroh-Wollin, Ulla. 2015. Från gammal man till den gamle mannen: Definitmarkering i fornsvenska nominalfraser med adjektivattribut. *Arkiv för nordisk filologi* 130: 101–138.

Stroh-Wollin, Ulla. 2016. The emergence of definiteness marking in Scandinavian—new answers to old questions. *Arkiv för nordisk filologi* 131: 129–169.

Stroh-Wollin, Ulla. 2018. Mysteriet med den väst- och sönderjyska bestämda artikeln æ. Paper presentation at Möte för nätverket för Nordisk syntaxhistoria 9.

Syrett, Martin. 2002. Morphological developments from Ancient Nordic to Old Nordic. *The Nordic Languages: An International Handbook of the History of the North Germanic Languages*, ed. by Oskar Bandle, Kurt Braunmüller, Ernst Hakon Jahr, Allan Karker, Hans-Peter Naumann, Ulf Teleman, Lennart Elmevik & Gun Widmark, 719–727. Berlin/Boston: De Gruyter Mouton.

Tartt, Donna. 2013. *The Goldfinch*. New York: Little, Brown and Company.

Tegnér, Esaias. 1962. *Om genus i svenskan*. 3rd ed. Stockholm: Nike-tryck.

Teleman, Ulf, Staffan Hellberg & Erik Andersson. 2010. *Svenska akademiens grammatik: 2 Ord*. Stockholm: Svenska akademien, Norstedts.

Terner, Erik. 1922. *Studier över räkneordet en och dess sekundära användningar förnämligast i nysvenskan*. Uppsala: Akademiska bokhandeln.

Thorsen, Peder K. 1901. Det danske Folkesprog i Sønderjylland. *Haandbog i det nordslesvigske Spørgsmaals Historie*, ed. by Franz von Jessen, 119–166. Copenhagen: De samvirkende sønderjydske foreninger.

Thráinsson, Höskuldur. 2007. *The syntax of Icelandic*. London: Barnes & Noble.

Thráinsson, Höskuldur, Hjalmar P. Petersen, Jógvan í Lon Jacobsen & Zakaris Svabo Hansen. 2012. *Faroese: An Overview and Reference Grammar*. 2nd ed. Tórshavn: Føroya Fróðskaparfelag.

Van Deusen, Natalie M. 2012. *The Old Norse-Icelandic Legend of Saints Mary Magdalen and Martha*. PhD dissertation, University of Wisconsin-Madison.

Van Gelderen, Elly. 2007. The Definiteness Cycle in Germanic. *Journal of Germanic Linguistics* 19(4): 275–308.

Viðarsson, Heimir F. 2007. "Þat uar langr time siþan hann hafdi messu heyrt": Lítil athugun á samspili þriggja málbreytinga í Miðaldaævintýrum. Reykjavík, University of Iceland, Ms.

Vieira, Renata & Massimo Poesio. 2000. An Empirically Based System for Processing Definite Descriptions. *Computational Linguistics* 26(4): 539–593. doi:10.1162/089120 100750105948.

Vincent, Nigel. 1997. The emergence of the D-system in Romance. *Parameters of Morphosyntactic Change*, ed. by Ans van Kamenade & Nigel Vincent, 149–169. Cambridge: Cambridge University Press.

Wallenberg, Joel C., Anton Karl Ingason, Einar Freyr Sigurðsson & Eiríkur Rögnvaldsson. 2011. *Icelandic Parsed Historical Corpus (IcePaHC)*. http://www.linguist.is/icelan dic_treebank.

Wessén, Elias. 1941. *Svensk språkhistoria I–III*. Stockholm: Almqvist & Wiksell.
Westergård-Nielsen, Christian. 1946. *Låneordene i det 16. århundredes trykte islandske litteratur*. Bibliotheca Arnamagnæana 6. Copenhagen: Ejnar Munksgaard.
Willemse, Peter, Kristin Davidse & Liesbet Heyvaert. 2009. English possessives as reference-point constructions and their function in the discourse. *The Expression of Possession*, ed. by William McGregor, 13–50. Berlin/New York: Mouton de Gruyter.
Yamamoto, Mutsumi. 1999. *Animacy and reference: A cognitive approach to corpus linguistics*. Amsterdam/Philadelphia: John Benjamins.
Zhao, Wei. 2014. A Survey of Studies of Bridging Anaphora. *Canadian Social Science* 10(3): 130–139.
Zuidema, Willem & Bart de Boer. 2014. Modelling in the language sciences. *Research Methods in Linguistics*, ed. by Robert J. Podesva & Devyani Sharma, 422–439. Cambridge: Cambridge University Press. doi:10.1017/CBO9781139013734.022.

Index

abstractness 140
accessibility
   accessibility marking scale 161, 162, 166, 168, 173
accessible 35, 161, 162, 166, 168, 173, 181, 183, 184, 203
accusative 87, 93, 94, 111, 116, 121, 140, 150–152, 155
adjective
   strong adjective 7, 43, 87, 164
   weak adjective 87
adverbial 88, 119, 144, 194, 195, 210, 211, 213
affix 56, 62
anaphora
   associative anaphora 14, 15
   direct anaphora 11, 14–17, 23, 24, 30, 31, 35, 37, 67, 87, 97, 132, 133, 140, 144, 150–153, 155, 157, 160, 161, 172, 179–181, 200, 203, 222, 223, 225, 228
   indirect anaphora 2, 10, 11, 14–17, 19–21, 23–27, 30, 35, 38, 58, 87, 89, 95–97, 132, 137, 158, 172–174, 176, 177, 179, 181–185, 189–191, 215, 222–225, 227, 228, 231
anaphoric
   anaphoric chain 161, 169, 172–175, 222, 224, 226
   anaphoric marker 13, 161, 169, 172, 173, 203, 227, 232
   anaphoric reference 26, 38, 41, 67, 152, 153, 155, 158, 223
   direct anaphoric context 22, 27, 33, 162, 163, 165, 167–170, 222, 233
   direct anaphoric marker 13, 203, 232
   direct anaphoric reference 26, 38, 67, 152, 155, 158, 223
   indirect anaphoric contexts 28, 175, 185, 190, 191, 232
   indirect anaphoric marker 13, 173, 227
   indirect anaphoric reference 26, 158
animacy
   animacy hierarchy 103, 131, 132
animate
   animate subjects 132, 156
annotation
   annotation level 85–89

article
   adjectival article 48, 52
   definite article 1–5, 7, 8, 10–17, 21–33, 35–39, 41–45, 47–58, 60–64, 66–68, 87, 91, 92, 99–103, 110–114, 118, 122, 124, 128, 132–135, 137, 139–142, 144, 150–153, 155–163, 168, 172, 173, 177, 179–182, 185–188, 190–192, 199, 202–204, 220–225, 227–229, 231–235
   indefinite article 1, 2, 4, 5, 9, 11, 17, 29, 36, 38–42, 57, 58, 64–69, 87, 92, 100–103, 109–111, 118, 124, 127, 128, 144–148, 156, 158, 159, 193, 194, 197, 199–210, 213–216, 218–223, 229–235
   generalized article 41, 42
   preposed article 4, 8, 48, 49, 51–53, 134, 186
   preposed definite article 3, 8, 42, 48–51, 53, 60, 87, 100, 134, 221
   incipient article 11, 13, 27, 28, 40, 68, 101, 156, 158
   incipient definite article 3, 11, 15, 25, 31, 37, 52, 55, 56, 67, 68, 92, 100, 124, 128, 132–134, 137, 140, 153, 162, 179–182, 185, 190, 191, 203, 222, 223
   incipient indefinite article 11, 40, 41, 67, 92, 100, 156, 194, 197, 199–201, 203, 204, 208, 215, 229, 230
   strong definite article 31, 168
   suffixed article 48, 51–53, 60, 134–136
   weak definite article 2

case
   case form 93, 112, 114, 118
   case reduction 4, 111, 112, 118
   case system 93, 95, 97, 110–114, 116, 120, 144, 156
cataphoric 40, 66, 68, 203
categorization 20, 97
classification tree analysis 144, 155
clitic 25, 45, 56, 162, 163, 165
cliticization 12, 45, 47, 48, 50, 63
cognate 32, 218
complementary distribution 4, 7, 8, 31, 33, 51, 60

concreteness
    concrete noun   59, 106
    abstract noun   37, 59, 99, 103, 140, 144, 153, 155
conditional   40, 41, 200, 217, 219, 230
context   2, 5, 7, 10, 14, 15, 17, 22–31, 33, 34, 36–43, 45, 47, 58–60, 62, 65, 67, 69, 85, 90, 97, 107–110, 114–118, 123, 124, 126–128, 131, 132, 137, 138, 157–159, 162, 163, 165, 167–170, 172, 174–179, 181, 183, 185, 188, 190–192, 200, 203–205, 210, 212, 213, 215–218, 220, 222, 223, 228, 230, 232, 233, 235
correlation   101, 117, 118, 120, 152
countability
    countable noun   144
    mass noun   37, 102, 140

dative   4, 87, 90, 91, 93, 94, 111, 116, 117, 120, 121, 140, 150–152, 155
declension   42, 43
definite
    definite form   4, 27, 28, 54, 62, 63, 96, 98, 103, 110, 114, 116, 127, 131, 156, 190, 191, 212, 228
    definite suffix   4, 8, 55, 59, 62, 63, 99, 159
    strong definite semantics   8, 32, 37, 221, 223, 225, 232
    weak definite semantics   37, 191, 222, 225, 232
definite description
    Long definite description   161, 162, 166–168
    short definite description   161, 162, 166–168
definiteness
    definiteness effect   122, 124
    double definiteness   4, 5, 7, 48, 51–53, 100, 134, 136
deictic
    deictic element   15, 25, 27, 28, 30, 56, 67, 159, 231, 232
demonstrative
    distal demonstrative   4, 22, 45, 51, 136, 161, 173
    proximal demonstrative   40, 54, 133, 134, 161
determiner   8, 24, 26, 29, 49, 53, 111, 133, 135, 162, 164, 168, 179, 234
dialect   13, 29–32, 49, 50, 60, 62, 81, 104

epithet   47, 167, 168
etymology   25, 38, 47, 49, 50, 63, 102

Faroese   1, 3–10, 51, 111, 193
free lexeme   3, 45, 163
frequency   52, 55, 58, 59, 98, 101, 106–108, 114, 118, 138, 144, 153, 158, 191, 199, 205, 207, 208, 210, 223

gender
    gender reduction   104, 105
    feminine   88, 93, 104–106, 108–110, 112, 140, 152, 153
    masculine   88, 93, 104–108, 110, 112, 139, 140, 152, 199, 233
    neuter   4, 88, 104, 105, 109, 110, 139, 140, 152, 199
genericity   192, 203, 235
genitive   4, 6, 50, 87, 93–95, 112, 116–118, 121, 138, 140, 144, 150, 151, 155
grammaticalization
    grammaticalization chain   13, 68, 133, 190
    grammaticalization model   58, 65, 67, 158, 159, 161, 163, 165, 167, 169, 171, 173, 175, 177, 179, 181, 183, 185, 187, 189, 191, 193, 195, 197, 199, 201, 203, 205, 207, 209, 211, 213, 215, 217, 219, 221, 229
    definite article grammaticalization   22, 25, 27, 28, 36, 41, 67, 111, 122, 156, 159, 172, 220, 221, 223, 228, 229, 231
    indefinite article grammaticalization   40, 41, 156, 193, 201, 202, 205, 214, 216, 221, 229

identifiability   103, 232
inalienable possession   177, 180, 222, 232
inanimate   54, 88, 89, 103, 104, 129–131, 140, 144, 156, 185, 199, 225, 226
indefinite
    indefinite pronoun   2, 10, 40, 205, 206, 216, 218, 231, 232
    indefinite subject   119, 124, 126
indefiniteness   39, 107, 109, 110, 139
inducible parts   18, 23, 176, 180
inference-based conceptual type   20–22, 176, 178, 179, 184, 225
inferences   21, 184
inflected form   4, 45, 162

INDEX 259

inflection
 double inflection 7, 116
 inflectional paradigm 4, 46, 50, 105
instrumentalis
insular language 3, 4, 7, 9, 111, 156, 193, 205

language acquisition 228
language universals
larger situation 11, 14–16, 23–25, 27, 28, 30, 31, 35, 38, 58, 59, 67, 95, 97, 123, 132, 138, 158, 185, 186, 190, 203, 225, 227, 228
lexeme 3, 9, 45, 86–88, 95, 96, 101, 163, 188
Low German 49, 64, 71, 72, 80, 111, 206, 207

marker
 specific marker 40, 41, 201, 204, 210, 211, 230, 231
 specificity marker 29, 197, 200, 214
meronymic
 meronymic relation 176, 179, 180, 185, 224, 225
 meronymic type 18, 176, 185
Middle Norwegian 70, 71, 73
Modern Danish 49, 57, 58, 62, 65, 99, 112, 233
Modern Icelandic 8, 43, 44, 49, 64, 112, 205
Modern North Germanic 3, 4, 8, 9, 42, 43, 45, 60, 101, 102, 127, 132, 164, 203, 235
Modern Swedish 40, 51, 56, 60, 99, 104, 112, 119, 163, 183, 194, 218
modifier
 adjectival modifier 7–9, 164, 165, 168, 186
morphological exponent 1, 3, 124
morphologization 1, 3, 11, 124
morphology 4, 7, 99, 232

negation 28, 40, 41, 88, 200, 216, 230
nominal 8, 13, 17, 18, 24, 56, 88, 95, 104–106, 108, 176, 177, 179, 183, 222
nominative 50, 87, 94, 105, 111, 114–118, 121, 132, 139, 140, 144, 150, 151, 155
Nordic language 70–73, 75, 100, 205
North Germanic 3–5, 8–12, 26, 30, 32, 37, 38, 41–45, 48, 49, 51, 60, 62, 64, 65, 67, 68, 70, 71, 73, 100–106, 110, 111, 114, 122, 127, 131, 132, 158, 160, 164, 172, 173, 177, 180, 186, 190, 192, 193, 203, 220–224, 228, 232, 235

noun
 abstract nouns 37, 59, 99, 103, 140, 144, 153, 155
 bare noun 3, 4, 6, 26, 38, 68, 87, 92, 112, 116, 133, 144, 150–153, 155, 180, 184, 186, 188, 189
 noun phrase 1, 3, 62, 74, 102, 111, 167, 221
 NPs 4, 5, 7, 9, 10, 17, 41, 51, 54, 61, 66, 74, 75, 91, 95, 97, 98, 100, 101, 103, 105, 107–109, 114–119, 121, 123, 124, 127–131, 134–138, 144, 150–152, 155, 156, 161–166, 168–170, 172, 175, 176, 178–186, 188, 189, 192, 194, 195, 197–199, 202, 203, 224, 225, 230, 233
 mass nouns 37, 102, 140
NPs
 full NPs 54, 161, 162

oblique 88, 112, 120, 121, 140, 144, 150, 155

paradigm 4, 15, 32, 44, 46, 50, 94, 104, 105, 111, 116
periodization 66, 70–72
plural
 plural form 9, 103, 116
 plural noun 9, 102, 103
 plural NPs 101, 118, 156, 203
polarity 216, 218, 230
possessive 2, 17, 22–26, 30, 38, 43, 44, 86–89, 137, 138, 176–181, 183–185, 222, 224–226, 231–233
possessor 88, 89, 117, 180, 185, 225
postposition 45–47, 49, 55, 160, 161, 208
pragmatic 13, 68, 110, 156, 235
predicative 34, 88, 144, 219
prepositional object 32, 54, 88, 110, 155
presentative
 presentative construction 119, 144, 195, 197
 presentative function 118
 presentative marker 40, 41, 107, 124, 193, 197, 203, 205, 210, 213, 214, 220, 230–232
pronoun 2, 10, 15, 17, 25, 26, 38, 40, 45, 86–88, 101, 104, 137, 138, 160–162, 168, 177, 180, 205, 206, 216, 218, 222, 225, 230–232
proportional statistics 90–92, 97, 124
Proto-Germanic period 3

quantifier 62, 193, 212

reference
  discourse reference 37, 87, 89
  generic reference 11, 27, 38, 87, 192, 202, 203, 220
  specific reference 42, 87, 163, 214, 218
  unique reference 11, 26, 27, 30, 32, 67, 87, 95, 138, 186
referent
  discourse referent 11, 13–17, 24, 28, 31, 34, 36, 40, 46, 64, 66–68, 110, 124, 127, 131, 134, 156, 158, 161, 165, 166, 168, 169, 172, 173, 176, 181, 185, 190, 193, 194, 197–200, 203, 214, 215, 218, 222–224, 227–230, 232–235
  human referents 104, 105, 129, 132, 180
  referent accessibility 158, 161, 172
  unique referent 2, 138, 159, 172, 186, 188–190
reflexive
  reflexive possessive 87, 138, 180, 183, 222, 225
regression 92, 93, 97, 139, 140
relative clause 37, 87, 88, 191
Romance Languages 25, 28, 44, 110, 204
runic 3, 45, 47, 54, 63, 64, 70, 72, 97
Runic Swedish 70, 72

salience 40, 132, 156, 197, 230
salient
  salient discourse referent 66–68, 124, 156, 197, 222, 229, 233, 234
  salient referents 41, 118, 224, 229, 230, 233
scheme-based conceptual type 20, 176
semantic
  semantic roles 17, 18, 177
Slavic languages 25, 110, 111, 204

source meaning 28, 29
specificity 29, 37, 39, 197, 200, 210, 214, 215, 222
subject function 139, 140, 144, 156
subjecthood 110, 120, 156
suffix 3, 4, 8, 45, 49, 55, 59, 62, 63, 85, 99, 159
synchronic 13, 132
syncretism 93, 111, 113
syntactic
  syntactic function 65, 121, 123, 153, 155, 229
  syntactic role 89, 101, 120–122, 128, 155

tag 85–91, 93–95, 97
temporal adverbial 210, 211, 213
textual
  textual deixis 15, 30, 67, 172, 191
  textual evidence 45, 47, 64
  textual information 28, 184, 191
thematic role 19, 176, 185, 190, 224, 225, 228
thematic types 23, 176, 177, 179, 182, 183, 185, 224
token 97, 101, 106
topical
  topicality 110, 124, 128, 161, 169, 172, 194, 197, 201, 214
totality 36, 102, 178, 234
typology 13, 14, 21, 29, 41, 121, 132, 176, 177, 179, 225

uniformity 2, 75, 231
unmarked 63, 111, 121, 122, 188, 190
utterance 23–25, 33, 34, 38, 86, 164, 228

variable 93, 140–142, 144–148, 151, 153, 155, 157
variant 54, 55, 63, 75, 118

weak adjectival declension 42, 43

Printed in the United States
by Baker & Taylor Publisher Services